This book is to be returned on or before
the last date stamped

T37

KU-517-821

SPECIAL SERVICES

Care in the
Community
Library Services

GREAT YARMOUTH
LIBRARY
(01493) 844551

added 12|03

ON LOAN TO

SSLY/APR

29. DEC 05

1 8 NOV 2008

-9. OCT. 1997

05. JAN 04

04. MAY 05

16. JUL 05

YAR. S

JABLONSKY

NORFOLK LIBRARY
AND INFORMATION SERVICE

NORLINK   3 0129

ITEM 015 918 775

CHURCHILL, THE GREAT GAME AND TOTAL WAR

CASS SERIES ON POLITICS AND MILITARY AFFAIRS
IN THE TWENTIETH CENTURY

Series Editor
MICHAEL I. HANDEL
U.S. Naval War College,
Newport, RI

1. *Leon Trotsky and the Art of Insurrection 1905–1917*
H. W. Nelson

2. *The Nazi Party in Dissolution: Hitler and the Verbotzeit 1923–1925*
David Jablonsky

3. *War, Strategy and Intelligence*
Michael I. Handel

4. *Cossacks in the German Army 1941–1945*
Sam Newland

5. *Churchill, The Great Game and Total War*
David Jablonsky

CHURCHILL,
THE GREAT GAME
AND
TOTAL WAR

DAVID JABLONSKY
U.S. Army War College

With a Foreword by Caspar W. Weinberger

FRANK CASS

First published 1991 in Great Britain by
FRANK CASS & CO. LTD.
Gainsborough House, Gainsborough Road,
London, E11 1RS, England

and in the United States of America by
FRANK CASS
c/o International Specialized Book Services, Inc.
5602 N.E. Hassalo Street, Portland, Oregon 97213

Copyright © 1991 David Jablonsky

British Library Cataloguing in Publication Data
Jablonsky, David
  Churchill, the great game and total war.
  1. Great Britain. Churchill, Winston S. (Winston Spencer),
  1874–1965
  I. Title
  941.082'092'4
  ISBN 0-7146-3367-4 (cased)
  ISBN 0-7146-4078-6 (pbk)

  Library of Congress Cataloging-in-Publication Data
Jablonsky, David.
  Churchill, the great game and total war / David Jablonsky.
      p.   cm.
  Includes bibliographical references.
  ISBN 0-7146-3367-4 (cased)
  ISBN 0-7146-4078-6 (pbk)
  1. Churchill, Winston, Sir, 1874–1965—Views on war. 2. Great
Britain—History, Military—20th century. 3. Great Britain—
History, Military—19th century. 4. World War, 1939–1945.
5. World War, 1914–1918. 6. War. I. Title.
DA566.9.C5J24 1991
941.084'090—dc20
[B]   89-25209 CIP

Now: RA,

*All rights reserved. No part of this publication may be reproduced
in any form or by any means, electronic, mechanical, photo-
copying, recording or otherwise, without the prior permission
of Frank Cass and Company Limited.*

CHU

Typeset by Williams Graphics, Llanddulas, North Wales
Printed and bound in Great Britain by
BPCC Wheatons Ltd, Exeter

NORFOLK LIBRARY AND INFORMATION SERVICE	
SUPPLIER	HEFFERS
INVOICE No.	339551
ORDER DATE	5.9.91
COPY No.	

To the memory of

MY GRANDFATHER

SANDERFORD JARMAN

1884–1954

Major-General, United States Army

Louisiana State University 1904

United States Military Academy 1908

I have eaten your bread and salt,
  I have drunk your water and wine,
The deaths ye died I have watched beside,
  And the lives that ye led were mine ...

I have written the tale of your life
  For a sheltered people's mirth,
In jesting guise — but ye are wise,
  And ye know what the jest is worth.

> Rudyard Kipling,
> *Barrack Room Ballads*
> *Departmental Ditties and Ballads*

CONTENTS

FOREWORD

Caspar W. Weinberger

A quarter of a century after his death, Winston Churchill still invokes the aura of strength and determination to overcome all odds that symbolized the spirit of the nation he led throughout the Second World War. Paradoxically, as this book convincingly demonstrates, this picture of the man who inspired the free world to win the fight for freedom in the greatest of all total conflicts, owes its existence to many characteristics of the late Victorian era into which Churchill was born in 1874. For it was during the waning years of Queen Victoria's reign that the future British Prime Minister developed his singular traits of character and formed his concepts of war and personal leadership which were to endure throughout his long life, which helped us all to keep our freedom, and which, I hope, will always inspire us.

PREFACE

Each person who comes into contact with the legacy of Winston Churchill has his own vision of the man. No one remains indifferent for long to the overwhelming personality of this British statesman and the gigantic drama of his life. I have been no exception. What follows, therefore, is a personal interpretation of Churchill and the late Victorian era in which he was raised, and of the effect that upbringing had on his ability to deal with the rapidly evolving complexities of total war in the first half of the twentieth century.

In arriving at this interpretation, I have relied primarily on Churchill's written words. After all, the British leader earned his living for much of his life by writing. Beginning with the *Malakand Field Force* and including his only novel, *Savrola*, this collection of articles and books spanning over half a century provided an incredibly rich and revealing lode, upon which I could not only build my conception of the man, but renew an appreciation of the English language in the hands of a master. At the same time, so many researchers have sifted through Churchill's speeches as well as his unofficial and official correspondence, that I have had no qualms about using secondary sources in this regard to round out my interpretation.

I am indebted to former United States Secretary of Defense, Caspar W. Weinberger, for taking time out from his busy schedule to pen a foreword for this book. Over the years, whether fighting as a combat infantryman in the South Pacific during the Second World War, or playing a major role in lifting America out of the Slough of Despond in the early 1980s, Mr Weinberger has consistently demonstrated the traits of character and leadership personified by Winston Churchill.

I am also indebted to Professor Michael Handel, United States Army War College, who introduced me to the endless variety of Churchill's character. Dr Handel, a lifelong student of the British leader, waged a constant campaign to ensure that I maintained an objective view of my subject. His efforts were, I'm afraid, futile. After years of studying Adolf Hitler and his fellow thugs, to climb and emerge on the grand open plateau of Churchill's life was truly to go from the ridiculous to the sublime.

David Jablonsky
Carlisle, Pennsylvania

1

INTRODUCTION

When I look back upon the years 1895 to 1900 I cannot but return thanks to the high gods for the gift of existence. All the days were good and each day better than the other.

Winston Churchill
Charles Eade (ed.), *Churchill by his Contemporaries*, p. 413

The longer you look back, the farther you can look forward.

Winston Churchill
William Manchester, *The Last Lion*, p. 12

...Oh! yet Stands the Church clock at ten to three?
And is there honey still for tea?
Rupert Brooke, "The Old Vicarage, Grantchester"

In March 1913, Sir Garnet Joseph Wolseley died and was buried in the crypt at St. Paul's near his benefactor, the Duke of Wellington. The regiments escorting the gun carriage in the funeral procession were chosen for their association with the general's military career, a reminder in slow march of his exploits in an era of warfare that would die forever the following year at the Marne. One after another, the units recalled a litany of martial glory from every corner of the British Empire.

Granted a commission by the Duke of Wellington in the last year of the Duke's life, Wolseley's ability, intellectual force and bravery, unusual even in an age of ostentatious courage, rapidly advanced him through the Service. By the time he was promoted to Lieutenant Colonel at the age of 26, he had served with distinction in myriad campaigns, suffering a crippling thigh wound in the Second Burmese War and losing an eye to a bursting shell in the Crimea. After the Crimean War, he fought in the Indian Mutiny, and in 1860 accompanied Lord Elgin's expedition to Peking during Britain's conflict with China. In 1862, he met with Robert E. Lee at the Confederate headquarters at Winchester shortly after the battle of Antietam. Both Lee and Chinese Gordon remained his personal heroes throughout his long life, their dissimilarities emphasizing the complexity of this quintessential Victorian soldier.

More battles and honors followed throughout the century. In 1870, Wolseley was knighted for his successful suppression of the Red River rebellion in Canada. In 1874, the year of Winston Churchill's birth, he led his troops into the small African city of Kumasi, now in central Ghana, to end the second Ashanti War. And as Governor of Natal at the end of the decade, he dealt equally successfully with unrest among both Zulus and Boers. The Zulu wars made a particular impression on the five-year-old Churchill, primarily because of lurid drawings in the newspapers. "I was very angry with the Zulus," he recalled later, "and glad to hear they were being killed."[1]

By that time, "All Sir Garnet" had become a popular phrase meaning that things were all right, all in order. In 1880, Wolseley returned to England to be hailed as "master of the small war," and to be good-naturedly caricatured as the "model of a modern Major-General" by W.S. Gilbert in *The Pirates of Penzance*.[2] The remainder of the century continued the succession of triumphs. In 1894, he was promoted to Field Marshal while commanding in Ireland, and in 1895 he began his tenure as Commander-in-Chief of the Imperial Army which lasted until his retirement in the first year of the new century.

Looking back after leaving the Service, Sir Garnet could see the results of the countless British battles and engagements that had occurred throughout the globe every day of Victoria's reign. On the world map, the British Empire was an all-engulfing red splash, three times the size of the Roman Empire, with London representing what Rome had once been − *caput mundi*, the head of the world. And to enforce the *Pax Britannica* throughout this empire, over 350,000 soldiers, including Indian sepoys, were scattered in 15 countries and territories around the world. The conflicts that secured those gains were limited in every sense, except for the individual British soldier who was given a small island for his birthplace and the entire world as his grave. As a result, the idea of a war for a nation's life in time of mortal peril was foreign to the Victorian era in Britain. But there were already signs of change in the Boer War that were undermining the idea that a nineteenth-century army would be equal to twentieth-century needs. How great those needs would become in total war could not be even remotely foreseen. For Wolseley, conflict remained a sublime and ennobling experience that could cleanse the nation. "England," he wrote at the time, "living under our present form of government can only be saved from annihilation by some such periodical upheaval as a great war."[3]

Churchill, of course, was not immune to such sentiments and to the lure of the Victorian wars and their heroes. In a letter to his mother concerning weekend plans away from school in January 1887, he confided excitedly that "Sir G. Womwell [the Sir George Wombwell who rode in the Charge of the Light Brigade at Balaclava] is going to take me to Drury Lane...."[4] And in 1892, he listened enraptured to Sir Garnet's lecture at Harrow on the Red River expedition. Three years later, as a result of

Wolseley's permission, he was under fire in Cuba as an observer in the Spanish War against that island's insurrectionists; and the following year he met socially with the old general before departing as a subaltern to India. By 1900, when Sir Garnet personally presided over Churchill's inaugural lecture on the Boer War at St. James Hall, the young man had passed through four different regiments and three different wars in the twilight of the Victorian era.[5]

It was a heady period with war a limited game for adventurous young Victorian patricians. And within those limitations were the fledgling British intelligence and espionage efforts known in India as early as the late 1830s as the "Great Game." In 1869, Sir Garnet had incorporated the need for those efforts into *The Soldier's Handbook.* "We are bred up to feel it a disgrace ever to succeed by falsehood ... and that truth always wins in the long run," he wrote. "These pretty little sentiments do well for a child's copy book, but a man who acts on them had better sheathe his sword forever."[6]

In 1901, Kipling immortalized these sentiments in the title character of *Kim,* who as "Friend of all the World" under the guidance of Mahbub Ali and Colonel Creighton of the British Secret Service, played "the Great Game that never ceases day and night, throughout India" against Tsarist Russia, "the dread Power of the North.'"[7] By that time, Churchill had already acquired in his adventures on the outposts of the British Empire a fascination for the "Great Game" of secret intelligence, cloak and dagger operations and espionage that would remain with him throughout his life.[8]

The "Great Game," like Victorian warfare would change in the new century. And Churchill would adjust to the changes. Nevertheless, he remained a Victorian who would have preferred to arrest time like David Copperfield and little Em'ly as children by the sea at Yarmouth when they made "no more provision for growing older, than ... for growing younger."[9] In later years, while enjoying himself at dinner with guests, Churchill would refill his glass, relight his cigar and quote Dr. Faustus in a phrase he could also have applied to the twilight of the Victorian age: "Let us command the moment to remain."[10]

But time could not be stopped. Once again there was Dickens, so avidly read by the young Churchill, who demonstrated in *Great Expectations* the futility of Miss Havisham's efforts to capture the moment by stopping the clock at twenty minutes to nine and leaving her home in the condition it was when her fiancé had left her on her wedding day. Time had worn relentlessly on despite her efforts: the wedding dress had withered on her enfeebled and shrunken body, and the bridal cake had long since succumbed to mold and rats. Churchill acknowledged that inevitability. In his only novel, *Savrola,* published in 1900, his protagonist peers through a telescope at a "beautiful world of boundless possibilities" but then becomes depressed as he contemplates a future cooling process which would reduce that world to a state as "cold and lifeless as a burned-out firework."[11]

To acknowledge, however, is not necessarily to accept. Throughout his long life, Churchill indicated in many ways his preference for "the palmy days of Queen Victoria," in which he had spent his formative years. There were, for instance, the Victorian expressions that studded his speech such as "I venture to say" and "I rejoice." And so many of his messages began with "Pray," such as "Pray give me" or "Pray do," that they were known to his subordinates as "Churchill's prayers." In a similar manner, some of his directives in World War II were so magisterial in tone that they became known in government circles by their opening words in the manner of papal encyclicals. One directive, for example, that began "Renown awaits the Commander who first ...." was simply titled "Renown Awaits."[12]

In addition, if he wished to know during that war whether his chauffeur was ready to drive him in his staff car, the question from the Prime Minister was invariably: "Is the coachman on his box?" And like his Victorian predecessors, Churchill as Prime Minister never called at Buckingham Palace or attended Parliament wearing anything but a frock coat. That continuity with the past extended to countries as well, and he strongly believed that "bad luck always pursues peoples who change the names of their cities." For him, Istanbul was always Constantinople and Sevastopol was Sebastopol. "Do try," he wrote to his Minister of Information in August 1941, "to blend in without causing trouble the word Persia instead of Iran."[13]

As he grew older, particularly after the war, Churchill often returned to the Victorian era, "eighty years which will rank in our island history with the age of the Antonines."[14] "I like to live in the past," he mused in June 1955. "I don't think people are going to get much fun in the future."[15] A visitor recalled walking into Churchill's office a month later after Harold Macmillan had been chosen over R.A. (Rab) Butler as the new Conservative leader to find the British statesman muttering: "Intelligent, yes. Good looking yes. Well-meaning yes. But not the stuff of which Prime Ministers are made." The visitor asked: "But would Rab have been any better?" Churchill gave him a blank look. "I was thinking of Melbourne," he said.[16]

Churchill, then, was a nineteenth-century man, a patrician product of the Indian Summer of the Victorian age. The late Victorian was, in turn, a product of a complex tension, combining a romantic and irrational outlook with a pragmatic and rational approach. Churchill was no exception. To this were added the various strands of personality and character traits that he developed before the turn of the century. The purpose of this book is to demonstrate how Churchill's development in the age of

Sir Garnet's limited wars paradoxically prepared him for leadership in an entirely different type of warfare in the modern era. In particular, the basic Victorian tension, while leading to some weaknesses and disadvantages, provided a firm base for his harnessing of the scientific and intelligence sinews of modern conflict, allowing him to play the nineteenth-century "Great Game" in the total wars of the twentieth century.

2

THE VICTORIAN FRAMEWORK

> I was a child of the Victorian era when the structure of our
> country seemed firmly set, when its position in trade and on
> the seas was unrivalled, and when the realisation of the greatness
> of our Empire and of our duty to preserve it was ever growing
> stronger.
>
> Churchill, *A Roving Commission*, p. x

TENSION

> He was at once tough and tender, a romantic and a realist....
>
> Violet Bonham Carter, *Winston Churchill.*
> *An Intimate Portrait*, p. 11

In dealing with "Victorianism," there is sometimes a tendency to define
it in terms of an era that was held together in unified form by distinctive
qualities in ideas, outlook, customs and general culture. This is certainly
an over-simplification for an historical period whose span of years is even
open to debate.[1] The variety of forms, institutions, and cultural expressions during the reign of Queen Victoria was enormous, with contradictions
and opposition being the rule rather than the exception. "Every line of
thought," one historian has noted of the period, "had its
countercurrent."[2] Exaggerated piety, for instance, was matched at times
by doubt and skepticism, optimism by pessimism. All this was true for
hundreds of other contradictions that emerged and receded in Victorian
England and that were mirrored in the intellectual life of the period. There
were scientists and rationalists like Darwin, Huxley and Spencer who
suffered all their lives from illness that defied not only cure but diagnosis
as well; novelists of domestic manners and morals like Bulwer-Lytton,
Thackeray and Dickens who suffered through unhappy marriages; and
moral critics like Carlyle, Eliot, Mills and Ruskin who skirted the borders
of sexual aberrations and improprieties.[3]

Those contradictions had a lasting impact on Churchill as he grew to
manhood in the last quarter of the nineteenth century. On the one hand,
there were romantic, emotional and irrational currents that swirled around
the late Victorians. On the other hand, there were the rocks of pragmatism,
rationality and earnestness upon which those currents constantly broke

only to regather again. Underlying the tension between those influences was the Victorian faith in progress which was, in one historian's estimate, "perhaps the most remarkable aspect of the age."[4]

The Rational Pragmatist

> Life is real! Life is Earnest!
> And the Grave is not its goal,
> Dust thou art, to dust returnest,
> Was not spoken of the soul.
>
> H.W. Longfellow, "Psalm of Life"

The idea of progress, of course, was not unique to England during the period. But its extreme practicality was. Victorians were pragmatists with a sound respect for common sense, a fact recognized as early as 1843 by Thomas Carlyle who presented the typical Englishman of the time as muddling through with a combination of horse sense, a disinclination to enter into speculation, and an ability to make the best of any situation. In 1856, the recurring theme of Buckle's bestselling *History of Civilization in England* was that only by increasing the influence of reason at the expense of emotion and unreflected faith, could progress continue to be achieved. And a decade later, Lecky's *Rationalism in Europe* emphasized a belief in reason, science and technology – all governed by pragmatic, enlightened self-interest.[5]

As a result of these trends, Churchill grew up in a period of enormous activity which stressed practical accomplishments as a principal goal in life. "Does it work?" would be a lifelong utilitarianistic question for him. After the First World War, in an article on Lloyd George, he praised the former Prime Minister "as the greatest master of the art of getting things done and of putting things through that I ever knew ...."[6] In such a context, ends would also justify the means. Thus, Churchill could refer approvingly to Arthur James Balfour's "cool ruthlessness where public affairs were concerned."[7] That approval extended to Herbert Asquith, another survivor of the Victorian age. "In affairs he had that ruthless side without which great matters cannot be handled," Churchill wrote. "When offering me Cabinet office in his Government in 1908, he repeated to me Mr. Gladstone's saying: 'The first essential for a Prime Minister is to be a good butcher ....' "[8]

Rationality was also an important concomitant of pragmatism. Churchill, for example, clearly indicated in his biography of his father that he viewed Lord Randolph's resignation in December 1886 from the Salisbury government as an unpremeditated and ill-advised emotional move conducted almost in a fit of pique at not getting his way on the Defence Estimates. For the young Victorian, there was a positive aspect to any coldly practical, rational approach, particularly under pressure.

That approach stood him in good stead in November 1899 when captured by the Boers in the South African war. Later, Churchill wrote of the incident: " 'When one is alone and unarmed,' said the great Napoleon in words which flowed into my mind in the poignant minutes that followed, 'a surrender may be pardoned.' "[9] That outlook could also act as an antidote to even the most primitive and unthinking type of emotionalism when combined with modern technology. In 1897, for example, while fighting with the Malakand Field Force on India's northwest frontier, Churchill referred only half-humorously to a native cut down by British fire as "a victim to that blind credulity and fanaticism, now happily passing away from the earth, under the combined influences of Rationalism and machine guns."[10]

That type of rationalism was also supported by Victorian earnestness, a recognition that human life was not a short materialistic interval between birth and death, but instead only a part of a spiritual pilgrimage in which man must consistently struggle against the forces of evil for grand purposes. The virtues required for that type of struggle were outlined in a series of books by Samuel Smiles with such titles as *Character* and *Thrift*, which were extremely popular in Churchill's youth.[11] Thus, there was Churchill, the young war correspondent recently captured by the Boers, exhorting British enlisted prisoners at Pretoria in December 1899 "to appear serious men who cared for the cause they fought for."[12] And there was the novice parliamentarian accepting advice from Lord Curzon on how to act in Commons. "The great thing is to impress the House with earnestness," Curzon wrote Churchill in May 1901. "They will forgive anything but flippancy."[13]

Idleness also had no part in morally earnest Victorian life. To begin with, there was the middle-class glorification of work as a supreme virtue. Only by means of that virtue, as Thomas Arnold pointed out, could true character be formed. Work was for the Headmaster of Rugby a sacred duty, and his public school became, in Carlyle's phrase, "a temple of industrious peace."[14] Moreover, work was also a practical means in Victorian society of exorcising both intellectual perplexity and psychological depression. Carlyle, for example, considered idleness to be "perpetual despair," not because it ushered in evil temptations, but because it opened the way to the "fatal nosology of spiritual maladies, so rife in our day."[15]

Churchill was not immune to such "maladies." Like the first Duke of Marlborough, he suffered from prolonged and recurrent fits of depression so familiar to him that he nicknamed the symptoms "Black Dog."[16] In the 1930s, Churchill described these symptoms in his biography of his illustrious ancestor whose "stress of soul and inward vexation were so great as to make him physically ill." After Blenheim in September 1704, Marlborough's "shining armour of serenity was heavy to wear."[17]

To cope with his "Black Dog," Churchill turned to work. Incessant activity was the key, he told Violet Asquith; without it he would relapse into "dark moments of impatience and frustration."[18] As a consequence, there was the bricklaying at Chartwell or the painting at Marrakesh. And when he was fired from office after the Dardanelles fiasco in 1915, the sudden cessation of work and authority was devastating. "Like a sea-beast fished up from the depths," he wrote, "or a diver too suddenly hoisted, my veins threatened to burst from the fall in pressure ...."[19]

Finally, Victorian earnestness included a pervasive authoritarianism that called for absolute obedience to God and the Queen down to more immediate superiors in the family and the military. This belief in obedience was essential to the Victorian concept of duty, no matter what else failed. God, George Eliot was reported to have said, was "inconceivable," immortality was "unbelievable," but duty was nevertheless "peremptory and absolute."[20] Moreover, duty was inextricably linked with glory in the Victorian era. That was the message in the poems that schoolboys learned even before they could read, whether it was *The Death of Nelson* or *The Charge of the Light Brigade*. In addition, the stories for Victorian children all had a point, a moral that normally encompassed dutifulness, if not unquestioning submission to orders. That sense of duty was implicit in a 1913 letter of Churchill's to a woman whose fiancé had been killed in a plane accident. Only a fellow Victorian could have understood the message of condolence. "To be killed instantly without pain or fear *in the necessary service of the country* when one is quite happy and life is full of success & hope," he wrote, "cannot be reckoned the worst of fortune."[21]

The Emotional Romantic

A man never mounts higher than when
he knows not whither he is going.

Oliver Cromwell

The late Victorian world was also marked by a romantic, emotional enthusiasm that bordered at times on the irrational – a world in which the positive morality of generous impulse could triumph, however momentarily, over pragmatic and rational self-control. "Nobility" in that environment lay in nature's pastoral forms, melodic music, and abstract images of the misery or goodness of man. To that were added, as the nineteenth century moved on, the images of grand mountain scenery and heroic men in heroic action against a backdrop of stirring and triumphant music. As a consequence, emotions such as love and pity were never far from the surface, providing as much optimistic hope for the human situation as scientific and materialistic progress.[22]

Churchill remained, in that context, an emotional Victorian romantic all his life. This was apparent in his paintings, with their broad strokes of light and color. "I seized the largest brush and fell upon my victim with Berserk fury," he wrote of his first painting experience after the First World War. "I have never felt any awe of canvas since."[23] As an artist, Churchill's knowledge of perspective was limited. Reflections on water would not always be in correct alignment with the objects reflected; and now and then a building façade would appear to spread rather than contract as it receded from the observer. But a more scientific approach would have destroyed that emotional, impulsive spontaneity that made his paintings so appealing. That was also why Churchill always used oil paint. Unlike watercolors, he pointed out in a revealing essay after some years of painting, there was no need with oils to be logical, building from white canvas to the darkest dark. Instead, he could strike anywhere, experimenting as he built pigment on layer by layer. "And always remember," he concluded, "you can scrape it all away."[24]

Like his paintings, there were no monotones in Churchill's writing or in any other of his activities. All was suffused with emotionalism which, stemming as it did from a patrician Victorian, knew no inhibitions. In World War II during a conference break at Chequers, for instance, one of his generals began playing "The Blue Danube" on a piano. To the amazement of the assembled military leaders, Churchill began to waltz alone dreamily around the floor. His tears could also flow at the slightest provocation, whether it was mention of a gallant act in combat or the thought of "invincible knights in olden days." "I've always been blubbery," he acknowledged in 1953.[25]

As with many of his fellow-Victorians, Churchill's emotions were channeled early on into aspirations with ideal objects, such as great causes or exalted pictures of human nature, that were often vague and at times nonexistent. In such cases, aspiration became an end in itself. Instead of an inspiring experience motivated by a desire to live on a higher plane, there was simply the desire to experience life passionately. Like Dorothea Brooke in Eliot's *Middlemarch*, Churchill would often pursue "some illimitable satisfaction, some object which would never justify weariness, which would reconcile self-despair with the rapturous consciousness of life beyond self."[26] In that context, lack of passion for him was inexplicable, cancelling out, as it did, such virtues as bravery. "He was quite fearless," he acknowledged of Arthur James Balfour; "but had no reason to fear. Death ... only involved a change of state, or at the worst a serene oblivion."[27]

High romantic aspirations were also a source of rationalization, not unfamiliar to Churchill: a "success in failure" philosophy. Far from damaging an ego, failure in that context could be used as proof of the venture's greatness, in comparison to any lesser goal that might be achieved easily. "Failure after long perseverance," a protagonist in *Middlemarch* comments, "is much grander than never to have a striving good enough to be called a failure."[28] It was a time of many undefined aspirations, in which man must move forward on endless brave and new adventures always hungry for new knowledge just over the horizon, beyond the sunset, always into new worlds. It was a time in which Churchill would always be at home, a time recognized by Tennyson, one of his favorite poets:

Come, my friends,
'Tis not too late to seek a newer world ...
We are not now that strength which in old days
Moved earth and heaven; that which we are, we are;
One equal temper of heroic hearts,
Made weak by time and fate, but strong in will
To strive, to seek, to find and not to yield.

THE ROMANCE OF HISTORY

History is what Alcibiades did and suffered.

Aristotle

During the entire Victorian period, there was a nostalgia for the past due in part to the rapidly changing present as well as the uncertainty of the future. That was, of course, not universal. Dickens, for example, demonstrated his feelings about romanticizing the past in *Dombey and Son* when Mrs. Skewton enthuses about "those darling bygone times ... with their delicious fortresses, and their dear old dungeons, and their delightful places of torture ... and everything that makes life truly charming!"[29] But there was generally an overwhelming interest in Britain's history. There were special railway trips to Stonehenge and Hadrian's Wall, and libraries stocked books on recent archeological finds in such places as Troy and Crete. That interest, as Churchill knew only too well, was also reflected in the public schools where the classics were taught in original Greek and Latin.

Moreover, in addition to the professional historians like Macaulay, there was a market for historical novels that lasted throughout the century. Some, like Sir Walter Scott in *Ivanhoe* looked longingly to an idealized, nonmaterial Middle Ages of stability and purity. Others, like Bulwer-Lytton in *The Last Days of Pompeii* performed a similar service for classical antiquity. And there were the more modern origins of England's imperial greatness in Charles Kingsley's *Westward Ho!* of 1855. All those trends continued during Churchill's formative years in the last quarter of the century with, as an example, Rudyard Kipling, who took children far back into England's past with *Puck of Pook's Hill* and *Rewards and Fairies.* At the same time, musicians like Vaughan Williams were examining

British folk music. Even A. Conan Doyle found it expedient toward the end of the period to enter the historical novel market with *The White Company*.[30]

At the center of these stories was the heroic man of action, fated to noble failure and Pyrrhic victories. At the age of 13 at Harrow, Churchill learned 1,000 lines of Macaulay that included Horatius from *The Lays of Ancient Rome*. Throughout his life, Churchill could recite those lines which never failed to invoke intense patriotic feelings in him. The Harrow School songs accomplished a similar function. In 1940, after attending the annual singing of those songs at Harrow, Churchill confided with some emotion to his son: "Listening to those boys singing all those well remembered songs I could see myself fifty years before singing with them those tales of great deeds and of great men and wondering with intensity how I could ever do something glorious for my country."[31]

Those men of action, whether real or fictional, were to be a source of referral and inspiration all of Churchill's life, part of the continuity of history. In August 1941, for instance, while crossing the Atlantic, he saw a film concerning Lord Nelson for the fifth time. Nevertheless, he was still deeply moved. "Gentlemen," he addressed the ship's company at the movie's conclusion, "I thought this film would interest you, showing great events similar to those in which you have been taking part."[32] And as a boy, Churchill "devoured" Stevenson's *Treasure Island*. In November 1895 at the age of 21, he returned to that book to capture his emotions when he saw the shores of Cuba for the first time. "I felt as if I sailed with Captain Silver," he wrote, "and first gazed on Treasure Island."[33] Cuba was the first of the adventures outside England that were to bring him fame before the turn of the century, primarily because they were so in keeping with the romantic milieu of the times. "To travel thousands of miles with money one could ill afford," Churchill acknowledged, "and get up at four o'clock in the morning in the hope of getting into a scrape in the company of perfect strangers, is certainly hardly a rational proceeding."[34]

The Imperial Romance

> It is not a sin in a historian to introduce a personal bias that can be recognized and discounted.
>
> Herbert Butterfield, *The Whig Interpretation of History*, p. 105

Churchill's view of history also stretched beyond the Victorian years. To begin with, there was Blenheim with its obelisks of victory, its grand vistas that created a sense of drama, and the great achievements carved ubiquitously in stone, woven in tapestries and painted on canvas. A monument, in short, to one man, John Churchill, first Duke of Marlborough, whose exploits fed into the unique Whig legend devised by the British in the intervening centuries to underpin their imperial ambitions. It was in that castle that Churchill was born, and it was among the patrician descendants of the great Whig aristocracy from Stuart and Georgian England that Churchill spent his formative years. It was thus no accident that he never deviated throughout his life from what J.H. Plumb has described as "that curious ideology of the Whigs, half truth, half fiction; half noble, half base."[35]

In pursuing that course, Churchill was doing no more than accepting the historical assumptions of his class. For him, English history was an evolutionary development by trial and error in which the Englishman's inherent national characteristics such as love of liberty and justice were gradually matched by the appropriate institutions of government. That process had begun in Saxon days out of whose dusk, for Churchill in the distant future, a purpose was steadily forming, "a new England, closer than ever before to national unity, and with a native genius of her own. Henceforward an immortal spirit stood forth for all to see."[36] From there, it was a quick leap to Elizabeth I who fulfilled England's special destiny by her victories abroad. That progress was imperiled by the Stuarts and Civil War; but those developments also proved providential, since Englishmen returned after an unpleasant experience with republicanism to their natural monarchical allegiance. There were, of course, problems with that initial return; but the Glorious Revolution of 1688 enshrined itself in Whig hagiography by bringing into existence the perfect relationship: a relatively docile monarchy served by a permanent parliament.[37]

From that time on, it was simply a matter of the freedom-loving English under the direction of the Whig squirearchy fighting and defeating Louis XIV and then Napoleon, while simultaneously fulfilling Britain's imperial destiny. There were setbacks and problems, of course, such as the loss of America and the threats posed to institutions by industrialization. But the Empire that emerged from those travails was the greatest and most just in history, founded on the richest and freest democracy the world had ever known. In that interpretation, to which Churchill fully subscribed, it was the play of time working on natural genius that produced Great Britain and its institutions. Finally, it was the landed Whig squirearchy, the "great Oaks" as Edmund Burke referred to them, who had been through the centuries England's natural rulers, the guardians of her destiny, and who had brought that miraculous historical development to fruition.[38]

The Romance of Imperialism

> We happen to be the best people in the world, with the highest ideals of decency and justice and liberty and peace, and the more of the world we inhabit, the better it is for humanity.
>
> Cecil Rhodes

> But it was when as an Imperialist he revived in the Tory party the inspiration of Disraeli and made the world-spread peoples of the British Empire realize that they were one, and that their future lay in acting upon this knowledge, that the life-work of Chamberlain entered its widest and loftiest sphere.
>
> Churchill on Joseph Chamberlain, *Great Contemporaries*, p. 75

British imperialism, in the late Victorian era, was an extension of the Whig version of England's development. Two years before Churchill's birth, Disraeli had confirmed that in his Crystal Palace address, in which he denounced the Liberals for viewing colonies simply from an economic viewpoint, ignoring "those moral and political considerations which make nations great, and by the influence of which alone men are distinguished from animals."[39] It was those higher considerations that caused earnest Victorians to venerate the soldiers on the Imperial frontier, to carry admiration for these men of action to the highest pitch. "They marshalled it," one historian has observed, "they defined it, they turned it from a virtue to a religion, and called it Hero Worship."[40]

The young Churchill, of course, was susceptible to the process. On 14 February 1885, he wrote to his father in India commenting on the death of Colonel Frederick Gustavius Burnaby, Royal Horse Guards who had been killed in action the previous month "sword in hand, while resisting the desperate charge of the Arabs at the battle of Abu Klea."[41] The letter demonstrated the public familiarity with the heroic Victorian men of action. Burnaby had ridden through Asia Minor to Persia, served as a war correspondent for *The Times*, and had undertaken a solo balloon flight from Dover to Normandy. It never occurred to the 11-year-old Churchill that his father would not have heard of the colonel.

But if the daily exploits of such heroes were not enough, there were always the fiction and nonfiction that dealt with every aspect of the heroic Empire. To begin with, there was the prolific pen of George Alfred Henty. In 1876, Henty published the first of his 80 novels on English and Imperial history. Whether it was with Clive or Sir Garnet in India, both published in 1884, or the 1894 adventures in the Punjab, young Victorians like Churchill could relive vicariously every British triumph throughout the Empire. In 1898, the year that Churchill observed Kitchener's victory over the Mahdi at Omdurman, it was estimated that Henty's annual sales were possibly as high as 250,000.[42] In addition, there were the male romances of H. Rider Haggard, which took place in exotic settings throughout the British Empire. Churchill read everything he could of Haggard's after his first encounter with *King Solomon's Mines* in 1884. And when one of his American aunts, who knew the author, took the young boy out of school to meet him, Churchill was overjoyed. "Thank you so much for sending me *Alan Quartermain*," he wrote Haggard afterward; "it was so good of you. I like A.Q. better than *King Solomon's Mines*; it is more amusing. I hope you will write a good many more books."[43]

Churchill was also exposed to a wide variety of nonfiction dealing with the popular Victorian man of action. Between 1852 and 1882, the increasingly literate British masses purchased 31 editions of Creasy's *Fifteen Decisive Battles of the World*, at least partially, according to Herbert Spencer, to "revel in accounts of slaughter."[44] Equal success awaited the Macmillan series entitled "The English Men of Action," each story of 250 pages being immediately sold out. By 1891, such stories were the staple of the popular press. That year, a new series entitled "Story of the VC: Told by those who have won it" appeared in the new *Strand Magazine* and enjoyed as much success as the new Sherlock Holmes short stories that also began in the magazine at the same time.[45]

Behind that Imperial heroism lay the tremendous moral force of the Queen, reaching its full power in Churchill's youth. Other sovereigns had more extensive political power than hers, and Franz Josef, at least, had as long a reign. But he left the Victorian era only a misty, nostalgic image of a capital city throbbing with the faintly decadent sounds of waltzes and operettas. Victoria, on the other hand, embodied all the virtues that Britain adopted as its own in the nineteenth century, extending them to every corner of the Empire.

As a consequence, the 11-year-old Churchill shared the Queen's indignation and that of the public when news was received of Chinese Gordon's death at Khartoum on 26 July 1885. Victoria's indignation, which was directed at the delays by the Gladstone Ministry in sending rescue forces to Gordon, spilled over into a message to the Prime Minister that was subsequently made public. "These news from Khartoum are frightful," she wrote, "and to think all this might have been prevented and many precious lives saved by earlier action is too frightful."[46] To Gordon's sister, the Queen wrote of her *"grief inexpressable* [sic]." Soon, the public perception was that Gladstone, the G.O.M. or Grand Old Man, had become the M.O.G. or Murderer of Gordon.[47] Algernon Charles Swinburne summed up the bitterness of needless death to the greatest of the Victorian Imperial heroes in a poem that ended:

> Forsaken, silent, Gordon dies and gives
> Example: loud and shameless Gladstone lives ....

Two years later, an excited Churchill attended the Queen's Golden Jubilee in London. "I can think of nothing else but Jubilee," he wrote his mother on 12 June 1887.[48] On 21 June, after visiting what he called "Buffalow Bill's" Wild West Show, Churchill stood among the cheering crowd as the Queen rode by on her coach, her head bowed with her hands folded on her lap, her cheeks glistening with tears. After her came the army, with exotically uniformed contingents from throughout the Empire marching in seemingly endless procession through the streets of London, many of them marked, as were streets throughout the cities and towns of Britain, by a roll call of Victorian Imperial victories and heroes. That night bonfires were lit on every hill between Land's End and Shetland.[49]

For Churchill, it was the monarchy that held the Empire together. "The cynical and the socialists may sneer after their kind," he wrote in 1897 of the Queen's role in the empire; "yet the patriot ... will observe, how much the influence of a loyal sentiment promotes the solidarity of the Empire."[50] That sentiment, of course, was not universal in the further reaches of the Empire, as Churchill discovered that same year as a member of Sir Bindon Blood's Malakand Field Force on India's northwest frontier. The impending action to crush the Swati revolt in that region was necessary, he wrote his brother in August, in order to punish those "who have dared violate the Pax Britannica."[51]

Churchill's commitment to that peace was primarily based on his perception of history. On the one hand, there was a peaceful, lawful and orderly life in a stable and prosperous England in which Parliament, a centuries-old constitution, civil liberties and common law all served to protect the citizen from the government. Elsewhere, there seemed to be a great number of countries buffeted by war, revolution, poverty and corruption, where citizens were normally at the mercy of autocratic, often despotic and corrupt, governments. "Yet perhaps," Churchill wrote in this regard after his Indian service, "if that unborn critic of remote posterity would remember that 'in the days of the old British,' the rice crop had been more abundant, the number of acres under cultivation greater, the population larger, the death rate lower, than at any period in the history of India — we should not be without a monument more generous than the pyramids."[52] It was a romantic, nationalistic outlook, in which history and the concept of progress bound the motherland to her colonies. And it was one that would remain with Churchill all his life. "I shall devote my life," he wrote his mother in December 1897, "to the preservation of this great Empire and to trying to maintain the progress of the English people."[53] A lifetime later during the Battle of Britain, Churchill reaffirmed:

that at all times according to my lights and throughout the changing scenes through which we are all hurried I have always faithfully

16

served two public causes which I think stand supreme – the maintenance of the enduring greatness of Britain and her Empire and the historical continuity of our Island life.[54]

The Man of Action

> 'Vehement, high and daring' was his cast of mind. The life he lived was the only one he could ever live; he must go on to the end.
>
> Churchill, *Savrola*, p. 32

> To die will be an awfully big adventure.
>
> J.M. Barrie, *Peter Pan*

History for Churchill was not a subject, as F.W. Deakin, one of his inter-war historical researchers, has pointed out, "but the sum of things; of 'recorded truths' to be grasped and reduced to an intelligible inner world."[55] Within that inner world, there was only the grand and the grandiose. Progress was measured through politics and war, rarely in terms of economic, intellectual and social issues. And always there were the legends and stories that had fired his youthful imagination, which he would only reluctantly disregard. At one point in preparing his *History of the English Speaking Peoples* prior to World War II, for instance, Churchill argued with Deaken as to whether or not King Alfred ever burnt the cakes, finally concluding that in times of crisis, myths were historically important and that King Alfred's cakes symbolized a myth of British resistance against foreign invasion.[56]

Churchill was always conscious of the continuity in his inner historical world and of his place in it. In June 1940, for example, his Chief of Staff urged him to delay sending troops to organize a redoubt in Brittany. "Certainly not," was the Prime Minister's immediate reply. "It would look very bad in history if we were to do any such thing."[57] And in December 1943, while recovering from pneumonia at Eisenhower's villa at Tunis, Churchill was reported to have recovered enough to mutter with his lifelong lisp: "I shupposhe it ish fitting I should die beshide Carthage."[58]

Like the great heroes of old, Churchill was at stage center in that inner world, at all times, as he had written of Pitt the elder, "a projection on to a vast screen of his own aggressive dominating personality."[59] Harry Hopkins, Roosevelt's envoy in the Second World War, recognized that early in the war. "Churchill ... always seemed to be at his Command Post on the precarious beachhead ...," he wrote; "wherever he was, there was the battlefront - and he was involved in the battles not only of the current war but of the whole past, from Cannae to Gallipoli."[60] That romantic outlook was captured in 1913 in an astonishingly prescient biographical sketch of Churchill:

17

He is always unconsciously playing a part – an heroic part. And he is himself his most astonished spectator. He sees himself moving through the smoke of battle – triumphant, terrible, his brow clothed with thunder, his legions looking to him for victory, and not looking in vain. He thinks of Napoleon; he thinks of his great ancestor. Thus did they bear themselves; thus, in this rugged and most awful crisis, will he bear himself. It is not make-believe, it is not insincerity; it is that in that fervid and picturesque imagination there are always great deeds afoot with himself cast by destiny in the Agamemnon role.[61]

Churchill believed that "a man's life must be nailed to a cross either of Thought or Action."[62] And there was no question of his choice. "The realm of thought alone," Violet Asquith noted, "always seemed to him to be an insufficient kingdom, cramping and cold."[63] That was why he was at the center of action during the 1911 Siege of Sidney Street or the 1926 General Strike. If his thoughts were of war, he must command troops; if he had disputes with bricklayers, he himself must build a wall. It was those needs that led him to India's northwest frontier in 1897 and to Khartoum in 1898; that caused him to board the ill-fated armored train in the Boer War, to take personal command of the defense of Antwerp in the First World War, and, but for George VI's intercession, to take part in the D-Day invasion. It was a world built upon the supreme value of action, of the conflict between good and evil, between life and death; but above all, upon battle, the romantic and irrational good fight for its own sake. "Whatever you may do," he declared to the demoralized French ministers in 1940, "we shall fight on forever and ever and ever."[64]

Churchill's world of action was also one of intuition. "Wherever intuition predominates," C.J. Jung noted in his *Psychological Types*, "a particular and unmistakable psychology presents itself .... The intuitive is never to be found among the generally recognized reality values, but is always present where possibilities exist."[65] And so it was with Churchill. One colleague described it as his "zigzag streak of lightning in the brain." And General Alanbrooke, his Chief of the Imperial General Staff (CIGS) for much of the Second World War, was constantly astonished at Churchill's "method of suddenly arriving at some decision as it were by intuition .... He preferred to work by intuition and by impulse."[66] Centuries earlier, Pascal in his *Pensées* had described the complexity of the elements on which the intuitive mind operates and concluded that that intuitive person "must see the matter ... at one glance, and not by a process of reasoning, at least to a certain degree." In his essay on painting, which he also likened to conducting a war, Churchill described a similar process. "There must be that all-embracing view," he wrote, "which presents the beginning and the end, the whole and each part, as one instantaneous impression retentively and untiringly held in the mind."[67]

From that intuitive process came many of the impulsive ideas which were to mark his actions throughout the years and which evoked an entire spectrum of responses all his life. On the one hand, there was Herbert Asquith who wrote in 1909 that "Winston thinks with his mouth."[68] On the other hand, there was General Smuts. "That is why Winston is indispensable," the South African told Churchill's physician in August 1942. "He has ideas .... Men of action live on the surface of things; they do not create."[69] And even President Roosevelt, another extroverted intuitive, remarked only half humorously that Churchill had "a hundred ideas a day, of which at least four are good."[70]

Ideas based on intuition, oriented on vague aspirations and freed from calculation may become opportunistic and seem impulsive to the nonintuitive. "On s'engage et puis ... on voit," was a dictum of Napoleon's certainly familiar to Churchill. Added to his impulsiveness was an admixture of enthusiasm and impatience. Throughout his life Churchill wanted results immediately on whatever project his fertile mind touched and, aware of his own overall inner consistency, was not troubled by charges of inconsistency leveled at him because of his many lesser impulses toward new enthusiasms. If he considered a course of action for a long period of time, particularly if he had conceived it alone and desired it passionately, then emotions engulfed him and he would convince himself that it must be possible. The next step, of course, was to use his incomparable invention, eloquence and high spirits to convince everyone else that his desired project was not only possible, but the only way open to mankind. Still, he always expected others to answer his passionate intensity with equal persistency. From that perspective, it was unfathomable to him, as an example, that Asquith and Kitchener would acquiesce to the Gallipoli campaign without really believing in it.[71]

The failure of that campaign, of course, led to Churchill's removal from stage center. "At a moment when every fibre of my being was inflamed to action," he wrote after the First World War, "I was forced to remain a spectator of the tragedy, placed cruelly in a front seat."[72] It was that sense of participation in great events that he would miss. Years before at Blenheim, Churchill had shot at a rabbit 80 yards away, causing only some fur to fly. When his companion asked him why he had shot at a target so obviously out of range, he replied: "I wished that hare to understand it was taking part in these proceedings."[73] Only by taking part in great proceedings could Churchill indulge his compulsive drive for decisive action, responding directly to a sense of events or issues with a visceral, passionate, often unaware, immediacy. "I like things to happen," he once admitted, "and if they don't happen I like to make them happen."[74] Before the turn of the century, he had captured that abiding passion in his only novel. "If I have done anything," Savrola tells Lucille, "to make the world more happy, more cheerful, more comfortable, let them recall the action."[75]

19

SCIENCE AND THE ROMANCE OF RATIONALISM

O God, if there be a God, save my soul, if I have a soul.
Anonymous Soldier before the battle of Blenheim.
Herbert Tingsten, *Victoria and the Victorians*, p. 41

We will go forward into a way of life more earnestly viewed,
more scientifically organized ... than any we have known.
Churchill's speech at the Manchester Free Trade Hall,
22 May 1909. R. Churchill, Vol. II, p. 313

In nineteenth-century England, the Victorian counter-currents of emotional romanticism and rational pragmatism crossed and found a popular blend in science and technology under an overarching banner of "progress." At mid-century, for instance, Charles Dickens scornfully dismissed as driveling idiots those who were concerned about railroad construction across the lagoon into Venice. Instead, he pointed out, they should be grateful for living in an era when iron was used for something positive like railroads instead of for driving screws into the skulls of innocent men. And in Rome, he rejoiced at telegraph wires passing "like a sunbeam through the cruel old heart of the coliseum."[76]

For the late Victorians, progress continued to be a natural and inevitable product of a rational, harmonious, teleological world. Everything seemed to be on the verge of being completely understood to the young Churchill. Years later, he recalled his wonderment of the period.

The Victorian Age was the age of ... growth and gathering in every land of all those elements and factors which go to make up the power of States .... Science had opened the limitless treasure-house of nature. Door after door had been unlocked. One dim mysterious gallery after another had been lighted up, explored, made free for all: and every gallery entered gave access to at least two more. Every morning when the world woke up, some new machinery had started running. Every night while the world had supper, it was running still. It ran on while all men slept.[77]

It was a time of ecstatic faith in science. In 1872, two years before Churchill's birth, Winwood Reade's *The Martyrdom of Man* became a best seller by describing a future without hunger and disease in which man would cross "the airless Saharas" of space, and the earth would become a Holy Land visited by pilgrims from throughout the universe. "Finally," Reade concluded, "man will master the forces of nature .... Man then will be perfect; he will then be a Creator; he will therefore be what the vulgar worship as a God."[78]

Churchill's faith in science was initially based on more pragmatic, first-hand experience with the benefits that science could bring in his father's home at Connaught Place, the first private house in London with electric lighting.[79] In school, he maintained an interest in science, not always matched by expertise. At the age of eleven, for instance, he wrote his mother of his enthusiasm for chemistry and how wonderful it was "that water is made of two gases namely hydrogdgen and nitrodgen I like it, only it seems so funny that two gases should make water [sic]."[80] At Harrow, Latin and Greek were still the staples of a gentleman's education. Nevertheless, as Churchill indicated in his midlife memoirs concerning his entrance exams for Sandhurst, science remained an abiding interest. "In this hand," he wrote of the exams, "I held only a pair of Kings – English and Chemistry."[81]

From early childhood on, then, Churchill wholly absorbed the Victorian faith in science and was always ready to accept innovation in that field. Like most Victorians of his class, his love of and regard for tradition did not spill over to matters of science. As Prime Minister, for instance, he directed that a hot-water system capable of providing baths for himself and his guests be installed at Chequers, a mansion embodying traditional Britain. And like most Victorians, Churchill accepted the extension of the scientific method into every activity. Throughout his formative years, he learned to observe, to experiment by hands-on experience and to deduce. It was a development that only fueled the contradictory currents in his Victorian character. To an essentially emotional romantic nature was added a lifelong belief in the efficacy of deductive reasoning. "Once you have seen a thing working," he commented to a colleague in middle age, "you know how it works."[82]

Churchill approached this faith in science with typical Victorian earnestness and optimism, aided in part by the positivist philosophy, popular in the late Victorian era, which sought to replace formal religion with belief in science and history. All this was reinforced by his encounter with the eighth edition of Reade's *Martyrdom of Man* in January 1897 while serving in India. "Christianity will be put aside as a crutch which is no longer needed," he wrote to his mother after reading the book, "and man will stand erect on the firm legs of reason .... One of these days ... the cold bright light of science and reason will shine through the cathedral windows ...."[83] Those sentiments remained essentially unchanged the following year after reading one of Mrs. Humphrey Ward's religious novels. "I was so thankful when the girl committed suicide," Churchill wrote to his mother from his posting in Egypt. "It would have been too cruel had she resigned her free spirit, covered her brain with cobwebs and become a Catholic."[84]

Such cold, hard rationalism did not keep Churchill from attributing his survival at the battle of Omdurman a month later to "the Almighty's amiability," or his escape from a Boer prison the following year to "that High Power which interferes in the external sequence of causes and effects ...."[85] Still, his skeptical approach to religion based on his positivist outlook concerning science and history was evident in his only novel published early in the new century. "He hoped for immortality," Churchill wrote of Savrola, "but he contemplated annihilation with composure."[86]

That secular faith was based on optimism. Progress was mankind's destiny and science and technology were the means to achieve that destiny. Late Victorian warfare did not break that optimistic linkage. Although the Gatling and the Maxim had been introduced, the Industrial Revolution had not begun to impact fully on weaponry. In fact, the eleventh edition of the *Encyclopedia Britannica* informed its readers during that period that "losses in battle are ... almost insignificant when compared with the fearful carnage wrought by sword and spear."[87] There were times, of course, when even the most optimistic might wonder. As he contemplated the thousands of Dervish dead after the battle of Omdurman, Churchill's mood was one of cynical, pessimistic fatalism. "Their end, however," he told his readers in the *Morning Post* in October 1898, "only anticipates that of the Victors, for Time, which laughs at Science, as Science laughs at Valour, will in due course brush both combatants away."[88]

Generally, however, Churchill continued to view the impact of science and technology on warfare with disinterested equanimity, if not optimism. As late as 1912, he demonstrated this inclination while hosting in his capacity as First Lord of the Admiralty the Prime Minister, Herbert Asquith, and his daughter on the Admiralty yacht *Enchantress*. Violet Asquith later described an incident with Churchill as the yacht sailed through the Mediterranean.

> As we leaned side by side against the taffrail, gliding past the lovely, smiling coastline of the Adriatic, bathed in sun, and I remarked: "How perfect!" he startled me by his reply: "Yes – range perfect – visibility perfect" – and details followed showing how effectively we could lay waste the landscape and blow the nestling towns sky-high. He was enthralled by the technology of naval warfare and his sense of its results in human terms was for the time being in abeyance.[89]

Churchill's response was just one manifestation of his wide-ranging interest in science. His Victorian mind had long outstripped the narrow utilitarian view of science and provided him with both an optimism that allowed him to foresee many possible, and some impossible, applications of science and technology, and an unlimited confidence in the ability of science to solve any technical problems. Moreover, as a Victorian, his scientific attitude would remain throughout his life the antithesis of the twentieth-century scientist, the specialist learning more and more about less and less. Churchill's interests were always too great to specialize in any one thing. For him, there must be wide freedom in the mind to range over all fields of discovery, and he was fond of quoting Gladstone's classic observation: "Expert knowledge is limited knowledge."[90]

THE PATRICIANS

In those days English Society still existed in its old form. It was a brilliant and powerful body, with standards of conduct and methods of enforcing them .... In a very large degree every one knew every one else and who they were .... Everywhere one met friends and kinsfolk. The leading figures of Society were in many cases the leading statesmen in Parliament ....

Churchill, *A Roving Commission*, p. 89

Winston is a man of simple tastes. He is always prepared to put up with the best of everything.

Lord Birkenhead. Manchester, *The Last Lion*, p. 26

Victorian England was governed by a small, select, homogeneous patriciate acting with enormous confidence to discharge not only what they considered their duty as superior citizens, but their right as well. That confidence was demonstrated at the very top in 1900 by the Queen who was returning on her yacht from a visit to Ireland. After a particularly violent wave had rocked the boat, the Queen summoned her doctor. "Go up at once, Sir James," she commanded, "and give the Admiral my compliments and tell him the thing must not occur again."[91] At a lower level in the aristocratic scale, the same type of confidence and presumption of privilege was demonstrated by Colonel Brabazon, a close friend of the Churchill family who befriended the young Churchill on many occasions. When the colonel, who affected a fashionable clumsiness with his r's, arrived late one evening at a railroad station and was informed that the train for London had just departed, his response was instantaneous. "Then bwing me another," he commanded the stationmaster.[92]

The general idleness of those patricians did not sit well with a growing middle class nourished on Samuel Smiles and the Victorian work ethic. Dickens' villains, for instance, included a large potpourri from the aristocracy ranging from Sir Milberry Hawk in *Nicholas Nickleby* to Sir Leicester and Lady Dedlock in *Bleak House*. Buttressed against them were heroes such as Pip in *Great Expectations*, who learned first hand of the corrupting power of unearned wealth. And while not hostile to the patrician class, Tennyson in *The Idylls of the King* emphasized the newness of the aristocracy at the round table, where nobility was a character trait, not a symbol of rank or birth. At the same time, Lewis Carroll peopled his fantasy lands with patricians who were at best muddlers and at worst tyrants screaming for decapitation at the slightest offenses. And finally, there were the endless parodies of the aristocracy by Gilbert and Sullivan in their Savoy Operas, particularly focusing on the idleness of that class which, like the House of Lords in *Iolanthe*, "did nothing in particular and did it very well."

All that notwithstanding, the dominance of the British patricians, with a social status determined by birthright, remained a fact of life during Churchill's formative years. If, for example, a peer committed murder, he was entitled to a trial by the House of Lords; and if condemned to the gallows, was hanged with a silken rope. Moreover, although the majority of the upper class was only related to peers because of primogeniture, that majority still retained the aristocratic life style, a large portion of which consisted of never lifting an unnecessary finger. It was said of Lady Ida Sitwell, in that regard, that not only was she ignorant of how to lace up her own shoes, but that she would have been humiliated by such knowledge. Churchill's cousin, the ninth Duke of Marlborough, displayed a similar trait. While visiting friends without his valet and thus without the concomitant services provided in terms of his toilet, the Duke complained that his toothbrush didn't "froth properly." His friends gently pointed out that toothpaste was necessary for the brush to foam.[93]

Churchill, himself, went his entire life without ever drawing his own bath or riding on a bus. His one experience with the Underground was a disaster. "That was during the General Strike," his wife later recounted, "when I deposited him at South Kensington. He went round and round, not knowing where to get out, and had to be rescued eventually."[94] He had a lifelong love of luxurious hot baths, taking pride not only in the amount of work he accomplished in them, but in his ability to turn the taps with his toes. And before and after the baths, for most of his life, there was someone to undress and dress him. "I doubt if he had ever packed his own clothes," Violet Asquith summed it up. "It was simpler far to ring a bell, and throughout his life the bells he rang were always answered."[95]

Part of the answering bells had to do with the "old boy network" that connected all parts of patrician society. Without it, Churchill could not have attended Harrow and Sandhurst and certainly could not have effected the key transfers to either General Blood's Malakand Field Force in India or Lord Kitchener's 21st Lancers in the Sudan. It was part of an age that could take for granted Lady Randolph Churchill's moving to South Africa with a fully equipped hospital ship in order to be close to her two sons then engaged in the Boer War.[96] Equally important, this network fed upon itself throughout an Empire that John Stuart Mill termed "a vast system of outdoor relief for the British upper classes." As a young subaltern, Churchill was comfortable in India. But he could have been so anywhere in the Empire, where he could have found himself if not among friends, at least with friends of friends. "The officers congregate about ... the club," Churchill noted of his stay at Bloemfontein in the spring of 1900, "and here I find acquaintances gathered together from all the sentry beats of the Empire, for the regular army usually works like a kaleidoscope, and, new combinations continually forming, scatter old friends in every direction."[97]

Adversity

> Winston is going back to school. Entre nous I do not feel very sorry for he certainly is a handful.
>
> Duchess of Marlborough to Lord Randolph Churchill,
> 23 January 1888, C.V., I, I, p. 154

> Their faults were many. Whose faults are few?
>
> Churchill, 26 May 1888 paper at Harrow entitled "Palestine in the time of John the Baptist." C.V., I, II, p. 165

Churchill received little affection or support from his parents in his early years to a degree that was remarkable even for the patricians of the late Victorian era. His adored mother lived a feckless life of endless parties and entertainment, only focusing an absent-minded attention on her young son during moments of crisis. Lord Randolph, on the other hand, seemed to be eternally disappointed in his son, constantly underestimating him. In his fifties, Churchill recalled how his father had observed him playing with soldiers and had asked him if he would like to enter the army some-day. "For years," he wrote, "I thought my father with his experience and flair had discerned in me the qualities of military genius. But I was told later that he had only come to the conclusion that I was not clever enough to go to the Bar."[98] It was an account told with typical deprecating and endearing humor. But there was no disguising the feelings of humiliation and inferiority. Later in life, Churchill told his son during Randolph's vacation from Eton: "I have talked to you more in this holiday than my father talked to me in his whole life ...."[99]

Only Churchill's nanny, Mrs. Everest or "Woom" as he called her, provided an outlet for his youthful emotions. "She had been my dearest and most intimate friend," he wrote, "during the whole of the twenty years I had lived."[100] "Woom" was a typical Victorian nanny, writing affectionate scolding letters to Churchill in school similar in tone and content to those received by David Copperfield from his beloved Peggoty. Throughout his young life, she provided him, as he wrote of the character in *Savrola* modeled after her, "with a devotion and care which knew no break."[101] When she died, Churchill and his brother, Jack, had a small memorial built for her grave; and for seventy years until his own death, Churchill kept a picture of "Woom" in his room.

But a nanny's affection could not substitute for that of parents; and the young Churchill, five years older than his brother, grew up in self-absorbed loneliness. As a result, all the forces of his vivid but developing personality were concentrated inward upon himself; and he was from infancy stage center in a platform of his own creation, a self-centered egocentric mechanism against the loss of self-esteem that remained with him all his life. "At dinner he talks and talks," one journalist wrote of him in 1898, "and you can hardly tell when he leaves off quoting his one idol, Macaulay, and begins his other, Winston Churchill."[102] Churchill would have been the first to confirm that judgment. His idea of an entertaining dinner, he once said, was to dine well and "to discuss a good topic – with myself as chief conversationalist." Once, after a meal, Churchill broke in on a point being made by his son, Randolph. When Randolph attempted to renew his line of argument, his father growled: "Don't interrupt me when I am interrupting."[103]

Within that self-absorbed world, Churchill remained in many ways a boy who never grew up, a leading character in a Dumas or Stevenson romance in which he was the writer, producer and actor. As much as any monarch conceived by a Victorian historian, poet or moralist, he believed it to be a splendid thing all his life to ride triumphantly after battle back through the cheering throngs. And as much as any of the heroes dramatized in nineteenth-century literature, he knew with unshakable certainty throughout his life what was handsome, noble, larger-than-life, worthy of pursuit and what, on the contrary, was ignoble, grey, thin, compromising – likely to lessen or destroy the grand play of color and movement in the universe.[104]

In addition, Churchill retained throughout his life the small boy's delight in making mischief, in showing off and in dressing up. He owned more hats than his wife, ranging from seamen's caps to his hussar helmet; and his closets were always full of costumes. For more formal occasions, there were his uniforms as RAF Air Commodore, as Colonel of the Queen's Own Fourth Hussars, as Lord Warden of the Cinque Ports, or as Elder Brother of Trinity House, England's first lighthouse and piloting authority, created in 1514 by Henry VIII. In Commons, he was not averse to sticking out his tongue or thumbing his nose at the opposition. Once during the Blitz, a young soldier was assembling an electric train at No. 10 for Churchill's first grandson when he became aware of the Prime Minister's presence. "You've got two locomotives," Churchill said. "Have you got two transformers?" The soldier nodded. "Good!" the British leader boomed, clapping his hands. "Let's have a crash!"[105]

The Adversarial Product

> How an under-esteemed boy of genius of noble character and
> daring spirit seized and created a hundred opportunities to rise
> in the world and add glory by his own merit and audacity to
> a name already famous.
>
> Randolph Churchill, Theme – Frontispiece,
> *Winston S. Churchill*, Vol. I

> He had a stout heart, an audacious spirit, colossal ambition,
> a late-maturing but massive brain.
>
> Randolph Churchill on his father upon Churchill's departure
> from Sandhurst. *Winston S. Churchill*, Vol. I, p. 232

Churchill was aware early on that there were important positive results
from his unhappy childhood. "Solitary trees, if they grow at all, grow
strong," he wrote of the vanquished Mahdi in 1898, "and a boy deprived
of a father's care often develops ... an independence and vigour of thought
which may restore in after life the heavy loss of early days."[106] In 1933,
he returned to the subject in the first of his volumes on his famous ancestor.
"It is said that famous men are usually the product of an unhappy
childhood," he wrote. "The stern compassion of circumstances, the
twinges of adversity, the spur of slights ... in early years, are needed to
evoke that ruthless fixity of purpose ... without which great actions are
seldom accomplished."[107] And again the subject was raised one evening
in December 1941 after President Roosevelt had spoken of his unhappy
childhood. "When I hear a man say that his childhood was the happiest
time of his life," Churchill replied, "I think, 'my friend, you have had
a pretty poor life.'"[108]

Certainly, as Anthony Storr has demonstrated, one result of the parental
neglect experienced by Churchill is a loss of self-esteem which can be
restored in part by developing a number of characteristics. The most
significant of these is intense ambition. "What an awful thing it will be
if I don't come off," Churchill wrote his mother in 1899. "It will break
my heart for I have nothing else but ambition to cling to ...."[109] It was
a compulsive, driving ambition displayed in the unabashed, unashamed
manner that only a Victorian patrician could have. "He has that scorn
of concealment," one journalist wrote in this regard of Churchill in 1908,
"that belongs to a caste which never doubts itself."[110] It was that openness and spontaneity that prevented enduring enmity to Churchill's
inordinate ambitions. "He is ambitious and calculating," one newspaper
account described him as early as 1898; "yet he is not cold – and that
saves him. His ambition is sanguine, runs in a torrent, and the calculation is hardly more than the rocks or the stump which the torrent strikes
for a second, yet which suffices to direct its course."[111]

Although there was a rational, pragmatic basis for Churchill's ambition, it typically contained an irrational, romantic strain in its extremes, totally divorced from a sober appraisal of his gifts and deficiencies or of his achievements. That element of unreality took shape in Churchill as, in his son's words, "a burning sense of personal destiny as vivid as that of the young Bonaparte."[112] As early as 1897, he wrote his mother from the Malakand field camp: "I have faith in my star – that is that I am intended to do something in the world."[113] And between then and 1900 on three different continents, Churchill asserted to three very different people his passionate conviction that he would one day be Prime Minister of England.[114] He never lost that conviction of his destiny – a key factor that allowed him to endure the exceptional vicissitudes of his career. Thus he could write at the beginning of World War I: "Everything tends toward catastrophe. I am interested, geared up and happy."[115] And when the second war came, he was equally serene. "I thought I knew a good deal about it all," he wrote, "and I was sure I should not fail."[116]

Despite this conviction of his destiny, Churchill was also dependent upon external sources of self-esteem. In January 1898, for instance, he wrote to his mother concerning the manuscript of *The Story of the Malakand Field Force*, seeking what she had not given him in his youth. "Write to me ... about the book and be nice about it," he wrote. "Don't say what you think, but what you think I should like you to think."[117] For Churchill, loyalty was essentially an uncritical aspect. He expected it from his friends, and he gave it unstintingly. In World War I, he was especially appreciative of the letters from his First Sea Lord, Admiral Fisher, which ended with variations of "Yours to a cinder," "Yours till hell freezes," or "till charcoal sprouts."[118] And when a former First Sea Lord, Admiral "Tug" Wilson refused to stay on at the Admiralty after Churchill's dismissal in that war, Churchill was genuinely moved. "It came as an absolute surprise to me," he wrote later: "and I do not mind saying that I felt as proud as a young officer mentioned for the first time in dispatches."[119] In later years, Violet Asquith touched on the passionate, almost irrational intensity of Churchill's conception of loyalty, pointing out that:

> when we differed our disagreement was all the more distasteful to him because I was his friend. He reproached me with his glowering look: "You are not *on my side*" – and took scant interest in the reasons which had brought me to this pass. Disagreement was, in any form, obnoxious to him, but when combined with personal affection it became a kind of treachery. He demanded partisanship from a friend, or (at the worst) acquiescence .... There was an absolute quality in his loyalty, known only to those safe within its walls .... In a friend he would defend the indefensible, explain away the inexplicable – even forgive the unforgiveable.[120]

To all his traits, particularly that of ambition, Churchill added an obstinate persistent nature coupled with a drive to persevere, no matter what the project. In 1894, for instance, a watch given to Churchill by his father fell out of his pocket into a deep pool formed by a stream. For the remainder of that day, Churchill dove for the watch without success. After other efforts, which included dredging operations over a two-day period, he hired 23 men from a nearby infantry detachment to dig a new course for the stream. He then obtained a fire engine and pumped the pool dry. After five days, Churchill recovered his father's watch.[121]

Persistency and perseverance require, in turn, a power to concentrate on the subject at hand – a trait Churchill began to develop in India, from where he wrote his mother in 1897 with obvious pleasure that he had "discovered a great power of application which I did not think I possessed."[122] It was a trait that was to mark him all his life. "Winston has always seen things in blinkers," Churchill's wife commented as late as 1945. "His eyes are focused on the point he is determined to attain. He sees nothing outside that beam."[123] An ability, in short, to achieve an extraordinary degree of concentration, amounting almost to an obsession. It was that intense single-mindedness that gave Churchill his incomparable power during crises. But his intense focus on one problem could also blur other problems that were part of the overall solution. "He deceives himself into the belief that he takes broad views," Lord Esher wrote of Churchill in 1917, "when his mind is fixed upon one comparatively small aspect of the question."[124] Violet Asquith recalled the self-absorbed concentration of Churchill's at a ball in which "he was impervious to his surroundings, blind and deaf to the gyrating couples, the band, the jostling, sparkling throng." At one juncture, she pointed out a woman to Churchill who replied: "Yes .... A great woman – sagacious – chaste," a choice of epithets that left Asquith breathless. "There were a hundred adjectives which could with truth have been applied," she wrote later. "... But ... it would have been impossible to discover three words which less described her. She was neither 'sagacious,' 'chaste,' nor 'great.' "[125]

The Public Schools

Rouse not the Berserkir rage that lies in them! Do you know their Cromwells, Hampdens, their Pyms and Bradshaws? Men very peaceable, but men that can be made very terrible.

Thomas Carlyle, *Past and Present*

As to the gentlemen, let them be solicitous to possess only strength and valour: let their motto be: – Hunt, shoot and fight: the rest is not worth a fillip.

Miss Ingram in *Jane Eyre*

So today – and oh! if ever
Duty's voice is ringing clear
Building men to brave endeavour –
Be our answer, "We are here."

Harrow School Song

The British public schools were an integral part of nineteenth-century English patrician life. The spirit of those select schools was captured in Thomas Hughes' *Tom Brown's Schooldays*, an 1856 fictional account of life at Rugby under that school's famous headmaster, Dr. Arnold. The book provided an ideal of life for two generations of British schoolboys, best summed up in Squire Brown's parting thoughts concerning Tom: "If he'll only turn out a brave, helpful, truth-telling Englishman, and a gentleman and a Christian, that's all I want."[126]

Underlying that ideal in Tom Brown was a tradition of manliness from the English squirearchy with its cult of games and field sports and its emphasis on physical strength and prowess. It was also a morally righteous manliness to be used against bullies – usually older, if not stronger – in defense of the small and the weak, the downtrodden fags that seemed to populate Hughes' Rugby. "I want to leave behind," Tom Brown stated in formulating his ambitions at Rugby, "... the name of a fellow who never bullied a little boy, or turned his back on a big one." Allied to this theme, but even more fundamental to the manly tradition, was the concept of combativeness, the love of a good fight. "After all," Tom Brown conjectures, "what would life be without fighting, I should like to know! From the cradle to the grave, fighting, rightly understood, is the business, the real, highest, honestest business of every son of man ...."[127] And if there were any doubt as to the necessity for that moral belief, Hughes outlined a deeper, social-Darwinistic meaning in a Sunday sermon of Dr. Arnold's that "brought home to the young boy for the first time the meaning of life: that it was no fool's or sluggard's paradise into which he had wandered by chance, but a battlefield ordained from of old, where there were no spectators, but the youngest must take his side, and the stakes are life and death."[128]

By the time Churchill entered Harrow in 1888, the manliness cult in the public schools had been augmented by the amateur ideal in the gamesmanship formulation of the new imperialism, as new generations of military men of action and civilian ruler-administrators were produced for the Empire. The essential linkage of sport and the wars to support that Empire was summed up in Sir Henry Newbolt's classic public school poem, "Vitaï Lampada."

There's a breathless hush in the Close tonight –
Ten to make and the match to win –
A bumping pitch and a blinding light,
An hour to play and the last man in.
And it's not for the sake of a ribboned coat,
Or the selfish hope of a season's fame,
But his Captain's hand on his shoulder smote –
"Play up! play up! and play the game!"

Years later, the former cricket player under native attack exhorts his colonial troops to greater deeds:

The sand of the desert is sodden red –
Red with the wreck of a square that broke;
The Gatling's jammed and the Colonel dead,
And the regiment blind with dust and smoke;
The river of death has brimmed his banks,
And England's far, and Honour a name;
But the voice of a schoolboy rallies the ranks:
"Play up! play up! and play the game!"[129]

Although not as bad as depicted in Kipling's *Stalky & Co.*, the public schools in Churchill's time were essentially totalitarian, operating almost subliminally as they molded the individual and made him want to identify with the group. Harrow was no exception. "I am all for the Public Schools," Churchill recalled in later life, "but I do not want to go there again."[130] Still, the school had its effect. At Harrow, Churchill shed his egocentric world view to some degree and began "to play the game." Most importantly, the school experience reinforced his determination to make himself physically and mentally tough, to mold himself in more courageous, heroic and manly terms than were naturally his in physique and temperament.

"I am cursed with so feeble a body," Churchill wrote his mother from Sandhurst in 1893, "that I can scarcely support the fatigues of the day ...."[131] His frustration was understandable. He stood five feet, six and a half inches at the time, with a chest measurement of 31 inches, inadequate by Sandhurst standards. He had extremely sensitive skin and suffered all his life from a difficulty, like his father, in pronouncing the letter "s." As a young man, he would walk up and down attempting to remedy this problem by rehearsing such phrases as: "The Spanish ships I cannot see for they are not in sight." Later on the lecture circuit, he began to cure his lisp and to lose the inhibitions that it had caused. "Those who heard him talk in middle and old age," his son commented later, "may conclude that he mastered the inhibition better than he did the impediment."[132]

Despite those physical disadvantages and a temperament that was not naturally courageous, Churchill emerged as a mentally tough, physically brave man. In fact, as Anthony Storr has demonstrated, it was precisely *because* he lacked the very mental and physical traits that were the quintessential staples of the British public schoolboy and the Victorian man of action, that Churchill persevered, forcing himself to go against his inner nature. It would be a lifelong and successful effort to compensate, to keep from "falling below the level of events."[133] At the age of 18, he nearly killed himself by jumping off a bridge at Bournemouth to avoid capture by his brother and cousin in a youthful game. In a similar manner, after dislocating his shoulder upon his arrival in India in 1896, Churchill participated with his weakened arm strapped to his side in the charge of the 21st Lancers at Omdurman, and continued to play in championship polo matches well into his fifties.

The history of Churchill's involvement in the late Victorian wars was also one of continual search for physical danger. "By a strange stroke of luck," he wrote exultantly from the Malakand Field Force in 1897, "I have dropped into the hardest fighting that the frontier has seen for many years."[134] In the spring of 1900, he deliberately risked his life to carry a relatively unimportant dispatch through Boer-occupied Johannesburg to Lord Roberts. It was a pattern that never altered in the new century, whether it was his reckless self-exposure in France during World War I or his fierce enjoyment of visits to the front in the next war. "Before things happen," Churchill confided in later life, "I have a feeling of apprehension. But when things begin I feel almost gay."[135]

Despite his unhappy years at Harrow, Churchill realized that the public school tradition had been a critical catalyst in his development. Nevertheless, he was not a frequent visitor over the years. In 1911, he took Birkenhead to Harrow only to be booed by the students over Irish Home Rule and the Parliament Bill. Thereafter, he claimed gratitude to the school only because of the school songs and the fact that it was at Harrow that he had learned the beauty of the English language. After Harrow was bombed in the 1940 Blitz, however, Churchill visited the school and acknowledged his debt. "Hitler in one of his recent discourses," the Prime Minister told the assembled students, "declared that the fight was between those who have been through the Adolf Hitler Schools and those who have been at Eton. Hitler has forgotten Harrow ...."[136]

THE VICTORIAN WARS

If a strong man, when the wine sparkles at the feast and the lights are bright, boasts of his prowess, it is well he should have an opportunity of showing in the cold and grey of the morning, that he is no idle braggart.

Churchill, *Malakand Field Force*, p. 315

The healthy, open-air life, the vivid incidents, the excitement, not only of realisation, but of anticipation, the generous and cheery friendships, the chances of distinction which are open to all, invest life with keener interests, and rarer pleasures. The uncertainty and importance of the present, reduce the past and future to comparative insignificance, and clear the mind of minor worries. And when all is over, memories remain, which few men do not hold precious.

Churchill, *Malakand Field Force*, pp. 252–253

During Queen Victoria's reign, at least one regiment of her army saw combat every year, fighting on five continents from Aden and Afghanistan to Zululand and the Zhor Valley. The ultimate sin in that period was cowardice, because such a trait in an Englishman was the most certain way to shatter the image of the colonial rulers and thereby the greatest threat to rule by consent. As a result, the basic assumption was absolute fearlessness; and the patricians who officered the military units on the Imperial frontier actually courted death by refusing to duck bullets and shells, brandishing cigars and swagger sticks instead of weapons. The quintessential embodiment of that concept was the Last Stand, the resistance of British troops to the last man. At the battle of Isandhewana, for example, every officer had a horse and could have escaped. All remained to die with their men. And in 1880 when a young officer and his eleven men were killed in Afghanistan while covering the retreat of an entire brigade, Wolseley was an admiring observer. Had not Horatius, as Macaulay had taught succeeding generations of Victorian children, held the Sublican Bridge over the Tiber in a similar manner two millenia before? "I envy the manner of his death," Sir Garnet wrote of the young officer. "... If I had ten sons, I should indeed be proud if all ten fell as he fell."[137]

The Sporting Game

You've heard of Winston Churchill –
This is all I have to say –
He's the latest and the greatest
Correspondent of the day.

Sung by T.E. Dunville, Lancashire Music Hall Comedian.
Young Winston's Wars, p. xxii

May we meet again, and soon, when the bugles are blowing and drums are beating and khaki is the colour we wear.

Ian Hamilton to Churchill, 25 April 1898
letter. C.V., I, II, p. 929

What has he done all his life?

Adolf Hitler on Churchill,
Frontispiece, *Churchill. The Making of a Hero*

Churchill's attitude toward war in the Victorian era was to a large extent governed by that period's dominant romantic outlook concerning the good fight. Conflict was a normal relationship between great powers, and war, a legitimate political option, was a game to be played very much in the public school spirit. "I shall do my best to play a good game," he wrote his mother from India in August 1897. He was more explicit to her the following month.

I mean to play this game out and if I lose it is obvious that I never could have won any other. The unpleasant contingency is of course a wound which would leave permanent effects and would while leaving me life – deprive me of all that makes life worth living. But all games have forfeits. Fortunately the odds are good.[138]

For Churchill, a primary motivation to "play the game," as has been indicated, was his desire to overcome his physical and psychological disadvantages. "I am more ambitious for a reputation for personal courage than [for] anything else in the world," he wrote early on in the Malakand Field Force campaign in 1897, and the remainder of his first combat experience was involved in achieving that goal.[139] It required constant test and examination. A matter, in other words, of finding situations which afforded "opportunities for the most sublime forms of heroism and devotion."[140] "I am glad," he wrote his mother, "to be able to tell you ... that I never found a better than myself as far as behaviour went"; no one, he pointed out a month later, would "be able to say that vulgar consideration of personal safety ever influenced me."[141]

There was also Churchill's emerging ambition which fueled his insatiable drive for fame and glory. His letters during the Indian and Sudan campaigns in 1897 and 1898, for example, were replete with concerns about awards and decorations. "I should like to come back," he wrote after his first combat action, "and wear my medals at some big dinner or some other function."[142] In Egypt the following year, he was still requesting information on his decoration for the India campaign in a letter that concluded: "I am possessed of a keen desire to mount the ribbon on my breast while I face the Dervishes here. It may induce them to pause."[143] And always there was the test of "the game." How men conducted themselves in crises was all-important. There would be no glory for those who forsook their stage in history. Those who observed would see to that. "I rode on my grey pony all along the skirmish line where every one else was lying down in cover," Churchill wrote early in the India campaign. "Foolish perhaps but I play for high stakes and given an audience there is no act too daring or too noble. Without the gallery things are different."[144]

Underlying that attitude was also the ideal of chivalry. Within that ideal and given the relatively small number of British casualties in the limited

Victorian conflicts, Churchill could indulge an almost Arthurian concern with the manner of death. In general, he could mourn the fact that "golden lads and girls all must, as chimney-sweepers, come to dust." But if the death was honorable, or in an honorable cause, he could still celebrate it as part of a chivalric necessity. "Lord Ava is seriously wounded," he wrote in February 1900 about the nobleman fatally wounded in the Boer War, "a sad item, for which the only consolation is that the Empire is worth the blood of its noblest citizens."[145]

It was this Victorian ideal of chivalry that also inspired Churchill's attitude toward an opponent. To begin with, as one who had been bullied and misused as a child, and as a public school product, he had an instinctive sympathy for the underdog. He passionately followed the Dreyfus affair from abroad, for example, and rejoiced in 1898 when Colonel Henry confessed that the key document relied upon to prove Dreyfus guilty was a forgery. "Bravo Zola!" he wrote home. "I am delighted to witness the complete debacle of that monstrous conspiracy."[146] In a similar manner, Churchill never painted the enemies in his Imperial conflicts in stark black, displaying instead a fairness and generosity, unusual even by Victorian chivalric standards. " 'Never despise your enemy' is an old lesson," he wrote of the 1897 Indian campaign, "but it has to be learnt afresh, year after year, by every nation that is warlike and brave."[147]

That lesson was borne home to Churchill the following year after the battle of Omdurman in his outrage at Lord Kitchener's orders to desecrate the Mahdi's tomb and decapitate the Dervish leader's corpse. "The civilization which can direct the shrapnel shell," he wrote in his dispatch to a London newspaper, "must not war with the dead, or strike at the living through their supernatural beliefs."[148] To his mother, he was more direct, writing of the vindictive Kitchener: "He is a great general but he has yet to be accused of being a great gentleman."[149] That outlook was reinforced by his experience as a captive in the Boer War, in which his captors treated him with fairness and in many cases with generosity, "a great surprise."[150] In later years, Churchill was drawn to General Smuts for many reasons, not the least of which was his romantic and chivalric perception of the South African as a gallant foe who had become a loyal and devoted subject of the King. The British statesman had always taken great pride in helping to establish a just and generous peace after the Boer War, and Smuts, like Botha, was living proof for him that magnanimity and good sense in victory would lead to goodwill.[151]

The Cruel Game

> Death stood before me, grim sullen Death without his lighthearted companion, Chance.
>
> Churchill, *London to Ladysmith*, p. 94

> The ethics of human destruction must necessarily be somewhat obscure.
>
> Churchill, 1898. R. Churchill, Vol. I, p. 409

> I submit that it is unfair as well as irrational to attribute cruelty and bloodthirstiness to soldiers who placed in a position where they have to defend their lives, use the weapons with which they are armed with skill, judgment, and effect.
>
> Churchill, 1898. R. Churchill, Vol. I, p. 410

Churchill's experience in nineteenth-century wars also confirmed a ruthless rationality and pragmatism in Victorian combat. Under the new imperialism, there was in all classes almost a religious faith in Britain as the great force for good in the world. That England could be in the wrong in any one of the countries splashed with red on the world map was almost inconceivable, particularly against itinerant natives. Those tribesmen would often mutilate the British wounded and dead, as Churchill discovered in India. In return, he noted, the British "do not hesitate to finish their wounded off .... I have not soiled my hands with any dirty work – though I recognize the necessity of some things."[152] It was also a necessity recognized by the British public. After all, there were lessons that must be taught. Thus, Churchill could describe in his best-selling account of the Indian campaign how the 11th Bengal Lancers formed a line across a plain on the northwest frontier and began a merciless pursuit of the enemy up a narrow valley:

> No quarter was asked or given, and every tribesman caught was speared or cut down at once. Their bodies lay thickly strewn about the fields, spotting with black and white patches, the bright green of the rice crop. It was a terrible lesson and one, which the inhabitants ... will never forget. Since then their terror of Lancers has been extraordinary.[153]

A ruthless rationality extended the use of military power in that type of warfare to noncombatants. "Of course, it is cruel and barbarous," Churchill acknowledged concerning the burning of native shacks in India as punishment for raids, "as is everything else in war, but it is only an unphilosophic mind that will hold it legitimate to take a man's life and illegitimate to destroy his property."[154] It was a rationale that could also be extended to weapons, such as the new Dum-Dum bullet fired from the Lee-Metford rifle. Churchill had nothing but praise for the expansive character of the new round, "a wonderful and from the technical point of view a beautiful machine," since it "tears and splinters everything before it, causing wounds which in the body must be generally mortal and in any limb necessitate amputation." Results and effectiveness were the ultimate criteria. "I would observe," Churchill concluded on the Dum-Dum, "that bullets are primarily intended to kill, and these bullets do their duty most effectively without causing any more pain to those struck by them, than the ordinary lead variety."[155]

That rational and pragmatic approach to weapons and technology gained further ascendancy as the young Victorian continued to encounter the realities of military life on the Imperial frontier. In late 1897, Churchill and a small group of British and Indian troops from the Malakand Field Force were being pursued by a band of Swati tribesmen. The leading warrior paused to slash at one of the British wounded, and Churchill, as he later recounted, decided to kill him.

> I wore my long Cavalry sword well sharpened. After all, I had won the Public School fencing medal. I resolved on personal combat à l'arme blanche. The savage saw me coming. I was not more than twenty yards away. He ... awaited me, brandishing his sword. There were others waiting not far behind him. I changed my mind about the cold steel. I pulled out my revolver, took ... most careful aim, and fired.[156]

In a similar manner, at Omdurman in 1898 during the initial charge of the 21st Lancers, Churchill used a 10-shot Mauser pistol instead of a saber. The choice was dictated by the necessity to strap his arm to his side because of his easily dislocated shoulder. Nevertheless, Churchill was grateful for the choice of the pistol, "the best thing in the world," which probably saved his life. As a result of the charge, "the most dangerous 2 minutes I shall live to see," the Dervish lines fell back "A.O.T. [arse over tip] ...." In those two minutes, 70 officers and men and 119 horses had been killed and wounded in a totally unnecessary charge. Once again, at least momentarily, rational pragmatism replaced irrational romanticism, as Churchill recounted two days later to his mother.

> I was very anxious for the regiment to charge back – because it would have been a very fine performance and men and officers could easily have done it while they were warm. But the dismounted fire was more useful, though I would have liked the charge – "pour la gloire" – and to buck up British cavalry. We got a little cold an hour afterwards and I was quite relieved to see that "heroics" were "off" for the day at least.[157]

After Omdurman, Churchill walked among the thousands of Dervish bodies stacked on the battlefield and found "nothing of the dignity of unconquerable manhood."[158] Those feelings were reinforced by a steadily mounting British casualty list that included many of his closest friends. "The realization came home to me with awful force," he wrote later, "that war, disguise it as you may, is but dirty, shoddy business which only a fool would undertake. Nor was it until the night that I again recognized that there are some things that have to be done, no matter what the cost."[159] Duty was something that late Victorians could understand. And with duty would come the romanticizing of what had to be done. The brave deeds of Omdurman, Churchill told his readers in the *Morning Post*, "brighten the picture of war with beautiful colours, till from a distance it looks almost magnificent, and the dark background and dirty brown canvas are scarcely seen."[160]

It required more effort to romanticize the Boer War. In South Africa, the British were not dealing with the Pathan and Omdurman tribesmen. This time it was the Boers with a panoply of modern weapons ranging from machine guns, which shredded the dense ranks of the Queen's army, to distant artillery known as Long Toms, which were emplaced far beyond the reach of the British cavalry, rapidly firing 40-pound, 4.7-inch shrapnel shells that dismembered men in the attack or in static positions. Added to this were the sandbagged entrenchments and the barbed wire. As British casualties mounted at such battles as Spion Kop and Vaal Krantz, regimental histories began to record phrases that would become setpieces for the total wars of the twentieth century. Battles became "enshrined forever" in history; engagements were "imperishable" and "immortal."[161]

Those changes were not lost on Churchill who, along with Gandhi, served at the battlefields along the Tugela River. "Colenso, Spion Kop, Vaal Krantz ... were not inspiring memories," he wrote. Spion Kop, in particular, was most revealing concerning the effects of artillery shrapnel on a 2,000-man British brigade crowded in a space "about as large as Trafalgar Square" on the bare top of the kop − "scenes ... among the strangest and most terrible I have ever witnessed."[162] After the relief of Ladysmith, Churchill went back through the Boer ridges above the Tugela and reflected how a month before, the taking of those positions had "meant honour or shame, victory or defeat, life or death ... and now they were ... dark jumbled mounds of stone and scrub with a few holes and crevices scratched in them and a litter of tin-pots, paper, and cartridge cases strewn about."[163]

The tone was too pessimistic for Churchill to sustain in an endeavor which still fitted Victorian standards of limited war. "In a word," he wrote later, "let no one despair of the Empire because a few thousand soldiers are killed, wounded or captured."[164] And at Diamond Hill on 14 June 1900, there was almost a palpable sense of relief when the British reverted to a cavalry charge, "a fine gallant manoeuvre, executed with a spring and an elasticity wonderful and admirable ... in troops who have been engaged ... in continual fighting with an elusive enemy ...."[165] As for the new technologies of war, Churchill also had a warning firmly grounded in the nineteenth century. "Battles now-a-days are fought mainly with firearms," he wrote, "but no troops ... can enjoy the full advantage of their successes if they exclude the possibilities of cold steel and are not prepared to maintain what they have won, if necessary with their fists.''[166]

The Great Game

> The cards I throw away are not worthy of observation or I should not discard them. It is the cards I *play* on which you should concentrate your attention.
>
> Churchill to Violet Asquith. *Winston Churchill. An Intimate Portrait*, p. 213

For the majority of late Victorian army officers, intelligence operations and assessments could not compare with frontline command. Moreover, even those officers who appreciated the value of tactical intelligence while operating in the field frequently failed to grasp the importance of strategic intelligence. Baden-Powell, the future founder of the Boy Scouts, typified the attitude at that time towards intelligence work. He had come to appreciate what he termed "jolly larks" as he played the "Great Game" on India's northwest frontier in the early 1880s. And for him, it always remained a matter of cloak and dagger, with the gentleman amateur far preferable to career professionals − a preference specifically outlined in his memoirs which contained an account of his intelligence exploits on the Dalmatian coast disguised as an eccentric butterfly collector. "The best spies," he declared, "are unpaid men who are doing it for the love of the thing."[167]

There was also the "sporting value" of amateur espionage that was not only part of the "Great Game," but the public school ethos of gamesmanship as well. Thus, for Baden-Powell, the life of Britain's amateur agents had "that touch of romance and excitement ... which makes spying the fascinating sport it is."[168] It was a belief on which the popular spy novels of the period were based. In A.E.W. Mason's *Four Feathers*, for instance, Harry Haversham disguises himself as a native in the Sudan to redeem an earlier failure to play up and to play the game. And in John Buchan's *Greenmantle*, Richard Hannay typified the Victorian who viewed war and espionage as vehicles for English sportsmanship. In one incident, Hannay is put out at not "playing the game" when he abuses the hospitality of one villain. At another point, he allows an enemy agent, bent on spreading anthrax throughout the British Army, to escape rather than shoot him in the back. Finally, there is another hero in the novel, Sandy Arbuthnot, who can be heard crying during a gigantic cavalry attack: "Oh well done our side!"[169]

That type of romantic and amateurish approach to intelligence appealed to Churchill. But his early combat experience also gave him a direct pragmatic appreciation of what intelligence operations could accomplish.

"The great advantage the insurgents have," he wrote from Cuba to his readers of the *Daily Graphic* in November 1895, "is the detailed and constant information which they receive." He then went on to describe how the insurgents disguised themselves to merge with the peasantry. "Hence, they know everything: the position of every general, the destination of every soldier, and what their own spies fail to find out their friends in every village let them know."[170]

In the Malakand Field Force, Churchill gained a greater appreciation of the "Great Game," but it was not until he served under Lord Kitchener in the Sudan that he began to understand the need for organized intelligence. Kitchener, the Sirdar of Egypt, had made a reputation as an intelligence officer in the early 1880s by probing deep into the desert disguised in Arab clothing. In the late summer of 1898, as he maneuvered in the Sudan, Kitchener focused his intelligence operations on the efforts of the Mahdi to draw together his Dervish hordes for a concentrated attack. "The Sirdar did not remain in ignorance of these preparations," Churchill recalled. "The tireless enterprise of the Intelligence Branch furnished the most complete information ...."[171]

And part of that enterprise belonged to Churchill. Early on 2 September 1898, he was patrolling with seven men on what came to be called Heliograph Hill when he spotted what he estimated to be "40,000 men — five miles long in lines with great humps and squares at intervals ...."[172] The thrill of the "Great Game" was overwhelming. "Talk of fun!" he wrote. "Where will you beat this? On horseback, at daybreak, within shot of an advancing army, seeing everything, and corresponding direct with Headquarters."[173]

THE VICTORIAN CONTINUITY

"Well, very long ago," the Badger said, "on the spot where the Wild Wood waves now, before ever it had planted itself and grown up to what it now is, there was a city — a city of people, you know .... They were a powerful people, and rich, and great builders. They built to last, for they thought their city would last forever."

"But what has become of them all?" asked the Mole.

"Who can tell," said the Badger. "People come — they stay for a while, they flourish, they build — and they go. It is their way. But we remain. There were badgers here, I've been told, long before that same city even came to be. And now there are badgers here again. We are an enduring lot, and we may move out for a time, but we wait, and are patient, and back we come. And so it will ever be."

Kenneth Grahame, *Wind in the Willows* (1908)

The late Victorians, regardless of class, did not consider their age to be stable and serene, normally envisaging themselves, instead, as living in turbulent and troubled times. A key ingredient of that lack of self-complacency was the depression of 1873–96 which, among other things, increased state intervention in social and economic affairs. That tendency toward collectivism meant, in turn, laws on almost every conceivable subject, a trend satirized in Gilbert and Sullivan's 1893 *Utopia Limited*, in which Captain Fitzbattleaxe invents the Rival Admirers' Clauses Consolidation Act, a formulation of standard operating procedures for any two gentlemen in love with the same lady.[174] For the aristocracy, the depression meant that the mid-century power of land was broken. "What between the duties expected of one during one's lifetime," Lady Bracknell complains in Oscar Wilde's 1898 *The Importance of Being Earnest*, "and the duties extracted from one after one's death, land has ceased to be either a profit or a pleasure. It gives one position, and prevents one from keeping it up."[175]

Already in 1886, Tennyson was revising the hope for the future, so eloquently expressed as a young man in "Locksley Hall," in the more thoughtful, less exuberant "Locksley Hall Sixty Years After."

> Gone the cry of 'Forward, Forward,' lost within a growing gloom,
> Lost, or only heard in silence from the silence of a tomb ...
> Forward then, but still remember how the course of Time will swerve,
> Crook and turn upon itself in many a backward streaming curve.

And there was Thomas Hardy who denied that man could control his own environment and determine his own destiny, one of the most cherished of Victorian beliefs. In *Tess of the d'Urbervilles*, published in 1891, chance and accident consistently change and thwart the plans and intentions of the principal characters. In addition, Hardy savaged the Victorian idea of just rewards. Tess is a good person who is executed for murder while her drunken father, the epitome of selfishness, vanity and laziness, lives a relatively happy life and dies without suffering in his bed.[176]

Even the new imperialism came in for questioning during this period. In 1835, Macaulay had written approvingly in his *Critical and Historical Essays* of the English who "have spread their dominion over every quarter of the globe ... have created a maritime power which would annihilate in a quarter of an hour the navies of Tyre, Athens, Carthage, Venice and Genoa together ...."[177] In 1897, however, at the time of Queen Victoria's Diamond Jubilee, Kipling sounded a warning that would have greater impact in a few years during the South African experience.

> Far-called, our navies melt away;
> On dune and headland sinks the fire:
> Lo, all our pomp of yesterday
> Is one with Nineveh and Tyre!

Such pessimism was too much for Churchill, briefly back in the country from India, who stated in a speech at Bath:

> There are not wanting those who say that in this Jubilee year our Empire has reached the height of its glory and power, and that we now should begin to decline, as Babylon, Carthage, and Rome declined. Do not believe these croakers, but give the lie to their dismal croaking by showing by our actions that the vigour and vitality of our race is unimpaired and that our determination is to uphold the Empire ....[178]

Churchill's reaction was typical of the dominant mood that continued to prevail as Victorian England moved into the Edwardian period. Some pessimism and rational doubt lingered, even in children's books such as *The Wind in the Willows*, but generally the romantic, optimistic and chivalrous concept of Imperial patriotism and warfare prevailed in the years prior to World War I. In 1912, three events occurred which confirmed that trend. The first was the opening of *Where the Rainbow Ends* which played to packed houses of parents and children at London's Savoy Theater. The play concerned two children, Rosamund and Crispian, who escape by magic carpet from the home of their wicked aunt and uncle to search for their shipwrecked parents in the Land Where the Rainbow Ends. On their way they are protected by St. George, who upon initial appearance is a disappointing grey-haired, soldierly old man. But when Rosamund explains, "I am an English maiden in danger, and I ask for your aid," there is a blinding flash and St. George is revealed in all his glory, complete with shining armor and sword.

Patriotism and empire were the basic themes. Crispian is a young naval cadet from Dartmouth. He has a pet lion cub who is fed on "Commonwealth Mixture for British Lion. Equal parts of Canadian, Australian and New Zealand iron, mixed with South African steel." The bottle containing this mixture is labeled "Poison to Traitors," and chokes the mean uncle of the children who has come after them and has been making fun of the British flag as "that little bit of bumptious bunting." At the end of the play, St. George exhorts the English to resist the Dragon King, who is attempting to corrupt them, and to join all nations to "fight aggression and foul tyranny." In conclusion, he cries out to the audience: "Rise, youth of England, let your voices ring/For God, for Britain and for Britain's King."[179]

The second event that year was the death of Captain Robert Scott and four companions while returning from the South Pole. One of the men, his feet gangrenous from frostbite, walked away from the group so as not to hold them up. Scott left letters and journals which he completed while waiting to die. To the mother of one of his companions, he wrote that "we are very near to the end of our journey and I am finishing it

in company with two gallant, noble gentlemen. One of these is your son."
And in another letter, he concluded that "we have been to the Pole and
we shall die like gentlemen."[180]

The third incident in 1912 was the sinking of the *Titanic*. Again, a basic
ingredient was chivalry and grace under pressure. Gentlemen escorted
ladies to lifeboats as though they were entering carriages. Colonel John
Jacob Astor helped his young bride in, "smiled, touched his cap and ...
turned back to his place among the men." One woman, having been helped
into a lifeboat, watched her escort lean against the rail, light a cigarette
and wave goodbye as her boat departed. "Walter, you must come with
me," another woman begged. "No," replied her husband, turning away,
"I must be a gentleman."[181]

Both the *Titanic* and the Scott expedition revealed an amateurishness
in reality that was also part of the Victorian cum Edwardian ethos. The
Titanic, for instance, had over 2,000 passengers and lifeboats for 1,100.
Moreover, only 651 people actually managed to board those lifeboats
despite the calm sea. In a similar manner, a Norwegian team under
Amundsen had a smooth and successful expedition to the South Pole and
back a month before Scott, primarily because its members were trained
professionals. Scott and his men, on the other hand, were by comparison
hopelessly amateurish; and his last message to the First Sea Lord suggested
an outlook in which heroism had become more important than intelligent
preparation, which in turn would have made heroism unnecessary. "After
all," Scott concluded in that message, "we are setting a good example
to our countrymen, if not by getting into a tight place, by facing it like
men when we were there."[182]

3

THE GREAT AND TOTAL WAR

> The true romantic is not the Byronic hero; he is the British soldier whose idea of a *beau geste* is to dribble a football into the enemy's trenches.
>
> John Buchan, *Homilies and Recreations*, p. 27

> Before the war it had seemed incredible that such terrors and slaughters, even if they began, could last more than a few months. After the first two years it was difficult to believe that they would ever end. We seem separated from the old life by a measureless gulf.
>
> Churchill, *The World Crisis 1916–1918*, Pt. 2, p. 509

> Merciful oblivion draws its veils; the crippled limp away; the mourners fall back into the sad twilight of memory. New youth is here to claim its rights, and the perennial stream flows forward even in the battle zone, as if the tale were all a dream.
>
> Churchill, *The World Crisis 1916–1918*, Pt. 2, p. 544

The First World War was a gradually evolving shock to the British majority who approached it with Victorian idealism and optimism compounded by romantic public school notions of chivalry and combat. "War declared by England," a schoolboy at Rugby, who was destined to die in battle in 1914, wrote in his diary on 5 August 1914. "Intense relief, as there was an awful feeling that we might dishonour ourselves."[1] That public-school ethos was dramatically illustrated by the young officers who "played the game" by leading their men unarmed while kicking a football across no-man's-land. The most famous episode, in that regard, was Captain W.P. Nivill's performance at the Somme. Nivill was a company commander who gave footballs to each of his platoon leaders and kept one for himself, offering a prize to the platoon that first kicked its ball into the German front line during the initial attack. It was not recorded if anybody won; but Captain Nivill was killed instantly.[2]

It was to be a war that cleansed the body politic, an ennobling, inspiring and uplifting experience of the kind Sir Garnet Wolseley had described in the previous century. Raymond Asquith, the Prime Minister's son, captured the feeling in his popular 1915 poem entitled "The Volunteer."

Here lies a clerk who half his life had spent
Toiling at ledgers in a city grey.
Thinking that so his days would drift away
With no lance broken in life's tournament,

All turned out well, however:

His lance is broken; but he lies content
With that high hour, in which he lived and died ....[3]

Disillusion crept in as the carnage mounted. But the horror of modern
warfare was generally concealed well into the conflict from the British
public by a conspiracy of silence in the form of stiff upper, if not sealed,
lips. That tendency was supported by the popular literature of the time.
There was, for instance, a rearguard fictional movement for most of the
war, in which a band of brothers continued to protect the weak and
vanquish the villains under the leadership of such heroes as Bulldog
Drummond and Major-General Hannay. In 1917, Conan Doyle ended *His
Last Bow*, the final volume of Sherlock Holmes, by observing that "a
cleaner, better, stronger land will lie in the sunshine" after the war.[4] And
that same year, Henry Newbolt's *Book of the Happy Warrior* was a major
publishing success as was E.B. Osborn's anthology of war poems entitled
The Muse in Arms which continued to stress war as a sporting game, in
that case rugby, in the best public school tradition.

There's a roar from the "touch" like an angry sea
As the struggle moves from goal
But the fight was clean as a fight should be
And they're friends when the ball has ceased to roll ...
Can you hear the call? Can you hear the call?
That drowns the roar of Krupp
But hark! Can you hear it? Over all –
Now, School! Now, School! "Play Up."[5]

All such literary efforts notwithstanding, however, the romantic outlook
on war for the actual participants normally did not survive the first shock
of modern combat. "I agree with you about the utter senselessness of
war," Raymond Asquith wrote his wife in July 1916 at the onset of the
Somme campaign and less than a year after the publication of his poem,
"The Volunteer." "The suggestion that it elevates the character is
hideous."[6] Churchill would later describe the death in that campaign of
the young Asquith, who "when the Grenadiers strode into the crash and
thunder of the Somme ... went to his fate, cool, poised, resolute, matter-
of-fact, debonair."[7] But for the majority of Britons by 1918, concepts
such as patriotism, chivalry and playing the game had become not so much
devalued, as simply irrelevant, suited for another age infinitely remote

from the reality of mud and blood, boredom and fear, and carnage and mutilation.

THE FIRST LORD

Prudence and audacity may be alternated but not mixed. Having gone to war it is vain to shrink from facing the hazards inseparable from it.

Churchill, *The World Crisis 1911–1914*, p. 281

Somewhere in that enormous waste of waters ... cruising now this way, now that, shrouded in storms and mists, dwelt this mighty organization.

Churchill, *The World Crisis 1911–1914*, pp. 226–227

Well, there is one thing at any rate they cannot take from you. The Fleet was ready.

Lord Kitchener to Churchill, *The World Crisis 1915*, p. 391

Churchill was First Lord of the Admiralty in the Asquith administration when World War I began. He had been First Lord since 1911. "This is a big thing," he commented on being appointed, " – the biggest thing that has ever come my way .... I shall pour into it everything I've got."[8] And he did. "He felt to the quick the traditional glamour of his new office," Violet Asquith remembered, "the romance of sea power, the part that it had played in our island history, the conviction that it was today the keystone of our safety and survival. He revelled in its technology and enjoyed its symbols."[9]

Part of Churchill's commitment stemmed from his perception of the threat. He had observed the German Army maneuvers of 1906 and 1909 with some skepticism, primarily because of the close packed nature of the exercises. "I had carried away from the South African veldt a very lively and modern sense of what rifle bullets could do," he wrote, "... and we felt sure we possessed a practical experience denied to the leaders of these trampling hosts ...."[10] The growing German naval threat, however, was another matter. Sea power, he pointed out, was different. Land power had "a cushion, a pad" called mobilization that made surprise difficult. But no such cushion existed for a fleet in being, which could offer an immediate, no-warning attack. As a consequence, Churchill threw himself into a response to the German build-up of 1912 – so much so that Lloyd George believed the Navy had become "an obsession" with him. "You have become a water creature," he told Churchill. "... You forget that most of us live on land."[11]

It was during that period of frenzied activity that Churchill made many technological innovations, beginning with the development and production of the 15-inch naval gun. He was also concerned with speed, and in consultations with scientists and military historians, began developing a Fast Division of Ships that would be able "to curl around the head of the enemy's line" and fire upon the leading warships, "throwing his whole formation into confusion." Churchill also discovered that oil fuel would be necessary for the new high-speed battleships; and in 1913, he carried through Commons the Anglo-Persian Convention, which ensured oil supplies for the Royal Navy free from the risks of foreign controlled private speculation. Soon, the entire navy was well on its way to converting from coal to oil, a development of great tactical importance. Finally, there was the impetus Churchill provided to naval air, despite strong institutional resistance from the navy bureaucracy. In 1913, the first torpedo was launched from a British aircraft; and that same year the Hermes, completely converted to carry airplanes, was extremely successful in the North Sea maneuvers. When hostilities began, the former critics of naval air began to clamor for greater activity; or as one naval air pioneer summed it up: "They have pissed on Churchill's plant for three years – now they expect blooms in a month."[12]

When the war came, the First Lord was ready and happy. "Is it not horrible to be built like that?" he wrote his wife on 28 July 1914. "The preparations have a hideous fascination for me."[13] And a few days later when war was declared, Lloyd George recalled Churchill's entrance into a gloomy cabinet meeting. "Winston dashed into the room radiant," he wrote, "his face bright, his manner keen, one word pouring out on another .... You could see he was really a happy man."[14] Part of Churchill's happiness was due to his decision on 26 July to order the fleet, which was assembled for review at Portland, not to disperse in view of the increasingly tense international situation. That decision was one of the decisive acts of the war, particularly because of the unnoticed dispatch of the fleet on the night of 29–30 July to its war station at Scapa Flow.

In later years, Churchill could be almost lyrical in his romantic description of that July night when the fleet moved northward, "squadron by squadron, scores of gigantic castles of steel wending their way across the misty, shining sea, like giants bowed in anxious thought."[15] But it was his rational, pragmatic reason for the decision, which he shared only with the Prime Minister, that provided the most insightful glimpse of Churchill's conception of readiness, decision-making and surprise. "My own part in these events was a very simple one," he wrote. "It was ... to make sure that the diplomatic situation did not get ahead of the naval situation, and that the Grand Fleet should be in its War Station before Germany could know whether or not we should be in the war, *and therefore if possible before we had decided ourselves.*"[16]

In addition to his movement of the Grand Fleet, Churchill made two other strategic contributions early in the war that clearly illustrated the romantic-rational tension bequeathed to him by his Victorian past. The first was his impulsive dispatch of a marine brigade to Ostend on 27 August with orders to give the unit's presence the fullest publicity. By 5 September, the momentous day in the Battle of the Marne when French troops from Paris were moving to strike at the flank of the German First Army, that army believed that its rear was seriously menaced, primarily due to the Ostend expedition. How much effect that belief had on the German command at that crucial stage is not definitely known. Nevertheless, the 5 September message that the "English are disembarking fresh troops continuously on the Belgian coast" must have placed insidiously enervating pressures on the German commanders as the Battle of the Marne reached its climax.[17]

The second strategic contribution was Churchill's dispatch of one marine brigade and two newly formed brigades of naval volunteers to Antwerp as the German bombardment of that city began on 28 September 1914. That reinforcement delayed but could not prevent the capitulation of Antwerp on 10 October. Yet as Liddell Hart has pointed out, the defense of that important port was the deciding factor in slowing the German advance down the Belgian coast, thereby defeating the second attempt to gain a decision in the West. It was the extra days gained by the Churchill expedition that allowed the transfer of the main British force from the Aisne to the new left of the Allied line. "While the heroic defense of Ypres ... was the human barrier to the Germans," Liddell Hart concluded, "it succeeded by so narrow a margin that the Antwerp expedition must be adjudged the saving factor."[18] Churchill would have agreed with the conclusion. "Ten days were wanted," he wrote, "and ten days were won."[19]

The situation at Antwerp was also ideally suited for someone who conceived of himself as an heroic man of action. Churchill arrived at the besieged port, resplendent in the uniform of Trinity House, reminding one witness of nothing more than "a scene in a melodrama where the hero dashes up bare-headed on a foam-flecked horse, and saves the heroine, or the old homestead, or the family fortune, as the case may be."[20] Soon, he was at the center of the fight for the city where he was observed by the London war correspondent of an Italian newspaper.

> In the battle line ... stood a man enveloped in a cloak and wearing a yachting cap. He was tranquilly smoking a large cigar and looked at the progress of the battle under a rain of shrapnel which I can only call fearful .... It must be confessed that it is not easy to find in all Europe a Minister who would be capable of smoking peacefully under that shell-fire. He smiled and looked quite satisfied.[21]

Churchill's reaction to the situation at Antwerp was an impulsive proposal that he resign his cabinet post and assume local command, a request that reduced the British Cabinet to roars of laughter when Asquith read Churchill's message out loud. "What amazed and shook me was the sense of proportion (or lack of it) revealed by Winston's choice," Violet Asquith wrote of the affair. "His desire to exchange the Admiralty ... seemed to me to be hardly adult. It was the choice of a romantic child."[22] The action at close range was irresistible to Churchill, and after his return from Antwerp, he continued to press the Prime Minister for permission to return to the front. "Having, as he says, tasted blood these last few days," Asquith wrote of Churchill, "he is beginning, like a tiger, to raven for more, and begs that he ... may be relieved of his present office and put in some kind of military command .... His mouth waters at the sight and thought of Kitchener's new armies."[23]

Such commands would not be his for over a year, and then only because of the Gallipoli disaster. Still, the romance of war and the joy of being at the center of important events continued to play an important role for the remainder of Churchill's tenure as First Lord, despite the casualties that emerged from the conflict. "I think a curse should rest on me because I am so happy," he wrote during the Gallipoli campaign in the spring of 1915. "I know the war is smashing and shattering the lives of thousands every moment and yet – I cannot help it – I enjoy every second I live."[24]

THE REMARKABLE TRINITY

The wars of kings were at an end; the wars of people were beginning.

Marshal Foch

Struggling forward through the mire and filth of the trenches, across the corpse-strewn crater fields, amid the flaring, crashing, blasting barrages and murderous machine-gun fire, conscious of their race, proud of their cause, they seized the most formidable soldiery in Europe by the throat, slew them and hurled them unceasingly backward .... The battlefields of the Somme were the graveyards of Kitchener's Army. The flower of that generous manhood ... was shorn away forever in 1916. Unconquerable except by death, which they had conquered, they have set up a monument of native virtue which will command the wonder, the reverence and the gratitude of our island people as long as we endure as a nation among men.

Churchill, *The World Crisis 1916–1918*, Pt. 1, pp. 195–196

What was the sense of capturing a hill in the heart of Germany at such heavy loss? Were there not many such hills?

Tory questions posed to Marlborough after the storming of the Schellenberg. *Marlborough*, Vol. IV, p. 40

In the nineteenth century, Clausewitz examined what he termed the "remarkable trinity" of the government, the people and the army, and concluded that the relationship between the elements of the trinity would vary according to a number of variables. What he had not anticipated was the industrial revolution, mass literacy and the gigantic surge forward in science and technology in all those areas that were to bring the elements of the trinity into a new relationship focused on total war. Churchill sensed the beginnings of that new relationship in the Clausewitzian trinity as a result of his experience in the Boer War. In a prescient speech in May 1901, he pointed out that

> a European war cannot be anything but a cruel, heart-rending struggle, which, if we are ever to enjoy the bitter fruits of victory, must demand, perhaps for several years, the whole manhood of the nation, the entire suspension of peaceful industries, and the concentration to one end of every vital energy in the country.

Earlier wars on the margin of the Empire were one thing, he concluded,

> but now, when mighty populations are impelled against each other, each individual severally embittered and inflamed – when the resources of science and civilization sweep away everything that might mitigate their fury, a European war can only end in the ruin of the vanquished and the scarcely less fatal dislocation and exhaustion of the conquerors. Democracy is more vindictive than cabinets. The wars of peoples will be more terrible than the wars of kings.[25]

The First World War required a total mobilization for which there was no example to guide the British government. It was a total war in the sense that its rigors were not just confined to front-line combatants, but to entire populations on what came to be called the "Home Front," no matter how distant from the battle area. For the people of Britain, as the war progressed, the conflict brought every aspect of their lives under an ever-increasing control and regimentation ranging from freedom of action and speech to employment and even diet. Churchill was intimately involved in many of the major issues that arose from the regimentation of the Home Front. As early as 1915, he was urging a more discriminate acceptance of volunteers in terms of civilian employment in war-essential industries; and during the conscription crisis of 1916, he fought against the compromise solution which "neither secured the numbers of men that would be needed, nor did it meet the new fierce demand for equalization of sacrifice."[26] But it was his head-on encounter with industrial unrest after joining Lloyd George's government in 1917 to head the Ministry of Munitions, that brought home to Churchill the importance of the people on the Home Front of total war. Typically, he answered many of the grievances with pragmatic, common-sense solutions that demonstrated to them their importance in the total effort. That effort, he told over 4,000 workers at the Ponders End munitions factory in October 1917, "was not a war only of armies, or even mainly of armies. It was a war of whole nations ...."[27]

The military, of course, was still a major element in the "remarkable trinity." But Churchill had recognized a fundamental problem between that element and the government during Britain's initial skirmish with total war in South Africa. "It is not enough," he wrote to Joseph Chamberlain in 1901, "for the Government to say 'we have handed the war over to the military: they must settle it: all we can do is to supply them as they require!' I protest against the view. Nothing can relieve the Government of their responsibility."[28]

That belief was reinforced by Churchill's pre-war problems as First Lord with the high-level naval bureaucracy, which prevented the formation of a naval general staff and prevented or slowed many of his cherished projects. But it was the Admiralty's resistance to the convoy system, in which the "means of salvation were forced upon them from outside and below," that in all probability confirmed Churchill's views.[29] The adoption of that system, as Churchill noted, was the result of a struggle

> between the amateur politicians, thrown by democratic Parliamentary institutions to the head of affairs ... and the competent, trained, experienced experts of the Admiralty .... The astonishing fact is that the politicans were right ... upon a technical professional question ostensibly quite outside their sphere, and the Admiralty authorities were wrong ... upon what was, after all, the heart and centre of their own peculiar job.[30]

The Admiralty's view on the matter was simply that the larger the number of ships that formed a convoy, the greater the chance of a German submarine attacking successfully and the greater the difficulty for the escort ships to prevent such an attack. Churchill, on the other hand, used imagination and pragmatic logic to seek out "what was overlooked in this high, keen and earnest consensus."

> The size of the sea is so vast that the difference between the size of a convoy and the size of a single ship shrinks in comparison almost to insignificance. There was in fact very nearly as good a chance of a convoy of forty ships in close order slipping unperceived between the patrolling U-boats as there was for a single ship; and each time this happened, forty ships escaped instead of one .... The concentration of ships greatly reduced the number of targets in a given area and thus made it more difficult for the submarines to locate their prey. Moreover the convoys were easily controlled and could be quickly deflected by wireless from areas known to be dangerous at

any given moment. Finally the destroyers, instead of being dissipated on patrol over wide areas, were concentrated at the point of the hostile attack, and opportunities of offensive action frequently arose.[31]

As he became more immersed in the total conflict of the First World War, Churchill became increasingly concerned that policy must dominate strategy at the highest leadership. "The distinction between politics and strategy," he wrote, "diminishes as the point of view is raised. At the summit true politics and strategy are one."[32] But the civilian apparatus for control at that level was lacking. After the Dardanelles campaign, Churchill pointed out that "no one had the power to give clear brutal orders which would command unquestioning respect. Power was widely disseminated among the many important personages who in this period formed the governing instrument."[33] And to Asquith, he wrote concerning Lord Kitchener in October 1915: "The experiment of putting a great soldier at the head of the War Office in time of war has not been advantageous. In the result we have neither a Minister responsible to Parliament nor a General making a plan."[34] But the key was responsible power. "I will never accept political responsibility," Churchill concluded, "without recognized regular power."[35]

Even the more highly controlled and centralized government under Lloyd George, who took office in 1916, was not adequate to the task as far as Churchill was concerned. By that time, the dispute between the military, or "brass hats," and the politicians, or "frocks," was public knowledge. In fact, it was the people who tipped the scales in favor of the "brass hats" in the dispute, since the general public impression was that the military leaders must be right on matters of war. That impression, as Churchill pointed out, however, "was not entirely in accordance with the facts, and facts, especially in war, are stubborn things."[36] The basic fact, as Churchill increasingly realized, was that the broad issues of total war were so complex and far-reaching that the coordination of ends, means and ways for the war effort could only be accomplished at the highest policy level. "The General no doubt was an expert on how to move his troops," he observed, "and the Admiral upon how to fight his ships .... But outside this technical aspect they were helpless and misleading arbiters in problems in whose solution the aid of the Statesman, the financier, the manufacturer, the inventor, the psychologist, was equally required."[37]

At the root of Churchill's concern with policy's relationship to strategy was the evolution of the bloody attritive trench warfare on the Western Front. "We should be ill-advised to squander our new armies," he wrote upon leaving office in 1915, "in frantic and sterile efforts to pierce the German lines. To do so is to play the German game." And that game at the tactical and operational level had undergone a fundamental change.

"We are ... in the unsatisfactory position," he concluded, "of having lost our ground before the defensive under modern conditions was understood, and having to retake it when the defensive has been developed into a fine art."[38] But it was the national strategic, long-range aspect of total war, which took into account both allied and enemy Home Fronts as well as the battle areas, that formed the underlying basis for Churchill's concern. That autumn, in explaining his resignation from the government to the Commons, the former First Lord underscored the linkage between that aspect of total war and the concepts of attrition and exhaustion that were emerging from the conflict.

> The old wars were decided by their episodes rather than by their tendencies. In this war the tendencies are far more important than the episodes. Without winning any sensational victories we may win the war. We may win it during a continuance of extremely disappointing and vexatious events. It is not necessary for us in order to win the war to push the German lines back over all the territory they have absorbed, or to pierce them .... Germany may be defeated more fatally in the second or third year of the war than if the Allied Armies had entered Berlin in the first.[39]

After his resignation from Asquith's coalition government, Churchill moved to the Western Front, where from January to May 1916 he commanded the 6th Battalion, Royal Scots Fusiliers located at the village of Ploegsteert on the Ypres–Armentières road. Churchill's command experience at "Plug Street" confirmed his ambivalence about war in the modern era. On the one hand, no matter how grim the troglodyte world of the trenches, there was the visceral, combative exultation that had not changed since the days of the Malakand Field Force. "My beloved," he wrote his wife in January, "... I have just come back from the line, having had a jolly day."[40] In that context, even the grimness of attritive warfare could be viewed through the romantic prism of death's grandeur in a Victorian "last stand." In a letter written while an offensive was in progress, Churchill referred to "the bloody & blasted squalor of the battlefield," noting of a battalion that had lost 420 men out of 550 in that battle: "I shd feel vy proud if I had gone through such a cataclysm."[41] On the other hand, there was the daily proof offered by the ongoing carnage of Verdun. "Do you think we should succeed in an offensive," he wrote his wife in April, "if the Germans cannot do it with all their skill & science?"[42] And that same month, he wrote to Birkenhead that Verdun seemed "to vindicate all I have ever said or written about the offensives by either side in the West."[43]

Churchill returned to the subject of Verdun in May 1916 after his release from the army. In an objective, pragmatic speech to Commons, he warned against a philosophy that within two months would result in the Somme campaign. "The argument which is used that 'it is our turn now,' " he said, "has no place in military thought. Whatever is done must be done in the cold light of science ...."[44] And later that month, he reminded his listeners in the Commons that every 24 hours nearly a thousand men, "Englishmen, Britishers, men of our own race, are knocked into bundles of bloody rags ...."[45] In August, Churchill followed up those speeches with a memorandum for Parliament outlining the British and German losses thus far at the Somme, using his military knowledge to help compute the horrific figures. "Nothing in the great operations on the Somme," he later concluded from those figures, "affords any promise of finality or of a definite decision .... We must, therefore, either find another theater or another method."[46]

Decisiveness must, in other words, be returned to the battlefield as it had been in Victorian times, but without the cost extracted thus far by machine age total war. And that, as Churchill concluded, depended on the element of surprise. Surprise was what allowed maneuver to dominate static warfare. That was the essence of Gallipoli which for him had not been so much a failure of surprise, as a failure to exploit surprise. If there were attritive battles, Churchill argued in an October 1917 memorandum, they should at the very least be complemented by maneuvers based on surprise. "They mutually aid each other," he concluded, "and it might well be that the results of the battle of Exhaustion would be reaped on the battlefield of Surprise."[47] Moreover, that harvest could also be aided by the use of all the elements of intelligence and science that made up the "Great Game," to which Churchill had been devoted since the beginning of the war and which he increasingly saw as a key to ending attritive trench warfare, so far removed from the glorious combat of his youth. "Battles are won by slaughter and manoeuvre," he wrote.

> The greater the general, the more he contributes in manoeuvre, the less he demands in slaughter. ... Nearly all the battles which are regarded as masterpieces of the military art ... have been battles of manoeuvre in which very often the enemy has found himself defeated by some novel expedient or device, some queer, swift, unexpected thrust or stratagem .... There is required for the composition of a great commander ... not only imagination, but also an element of legerdemain, an original and sinister touch, which leaves the enemy puzzled as well as beaten. It is because military leaders are credited with gifts of this order ... that their profession is held in such high honour. For if their art were nothing more than a dreary process of exchanging lives, and counting heads at the end, they would rank much lower in the scale of human esteem.[48]

THE GREAT GAME

Royalty and Prime Ministers must never be taken by surprise.
Admiral Sir Hugh Sinclair,
Brigadier Menzies' predecessor as "C"

The importance of secrecy and the consequences of leakage of
information in war are here proclaimed.
Churchill, *The Second World War*, Vol. IV, p. 253

Churchill was drawn into the "Great Game" during the First World War
by his romantic perception of a world of cloak and dagger, in which reality
often matched his fertile imagination. "In the higher ranges of Secret
Service work," he wrote, "the actual facts in many cases were in every
respect equal to the most fantastic inventions of romance or melodrama.
Tangle within tangle, plot and counter-plot, ruse and treachery, cross and
double-cross, true agent, the bomb, the dagger and the firing party were
interwoven in many a texture so intricate as to be incredible and yet
true."[49] The link between fiction and reality was illustrated by the case
of Somerset Maugham who was recruited as a secret agent in 1915 and
dispatched to Switzerland under the pretext of writing a play "in the peace
and quiet of a neutral country." Maugham's experience in that country
soon provided ample material for the first of his semi-autobiographical
short stories about the secret agent Ashenden which were, as Maugham
admitted, "on the whole a very truthful account of my experiences." Too
truthful. At one point, Churchill, who was a friend of the author, pointed
out that many of the stories were in violation of the Official Secrets Act.
As a result, Maugham burned the manuscripts of 14 stories and waited
until 1928 to publish the remainder.[50]

Churchill's involvement in the "Great Game," however, also demonstrated that rational pragmatic side to his character that had emerged from
the Victorian era. As Home Secretary in 1910–11, for example, he contributed to the growth of the home department of the Secret Service
Bureau. During that period, the young Cabinet member served as first
chairman of the Aliens Subcommittee of the CID and approved the
preparation of a secret register of aliens from potential enemy countries.
Equally important, Churchill was instrumental in the authorization of
general warrants that allowed on a recurring basis the interception of
correspondence pertaining to any person on or added to the secret register.
Those activities were tied, in part, to invasion scares, which over the years
had spawned a large number of popular fictional accounts, beginning in
the Victorian era with the prototypal invasion story *The Battle of Dorking*,
and reaching cottage industry proportions in the Edwardian period with
such enormously popular stories as *The Riddle of the Sands*.[51]

Churchill's response as First Lord of the Admiralty to the overblown romance of those scares was equally hardheaded and practical. He was an active member of the Invasion Committee. In 1913, he prepared a series of papers for that body, outlining possible German courses of action in wartime, using his fertile imagination to stimulate thought and to expose weak points in the defense arrangements of the Admiralty War Staff. To that end, he also initiated a series of war games "in which, aided by one or the other of my naval advisers, I took one side, usually the German and forced certain situations."[52] One of those situations was the landing of German troops, aided by secret agents, on Britain's east coast just at the time when a British force was moving to the Continent to form the left flank of the French Army. Churchill's detailed scenario included rioting in London to prevent the departure of more troops after the Germans had landed, as well as a description of three German divisions fighting their way through the London suburbs.[53]

Throughout World War I, Churchill continued to apply that type of imaginative approach to the ever-expanding parameters of the "Great Game." The advent of wireless communication opened up an entirely new field of signal intelligence (Sigint), the impact of which the First Lord grasped immediately. Once again, he was on Heliograph Hill as the enemy approached. Only now he could actually listen to the conversation as the messages were plucked from the air. The science and technology that spawned Sigint also caused the attritive stalemate of total war on the Western Front. Ironically, part of the cure for that stalemate lay in the cause — a fact that Churchill, with his ultimate Victorian perception of science as a means of progress, realized from the first bloody encounters in the trenches. As a result, he devoted much of his efforts in the "Great Game" throughout the war to creating the means for technological surprise. Finally, the immensity of total war honed Churchill's already keen appreciation from Victorian days of tactical intelligence, while expanding his knowledge and appreciation of the need for operational and strategic intelligence. By the end of the conflict, he was a voracious consumer of any information that could support the "Great Game" at all levels of war.

Sigint

So now the Admiralty wireless whispers through the ether to the tall masts of ships, and captains pace their decks absorbed in thought.

Churchill, *The World Crisis 1911–1914*, p. 45

Early British codebreaking successes in World War I began Churchill's lifelong enthusiasm for Sigint. Those successes were due to three incredible code windfalls from around the world. The first was the seizure of the *Handelsverkehrsbuch* (HVB), a code used primarily by the German navy to communicate with merchant ships, but also employed within the High Sea Fleet. Although the code was seized by the Royal Australian Navy from a steamship near Melbourne in August 1914, the Germans continued to use it until March 1916. The second and more important windfall was the *Signalbuch der Kaiserlichen Marine* (SKM) provided by the Russians. On 6 September, Churchill received the news from the Russian naval attaché that the German light cruiser *Magdeburg* had gone down in the Baltic, and that the Russians had picked up a German crew member with the cipher and signal books, in Churchill's words, "clasped in his bosom by arms rigid in death ...." By mid-October, "these sea-stained priceless documents" were in the First Lord's hands.[54] The SKM was studied in Whitehall where, as Churchill noted, "self-effacing industry and imaginative genius reached their highest degree," affording Britain "the incomparable advantage of reading the plans and orders of the enemy before they were executed."[55] Two months later, a British trawler found a lead-lined chest from a sunken German destroyer in its nets. Among the papers in the chest was the last of the three German naval codes, the *Verkehrsbuch* (VB).

The combination of the various code books brought new successes which, in turn, encouraged the enthusiastic First Lord to make new organizational efforts. On 8 November 1914, Churchill issued a memorandum, for which he devised a new formula, "Exclusively Secret," appointing Sir Alfred Ewing "to study all decoded intercepts, not only current but past, and to compare them continually with what actually took place in order to penetrate the German mind and movements and make reports."[56] The sheer volume of Sigint, of course, soon rendered Churchill's instructions ludicrous. Nevertheless, the charter did demonstrate Churchill's imaginative appreciation of a basic Sigint premise: "the great majority of decodes were of messages of a routine and humdrum nature, meaningless in themselves, but, when carefully collated and compared, capable of revealing matters of far greater significance than their own individual content."[57]

That same month, however, Churchill also appointed a new Director of the Intelligence Division (DID) who quickly solved the problem. The Director was Captain William Reginald "Blinker" Hall, whose nickname devolved from a habit of high-speed blinking combined with a pronounced facial twitch. In between blinks, Hall also possessed an unusually intense and piercing gaze, which Compton Mackenzie described as "a horn-rimmed horny eye" that could make the object of that scrutiny feel "like a nut about to be cracked by a toucan."[58]

Nevertheless, even the new DID had to guard against Churchill's overpowering eloquence and enthusiasm for hostile dialectic. Hall recalled one such episode late at night, in which Churchill not only attempted to bring the Intelligence Director around to his point of view, but seemed genuinely unaware of the effect his filibustering had. At one point, Hall felt himself being seduced by the First Lord's argument, and remembering the incident of the broken shards in *Kim*, in which the young boy is taught to resist hypnosis as part of the "Great Game," the DID began to mutter: "My name is Hall, my name is Hall." Churchill broke off his argument and looked at Hall with a frown. "What's that you're muttering to yourself?" he demanded. "I am saying to' myself," the Intelligence Director responded, "that my name is Hall because if I listen to you much longer, I shall be convinced it's Brown." Churchill began to laugh. "Then you don't agree with what I've been saying?" he said. "1st Lord," Hall said, "I don't agree with one word of it, but I can't argue with you; I've not had the training."[59]

The combination of Hall and Churchill soon meant an expansion of Sigint and a new crop of naval cryptographers. By the end of 1914, Ewing had five permanent staff under him, initially placed by Hall in Room 40 of the Admiralty Old Building and, as their numbers grew, in a series of adjoining rooms, but still known collectively by the innocuous collective title "Room 40 O.B." Churchill's enthusiasm for this new organization was quickly justified. On 14 December, Room 40 warned of an impending raid by German battle cruisers on British east coast towns combined with a minelaying operation off the Yorkshire coast. The Naval Chief of Staff, however, wrongly concluded without consulting Room 40 that the German High Seas Fleet would not support the raid. In actual fact, the fleet had been ordered to provide such support from the middle of the North Sea. Unaware of that, the Admiralty ordered only a part of the British Grand Fleet south from Scapa Flow to lay a trap for the German raiders.[60]

On the morning of 16 December, as Churchill lay soaking in his bath at the Admiralty, an officer came hurrying in from the War Room with the news that German battle cruisers were bombarding the coastal town of Hartlepool. Pulling on his clothes, the First Lord ran downstairs to the War Room and after conferring with the First Sea Lord and other officers, ordered the trap to be sprung. His sympathy for Hartlepool, as he later described it, was mingled with "the anodyne of contemplated retaliation."[61] But even that was denied. Through a series of comic opera signaling errors combined with poor visibility and a latent discovery of the German High Sea Fleet in the North Sea, the German raiders were allowed to escape the trap. "All concerned," an enraged First Sea Lord wrote, "made a hash of it."[62]

The German raids illustrated for the first time to Churchill the problems of modern intelligence in a total war involving the full support of the people.

Naturally there was much indignation at the failure of the Navy to prevent, or at least to avenge, such an attack upon our shores .... However, we could not say a word in explanation. We had to bear in silence the censures of our countrymen. We could never admit for fear of compromising our secret information where our squadrons were, or how near the German raiding cruisers had been to their destruction.[63]

There was, however, a reassuring side to the encounter. "The indications upon which we had acted," Churchill noted, "had been confirmed by events. The sources of information upon which we relied were evidently trustworthy."[64] So long as Room 40 could continue its successful decryption efforts, there would always be a forewarning of any German move into the North Sea. This meant, in turn, that it was no longer necessary for the Admiralty to keep the Grand Fleet in a constant state of complete readiness, nor were the sweeps by that fleet of the North Sea required on a continual basis. The implications for the fleet as well as for the British people were not lost on the First Lord.

Without the cryptographers' department ... the whole course of the naval war would have been different. The British Fleet could not have remained continuously at sea without speedily wearing down its men and machinery. Unless it had remained almost continuously at sea, the Germans would have been able to bombard two or three times a month all our East Coast towns ... and returned each time safely, or at least without superior attack, to their home bases .... The nation would have been forced to realize that the ruin of its East Coast towns was as much their part of the trial and burden as the destruction of so many Provinces to France.[65]

Churchill's faith in Room 40's ability was confirmed the following month in the Battle of the Dogger Bank. At noon on 23 January 1915, the former Sea Lord, Admiral "Tug" Wilson, who had begun work in the Admiralty the previous October without any formal post, burst in unannounced upon Churchill, still excited about the latest decrypts from Room 40. "First Lord," he announced, "those fellows are coming out again." "When?" was Churchill's response, to which Wilson replied: "Tonight. We have just got time to get Beatty there."[66] After listening to Wilson's analysis of the decrypts and the calculations for the interception of the German fleet, Churchill dispatched the messages that began to move Admiral Beatty's ships out to sea. That night at a dinner at the French Embassy, as he later recalled, the First Lord's faith in the Sigint of Room 40 allowed his romantic imagination free rein as he contemplated the next day's events.

One felt separated from the distinguished company who gathered there, by a film of isolated knowledge and overwhelming inward preoccupation. In December we had hardly credited our sources of information. All was uncertain. It had even seemed probable that nothing would occur. Now with that experience wrought into one's being, only one thought could reign – battle at dawn! Battle for the first time in history between mighty super-Dreadnought ships! And there was added a thrilling sense of a Beast of Prey moving stealthily forward hour by hour towards the Trap.[67]

Churchill was in the War Room before daylight the next morning. Just after 8 a.m., a telegram intercepted from the German fleet indicated that the enemy was off the Dogger Bank. The First Lord followed the subsequent action minute by minute in an agony of "cold excitement" from the silence of the War Room. For participants in any combat, as he well knew, there was the noise, confusion, and the physical and mental effort that kept a man of action focused on the unfolding battle. "But in Whitehall," he still wrote in frustration years after the Battle of the Dogger Bank,

> only the clock ticks, and quiet men enter with quick steps laying slips of pencilled paper before other men equally silent who draw lines and scribble calculations, and point with the finger or make brief subdued comments. Telegram succeeds telegram at a few minutes' interval as they are picked up and decoded ... and out of these a picture always flickering and changing rises in the mind, and imagination strikes out around it at every stage flashes of hope or fear.[68]

By noon, the battle was over; and although one of the four German battle cruisers had been sunk, there had been a combination once again of mixed signals and missed opportunities at the operational level. For Churchill, it was just one more piece in a mosaic depicting how wide the gap could be between accurate, timely strategic intelligence and successful use of that intelligence at the operational level. "Thus for the second time," he summed up the Dogger Bank action, "when already in the jaws of destruction, the German Battle Cruiser Squadron escaped."[69]

Science and Technology

> Thus ended the battle of Omdurman – the most signal triumph ever gained by the arms of science over barbarians.
>
> Churchill, *The River War*, p. 300

> Tanks are not opposed to infantry: they are an intimate and integral part of the infantryman's strength ....
>
> Churchill to Lloyd George, September 1918. Gilbert, IV, p. 146

Death stands at attention, obedient, expectant, ready to shear
away the peoples *en masse*; ready, if called on, to pulverize,
without hope of repair, what is left of civilization. He awaits
only the word of command. He awaits it from a frail, bewildered
being, long his victim, now – for one occasion only – his
master.

Churchill, *The Aftermath*, p. 483

Churchill's natural interest in scientific gadgetry deepened as World War
I progressed. Increasingly, he saw science and technology as a means to
break the military deadlock, much as innovations ranging from the scythed
chariot and the stirruped cavalry horse to the long bow and the Maxim
gun had enabled armies to achieve surprise and win unexpected victories
in the past. "Machines save lives," he asserted in the March 1917 Army
Estimates debate, "machine-power is a substitute for man-power ...."
Unless new devices were developed, he continued, "I do not see how we
are to avoid being thrown back on those dismal processes of waste and
slaughter which are called attrition."[70] At the end of the year, Churchill
reflected on allied progress with "new devices" and the fact that the
Germans appeared bent on resuming the offensive. "Let them traipse
across the crater fields," he wrote. "Let them rejoice in the occasional
capture of placeless names and sterile ridges; & let us dart here & there
armed with science and surprise ...."[71]

Churchill could be ambivalent about scientific inroads into personal
combat, lamenting that modern warfare should turn "to chemists in spec-
tacles, and chauffeurs pulling the levers of aeroplanes or machine
guns."[72] Nevertheless, there was also a ruthless pragmatism that overwhelmed any residual romanticism in terms of dealing with changes caused
by scientific and technological innovations and breakthroughs. "I am
strongly pressing," he wrote in 1917, "that the cavalry shd be put by
regiments into the tanks .... The future life of this arm after the war
depends upon their discarding the obsolete horse & becoming associated
with some form of military machinery having a scientific & real war
value."[73] And although he considered such German innovations as
poison gas to be "scientific barbarism," he was opposed to turning back
the technological clock if there was an allied advantage. In April 1918,
for example, when the International Red Cross attempted to use its
influence to end the use of poison gas in the war, Churchill responded
that he was "in favour of the greatest possible development of gas warfare, and of the fullest utilization of the winds, which favour us so much
more than the enemy ...."[74]

Churchill's attitude to the role that scientific and technological surprise
could play in the modern "Great Game" was demonstrated in his interaction with the evolution of the tank in World War I. In the beginning, his
restless imagination concentrated on protecting his fledgling Royal Naval

Air Service with an armored machine possessing large driving wheels and rollers in front to crush both barbed wire and trenches. It was not until 1915, because of the failure of those experiments coupled with the persuasive advocacy of several army officers, that Churchill advocated a tank with a caterpillar system which could advance into German lines, "smashing away all the obstructions and sweeping the trenches with their machine-gun fire ...."[75] Nevertheless, he never claimed primary proponency. He acknowledged that a 1903 H.G. Wells article "had practically exhausted the possibilities in this sphere." Moreover, there was also the small band of armor pioneers in the British Army. "There never was a moment when it was possible to say that a tank had been 'invented,'" Churchill wrote later. "There never was a person about whom it could be said 'this man invented the tank.'"[76]

In any case, Churchill quickly learned as First Lord of the Admiralty that the process of inventing was only part of the problem in the complex power hierarchy of total war. In 1915, for instance, he tied the lack of progress in tank development directly to government indifference. "The problem," he wrote, "of crossing two or three hundred yards of open ground and of traversing ... barbed wire in the face of rifles and machine guns ... ought not to be beyond the range of modern science if sufficient authority ... backed the investigation. The absence of any satisfactory method cannot be supplied by the bare breasts of gallant men."[77] And after the war, Churchill returned to the subject when he credited the armor pioneers in the British officer corps with seizing the idea of the tank and even presenting specific proposals before the War Office. "These officers," he noted, "had not however the executive authority which alone could ensure progress and their efforts were brought to nothing by the obstruction of some of their superiors. They were unfortunate in not being able to command the resources necessary for action, or to convince those who had the power to act."[78]

With authority must come coordination extending from the lab to the trenches. "A hiatus exists between inventors who know what they could invent, if they only knew what was wanted," Churchill wrote in 1916, "and the soldiers who know, or ought to know, what they want and would ask for it if they only knew how much science could do for them."[79] That belief was reinforced by his experience with the Stokes gun, a handheld mortar whose design was based on a front line need for immediately responsive, short range indirect fire to be used in attacks on trenches at close quarters. "All the ideas on which this scheme rests," he wrote after the demonstration, "have come from officers who have been themselves constantly engaged in trench warfare. In order to give a fair chance to such a method of attack, it is necessary that it should not be attempted until it can be applied on a very large scale."[80]

With that last injunction, Churchill returned to his primary motive for the use of science and technology in the "Great Game": surprise. As early as December 1915, he analysed the importance of that element in any armor attack, emphasizing that surprise "consists in novelty and suddenness."[81] But that novelty, he soon realized, could be dissipated quickly. Less than a year later at the Somme, 35 tanks were dispersed in small, ineffective groups along the entire front of the Fourth Army as it attacked. Lloyd George informed Churchill just prior to the assault. "I was so shocked at the proposal to expose this tremendous secret to the enemy upon such a petty scale," Churchill remembered, " ... that I sought an interview with Mr. Asquith."[82] But to no avail. The attack was a limited success which, in Churchill's opinion, "recklessly revealed to the enemy a secret that might have produced allied victory in 1917."

> The immense advantage of novelty and surprise was thus squandered while the number of the tanks was small, while their condition was experimental and their crews almost untrained. This priceless conception ... was revealed to the Germans for the mere petty purpose of taking a few ruined villages .... The enemy was familiarized with them by their piecemeal use ....[83]

On 9 November 1916, less than a month after the piecemeal British armor attack at the Somme, Churchill summed up in a memorandum to the government what was by then an axiom for him concerning technological surprise. "Don't familiarize the enemy by degrees with these methods of attack. Apply them when all is ready on the largest possible scale, and with the priceless advantage of surprise."[84] Later, as he looked back on the war, his thinking on the subject was reinforced by his study of the Eastern Front where, in at least one incident, technological surprise had been sacrificed to reinforce a deception operation. In April 1915, German forces were withdrawn from the Western Front to participate in the Gorlice–Tarnow offensive that was to begin on 2 May. To cover the withdrawal, "lively activity" was prescribed for the Western Front, the most formidable being the gas attack at Ypres that began on 22 April. Although gas had been used in a minor role with artillery shells, the attack at Ypres involved for the first time the continuous discharge of gas from cylinders. "The precipitate exposure of this deadly device at a time when no German reserves were at hand to exploit its surprising effects," Churchill observed, "was one of the debts which the Western allies owed to the Eastern Front."[85]

Such scientific and technological advances by the enemy were also never very far from Churchill's thoughts during the war. The U-boats, in particular, were a major problem, but at least they were under his jurisdiction. "Let every resource and invention be applied," he exhorted, as he would for the Battle of the Atlantic over a quarter of a century later. "Let the anti-submarine war claim priority and dominance over every other form of British effort."[86] After the war, he summed up the success of the collaborative effort that he had directed. "A close and fruitful union between the scientist, the inventor, and the submarine officer was established, the best brains of the navy were concentrated on the problem, and no idea, technical or tactical was spurned by the Admiralty Staff."[87]

That type of effort was also required wherever Churchill perceived the need for scientific and technological countermeasures. Science must be organized for technological surprise or that surprise might be reversed. "One of the most serious dangers that we are exposed to," he wrote the Prime Minister in 1915, "is the possibility that the Germans are ... preparing ... surprises, and that we may at any time find ourselves exposed to some entirely new form of attack. A committee of engineer officers and other experts ought to be sitting continually at the War Office to formulate schemes and examine suggestions ...."[88] In another case, Churchill received intelligence that the Germans were planning to send Zeppelins over England at such high altitudes that British planes could not reach them. "Apparently this calculation is at present well founded," he wrote. "If that is so, we ought to find without delay a means of sending aeroplanes up to even greater heights at night."[89] In addition, there were always the enemy reactions to British technological advances that must be considered. Shortly after the piecemeal armor commitment at the Somme, Churchill recommended in a memorandum marked by its rational, deductive scientific approach, that an Anti-Tank Committee be established "to study the methods by which tanks can be defeated."

> This body should work in the closest harmony with those concerned in the production and design of tanks, each striving to defeat the other, exchanging information and perfecting their methods. It is not to be supposed that the Germans will not develop tanks in their turn. We have the enormous advantage of being able to experiment on ourselves with them, and to find out the best ways by which they may be defeated.[90]

In the end, however, the Germans found no counter to properly planned allied tank offensives. At the Battle of Cambrai on 20 November 1917, for instance, General Byng used massed armor combined with tactical and operational surprise to achieve a decisive breakthrough in the German lines. "All the requisite conditions were at last accorded," Churchill wrote. "The tanks were to operate on ground not yet ploughed up by artillery, against a front not yet prepared to meet an offensive. Above all, Surprise! The Tanks were themselves to open the attack."[91] In fact, surprise was also achieved because of the synergistic effects of technological progress in other areas such as the science of gunnery. By the autumn of 1917, as a consequence, artillery did not require preliminary registration to be on target, and the British were able to open accurate, pre-planned fire at H-Hour.

The following August, General Rawlinson's great armored attack met with equal success. There were nearly 600 tanks involved, assisted not only by a thick morning mist, but by special noise barrages and artificial fog as well. In addition, there were 120 brigades of British artillery of all types ready to fire, but only after the attack commenced. "Everything was subordinated to the surprise of the tank attack," Churchill commented in this regard.[92] When the British tanks moved forward in the half light of the dawn, the Germans were unable to resist. "The essence of the whole plan was surprise," Churchill reemphasized later, and for him that surprise was due to Rawlinson's imaginative combination of new technology and doctrine. "It was, truly, *his* victory, and that of the Fourth Army which he directed," he continued. "He had put aside old fashioned ideas, he had used new weapons as they should be used, he had reaped swift and rich reward."[93]

Unlike Rawlinson, however, the majority of the Anglo-French commanders, in Churchill's judgment, had been captured by technology instead of harnessing it for novel, imaginative use that restored surprise and thus maneuver to warfare. Ultimately, however, as Churchill also pointed out, scientific and technological innovations that were provided from above to Marshals Haig and Foch in the summer of 1918 managed to bring victory.

> Both were now provided with offensive weapons, which the military science of neither would have conceived .... The Goddess of Surprise had at last returned to the Western Front. Thus both Haig and Foch were vindicated in the end. They were throughout consistently true to their professional theories, and when in the fifth campaign of the war the facts began for the first time to fit the theories, they reaped their just reward.[94]

THE INTERWAR YEARS

> Surely, Germans, for history it is enough!
> Churchill, *The World Crisis 1916–1918*, Pt. 2, p. 544

> By the time he arrived at the highest command he was passing the prime of life .... The early successes and repeated advancement ... were followed by lengthy intervals of stagnation.
> Churchill, *Marlborough*, Vol. I, p. 85

Churchill's attitude toward conflict remained ambivalent in the years after 1918 despite the experience of total war. That ambivalence was a legacy of his Victorian background. On the one hand, there was the rational, pragmatic, pessimistic participant who had seen the familiar Victorian-cum-Edwardian edifice crumble as a result of the changes wrought by total war on all three elements of the Clausewitzian trinity. On the other hand, there was the emotional, romantic optimist who still thrilled to the drum beat of war, the gadgetry of weapons and the fascination of combat, and who could still see progress as a final product, no matter how dismal the way stations appeared.

The Nature of War

Cooks use recipes for dishes and doctors have prescriptions for diseases, but every great operation of war is unique .... There is no surer road to ill-success in war than to imitate the plans of bygone heroes and to fit them to novel situations.

Churchill, *Marlborough*, Vol. I, pp. 114–115

Churchill had no more illusions about the effect of the Great War on the victors than he had about its effect on the vanquished. "The shadow of victory is disillusion," he wrote. "The reaction from extreme effort is prostration. The aftermath even of successful war is long and bitter."[95] That disillusion was evident throughout the interwar period, in which he often returned in his writings and speeches to the attritive slaughter of the trenches where combat had been "reduced to a business like the stockyards of Chicago."[96] And in 1922, his notes for an election speech began:

What a disappointment the Twentieth Century has been
How terrible & how melancholy
is long series of disastrous events
wh have darkened its first 20 years.[97]

It was natural in those circumstances that Churchill's thoughts would return to the "palmy days" of his youth. "Winston waxed very eloquent on the subject of the old world & the new," one friend noted in her diary in January 1920, "taking up arms in defence of the former ...."[98] But there was no immediate comfort or direction for him from the past in terms of the unprecedented cataclysm through which Britain had passed. "The Muse of History to whom we all so confidently appeal has become a Sphinx," he wrote. "A sad half mocking smile flickers on her stone war-scarred lineaments."[99] In a long and bitter discourse touched with longing, Churchill lashed out at the era of his youth. "How those Victorians busied themselves and contended about minor things!" he wrote. "... They never had to face as we have done, and still do, the possibility of national ruin. Their main foundations were never shaken."[100] That was not a past, he believed, that could help in the cold grey dawn of total war. Commenting on the effect of the new era on John Morley, the statesman whom he considered a quintessential Victorian, Churchill found that Morley "was dwelling in a world which was far removed from the awful reality."

At such a juncture his historic sense was no guide; it was indeed an impediment. It was vain to look back to the Crimean War, to the wars of 1866 and 1870, and to suppose that any of the political reactions which had attended their declaration or course would repeat themselves now. We were in the presence of events without their equal or forerunner in the whole experience of mankind.[101]

It was those unprecedented "events" that preoccupied Churchill in the post-war world. In researching his multi-volume biography of the First Duke of Marlborough during this period, he examined the restraints in earlier centuries, within which, under the structure of Christendom, even warring nations had acted. "In the twentieth century," he wrote sarcastically, "mankind has shaken itself free from all those illogical, old-world prejudices, and achieved the highest efficiency of brutal, ruthless war."[102] There were, of course, as Churchill came to realize, fundamental changes in modern society behind the abandonment of the old restraints that had led inexorably to total war in which the "entire population in one capacity or another took part ...."

> The organisation of mankind into great States and Empires and the rise of nations to full collective consciousness enabled enterprises of slaughter to be planned and executed upon a scale, with a perseverance, never before imagined. All the noblest virtues of individuals were gathered together to strengthen the destructive capacity of the mass. Good finances ... made it possible to divert for considerable periods the energies of whole peoples to the task of Devastation. Democratic institutions gave expression to the will-power of millions. Education ... rendered each person serviceable in a high degree for the purpose in hand. The Press afforded a means of unification and of mutual encouragement .... Lastly, Science unfolded her treasures and her secrets to the desperate demands of men and placed in their hands agencies and apparatus almost decisive in their character.[103]

The effect of those changes on combat, Churchill observed as he looked back during the first decade after the First World War, was the "obliteration of the personal factor in war, the stripping from high commanders of all the drama of the battlefield, the reducing of their highest function to pure office work ...." For him, the modern commander had become "entirely divorced from the heroic aspect by the physical conditions which have overwhelmed his art."

> No longer will Hannibal and Caesar, Turenne and Marlborough, Frederick and Napoleon, sit their horses on the battlefield and by their words and gestures direct and dominate ... the course of a supreme event. No longer will their fame and presence cheer their struggling soldiers. No longer will they share their perils, rekindle

their spirits and restore the day. They will not be there. They have been banished from the fighting scene, together with their plumes, standards and breast-plates.[104]

The general in such an environment was for Churchill no more than a "high-souled speculator," who would in the future "sit surrounded by clerks in offices, as safe, as quiet and dreary as Government departments, while the fighting men in scores of thousands are slaughtered or stifled over the telephone by machinery."[105] It would be efficient, but not heroic. "My gardener last spring," Churchill commented in that regard, "exterminated seven wasp's nests .... It was his duty and he performed it well. But I am not going to regard him as a hero."[106] It would be, as Churchill envisioned it, a pale, lifeless, unromantic, unemotional world of the masses, without the splash of color and the verve of great deeds and individual heroism.

The heroes of modern war lie out in the cratered fields, mangled, stifled, scarred; and there are too many of them for exceptional honours. It is mass suffering, mass sacrifice, mass victory. The glory which plays upon the immense scenes of carnage is diffused. No more the blaze of triumph irradiates the helmets of the chiefs. There is only the pale light of a rainy dawn by which forty miles of batteries recommence their fire, and another score of divisions flounder to their death in mud and poison gas .... The wars of the future will be even less romantic and picturesque.[107]

War, in short, had "been stripped of glitter and glamour." If war should come again, Churchill reflected bitterly, "poets will not sing nor sculptors chisel the deeds of conquerors. It may well be that chemists will carry off what credit can be found," in a competition "to kill women and children and the civil population generally, and victory will give herself in sorry nuptials to the diligent hero who organizes it on the largest scale."[108] Once again it was the scale. Mass, impersonal death meant the end of the very basis for Victorian wars. Looking back on the battle of Omdurman after the First World War, Churchill commented in sorrow on the passing of that "sporting game" under the new rules of total war:

This kind of war was full of fascinating thrills. It was not like the Great War. Nobody expected to be killed. Here and there in every regiment or battalion, half a dozen, a score, at the worst thirty or forty, would pay the forfeit; but to the great mass of those who took part in the little wars of Britain in those vanished light-hearted days, this was only a sporting element in a splendid game. Most of us were fated to see a war where the hazards were reversed, where death was the general expectation and severe wounds were counted as lucky escapes, where whole brigades were shorn away under the steel flail

68

of artillery and machine-guns, where the survivors of one tornado knew that they would certainly be consumed in the next or the next after that.[109]

In *A Farewell to Arms*, Ernest Hemingway declared that "abstract words such as glory, honor, courage, or hallow were obscene beside the concrete names of villages, the numbers of roads, the names of rivers, the numbers of regiments and the dates." For Churchill, however, the Great War could not destroy the meaning of such abstractions which remained for him permanent and reliable, no matter what had transpired in the troglodyte world of the Western Front. One day after that conflict, someone remarked in his presence that nothing was worse than war. "Dishonour," Churchill immediately replied in full voice, "is worse than war − slavery is worse than war."[110]

It was not that Churchill failed to see the conditions of modern war, even as he experienced them. "Never for a moment," he could write to his wife in May 1917, "does the thought of this carnage & ruin escape my mind ...."[111] But he would not allow the squalor to fully penetrate his inner Victorian core. His romantic perception of what conflict had been and therefore what it should be remained a dominant counterweight to his realistic assessment of total war. It was a perception so powerful that it influenced even the disillusioned like Robert Graves and Siegfried Sassoon. Sassoon later recounted how he wondered if Churchill, during their September 1918 meeting, had been entirely serious when he said that "war is the normal occupation of man." Churchill had gone on to add "war − and gardening" as a qualifier. "But it had been unmistakable," Sassoon concluded, "that for him war was the finest activity on earth ...."[112]

It was, of course, not as simple as Sassoon described. Churchill's description, for instance, of the French General Mangin reflected the ambiguity of his feelings. On the one hand, there was the incredibly brave and resourceful general personally leading the men at Verdun and along the Chemin des Dames "like a hungry leopard." On the other hand, there was "Mangin the Butcher," relieved temporarily for the losses his leadership had inflicted on his own troops. In a similar manner, there was his mixed analysis of General Hubert Gough, the Fifth Army Commander. "He was a typical cavalry officer, with a strong personality and a gay and boyish charm of manner," Churchill wrote. "A man who never spared himself or his troops, the instrument of costly and forlorn attacks, he emerged from the Passchendaele tragedy pursued by many fierce resentments."[113]

But generally, despite his disillusionment, Churchill could still find the heroic men of action as he looked back on the Great War. There was, for instance, Bernard Freyberg, the New Zealander, whom he had befriended as a Sub-Lieutenant at the beginning of the war, commanding elements of four divisions in 1918 while successfully holding a front of 4,000 yards. And there was General Tudor and his Ninth Division, whom he visited just before the Ludendorff offensive in March 1918. "The impression I had of Tudor," Churchill wrote, "was of an iron peg hammered into the frozen ground, immovable. And so indeed it proved." Before he left the battlefield that day, Churchill turned and once again looked back on the men of the Ninth Division. "I see them now, serene as the Spartans of Leonidas on the eve of Thermopylae."[114]

Strength, in other words, even in total war was not enough for Churchill. There must also be the valor and steadfastness that he had known in his early years in a previous era. Marshal Foch, in this view, despite disastrous errors was redeemed by his "obstinate combativeness." "He was fighting all the time," Churchill wrote of Foch, "whether he had armies to launch or only thoughts."[115] Such characteristics, Churchill came to believe, were even more important at the political level of total war, when national survival was the stake. That lesson was provided by Georges Clemenceau, whom he met many times during the war and who, he considered, "embodied and expressed France. As much as any single human being, miraculously magnified, can ever be a nation, he was France."

It was the fiery French Premier's indomitability and willingness to take any measures on both the Home Front and the fighting front in order to emerge triumphant that most impressed Churchill. "Happy the nation," he wrote of Clemenceau, "which when its fate quivers in the balance can find such a tyrant and such a champion." And in a passage that presaged his own emergence in the spring of 1940, Churchill described Clemenceau's final call to public life, which marked the beginning of the end for France's misfortunes: "He returned to power as Marius had returned to Rome; doubted by many, dreaded by all, but doom-sent, inevitable."[116]

In the 1930s as he researched and wrote his history of Marlborough, Churchill returned again and again to his ancestor's "combination of mental, moral, and physical qualities adapted to action which were so lifted above the common run as to seem almost godlike." His studies renewed his faith in the man of action, whose every word "was decisive. Victory often depended upon whether he rode half a mile this way or that."[117] Such a man could make a difference in any type of conflict, particularly if he combined valor with common sense. In the fourth volume of his biography, Churchill lingered over the aftermath of the battle of Elixem in which Marlborough had pierced the Lines of Brabant with almost no Confederation casualties. Even as the battle neared its end, his grateful troops responded with spontaneous mass affection. As he rode up sword in hand to take his place in the final cavalry charge, the soldiers and their officers broke into cheering, extremely unusual considering the formal military etiquette of the times. And afterwards, when Marlborough moved along the front of his army, the veterans of Blenheim, as Churchill described it, "cast discipline to the winds and hailed him everywhere with proud delight."[118]

Surely there was still room in modern warfare for men like Duke John who in order to seal the victory at Ramillies, personally led a cavalry charge on the left wing, in Churchill's words, "transported by the energy of his war vision and passion."[119] In October 1940, that was still a concern as the Prime Minister attempted to bring Major-General PCS Hobart back to active duty against the resistance of the General Staff. "I am not at all impressed by the prejudices against him in certain quarters," he minuted. "Such prejudices attach frequently to persons of strong personality and original view." This was a time, Churchill added, "to try men of force and vision and not to be exclusively confined to those who are judged thoroughly safe by conventional standards." The minute continued:

> We are now at war, fighting for our lives, and we cannot afford to confine Army appointments to persons who have excited no hostile comment in their career. The catalogue of General Hobart's qualities and defects might almost exactly have been attributed to most of the great commanders of British history. Marlborough was very much not the conventional soldier, carrying with him the goodwill of the Service. Cromwell, Wolfe, Clive, Gordon, and in a different sphere Lawrence, all had very close resemblance to the characteristics set down as defects.[120]

It was a perceptive use of history for a man whose belief in historical continuity had been momentarily suspended by the advent of total war. Already in 1929, however, Churchill was referring to history "as a guide to present difficulties" to Katherine Asquith. "How strange it is," he wrote, "that the past is so little understood and so quickly forgotten. We live in the most thoughtless of ages. Every day headlines and short views."[121] And in the following decade as he moved back and forth in the late seventeenth- and early eighteenth-century life of his ancestor, Churchill began to appreciate the totality of the stakes in the more limited warfare of Marlborough's time. The battle of Blenheim, for instance, had changed the political axis of the world at that time. If that battle had been lost, he concluded, the "collapse of the Grand Alliance and the hegemony of France in Europe must have brought with them so profound a disintegration of English political society that for perhaps a century at least vassalage under a French-inspired king might well have been our fate."[122] Even attritive warfare had its characteristics of continuity. In fact, as Churchill concluded, the "spectacle of one of the battlefields of Marlborough, Frederick, or Napoleon was ... incomparably more gruesome than any equal sector of the recent fronts in France or Flanders."[123] In that light, World War I became for Churchill part of the grand historical pattern of Britain.

71

For the fourth time in four successive centuries she had headed and sustained the resistance of Europe to a military tyranny .... Spain, the French Monarchy, the French Empire and the German Empire.... During 400 years England had withstood them all by war and policy, and all had been defeated and driven out. To that list of mighty sovereigns and supreme military Lords which already included Philip II, Louis XIV and Napoleon, there could now be added the name of William II of Germany.[124]

His renewed faith in historical continuity caused Churchill to face up rationally and pragmatically to the prospect of future total wars. "The story of the human race is War," he wrote. " ... But the modern developments surely require severe and active attention."[125] In looking back on World War I in that regard, Churchill acknowledged that any romantic predilections in total war had to be supported by large doses of realistic, tangible support. "Foch's famous war cries, 'Allez à la bataille,' 'Tout le monde à la bataille,' " he commented, "would have caused no more meaning to history than a timely cheer, but for the series of tremendous drives and punches with which the British armies ... trampled down the ... German military might ...."[126]

But a world without emotional romanticism, without heroics and heroic men of action did not have to be the fate of total war. "There is a sense of vacancy and of fatuity, of incompleteness," he wrote as he observed disillusioned Britain in the interwar years. "We miss our giants." If the British people, Churchill warned, quit "the stern, narrow high-roads which alone lead to glorious destinies and survival," there would be nothing left but a "blundering on together in myriad companies, like innumerable swarms of locusts, chirping and devouring towards the salt sea ...."[127] Despite modern forces and trends, despite the stark realities of modern life and warfare, there must still be the indefinable, romantic aspirations of Victorian times. Britain had emerged victorious from the Great War on a new and higher plateau, Churchill concluded,

but the scenery is unimpressive. We mourn the towering grandeur which surrounded and cheered our long painful ascent. Ah! if we could only find some new enormous berg rising towards the heavens as high above our plateau as those old mountains down below rose above the plains and marshes! We want a monarch peak, with base enormous, whose summit is for ever hidden from our eyes by clouds, and down whose precipices cataracts of sparkling waters thunder.[128]

The Remarkable Trinity

> I became accountable for an operation the vital control of
> which had passed to other hands.
>
> Churchill, *Thoughts and Adventures*, p. 7

> Those who are charged with the direction of supreme affairs
> must sit on the mountain-tops of control ....
>
> Churchill, *Thoughts and Adventures*, p. 7

For Churchill, certain facts emerged from the First World War, "solid, inexorable, like the shapes of mountains from drifting mist," concerning the interaction in total war between the government, people and the military — the elements of Clausewitz' "remarkable trinity." To begin with, there was the total involvement of the people. "It is established that henceforward whole populations will take part in war," he wrote, "all doing their utmost, all subjected to the fury of the enemy."[129] That type of participation must be encouraged, Churchill believed. If nation states were to emerge triumphant from total war, the entire populace must remain in support of the government. In such an environment, with a nation at arms, satire and criticism had no place for him, no matter how talented the source. "When nations are fighting for life," he wrote of George Bernard Shaw,

> when the Palace in which the Jester dwells not uncomfortably, is
> itself assailed, and everyone from Prince to Groom is fighting on
> the battlements, the jester's jokes echo only through deserted halls,
> and his witticisms and commendations, distributed evenly between
> friend and foe, jar the ears of hurrying messengers, of mourning
> women and wounded men.[130]

National passions, then, had to be kindled and controlled, the latter not always an easy task. On the one hand, the national will of the Home Front could not be separated from the conduct of the war itself, no matter how powerful the military resources in the field. The Ludendorff offensive, Churchill believed in that regard, was decisive in the defeat of Germany, not because the German military was radically weakened by its failure. But the halting of that offensive, as he pointed out, "coming at the moment when the German national spirit was enfeebled by its exertions during four years and the cumulative effects of the blockade, led to the ... sudden final collapse of German resistance in November 1918."[131]

On the other hand, national passions coupled with scientific and technological developments encouraged the end to limitations on conflict. "It is established," Churchill concluded, "that nations who believe their life is at stake will not be restrained from using any means to secure their

73

existence."[132] That development, in turn, compounded the problem of conflict termination for the political leaders who had aroused the populace for total war in the first place. "The peoples, transported by their sufferings and by the mass teachings with which they had been inspired," Churchill wrote as he began his memoirs of what he considered to be the second part of the twentieth-century Thirty Years War, "stood around in scores of millions to demand that retribution should be exacted to the full. Woe betide the leaders now perched on their dizzy pinnacles of triumph if they cast away at the conference table what the soldiers had won on a hundred blood-soaked battlefields."[133]

Churchill's views on the role of the government in total war also crystalized during the interwar period. At the very top, he maintained a romantic faith, coupled with a pragmatic appreciation of usefulness, in the monarchy, "one institution ... which, so far from falling into desuetude or decay, has breasted the torrent of events, and even derived new vigour from the stresses."[134] That was equally true for parliamentary institutions which "had proved themselves as serviceable for waging war as for maintaining freedom and progress in times of peace."[135] It was a deeply felt Whig belief, from which he never deviated despite the inroads of modern war. "Half our mistakes and many of our misfortunes," he wrote, "could have been avoided if the great issues of war policy and strategy could have been fought out across the floor of the House of Commons in the full light of day."[136] That belief was reinforced by pragmatic evidence from the past as he worked on the Marlborough biography while languishing in the political wilderness of the 1930s. For all his great victories, Churchill wrote of his ancestor's operations in 1709, "at the moment when his work should have given him the greatest authority, and when that authority might have been most beneficiently exercised, he found himself alone, with no party and no country at his back."[137]

Churchill's work with Marlborough's history also underscored his observations from the recent war on the direct connection between success in battle and support on the Home Front. There were, for example, Marlborough's military failures in 1705. Churchill described in detail how those failures, coupled with the general election that year, which had cost the Tories critical seats, dramatically increased the political pressures on his ancestor for military success that were not relieved until the victory of Ramillies the following year. That victory also reinforced Churchill's appreciation of a government's role in recruiting allies as well as the effect of military success on that role. The lack of complete allied participation was a recurring problem for Marlborough throughout his career as he attempted to coalesce the disparate Dutch, British, and German forces that formed the core of the Grand Alliance. "It was never in his power to give orders which covered the whole field of the war," Churchill wrote, "and in many quarters ... his command was disputed, divided, or merely nominal."[138]

The role of a government in recruiting allies, Churchill realized in looking back on the First World War, was even more important in total war. "The manoeuvre which brings an ally into the field," he wrote, "is as serviceable as that which wins a great battle."[139] That was, of course, particularly true of the United States' entry into the war, an event captured in microcosm by Churchill in his description at the Chemin des Dames in May 1918 of the "impression made upon the hard-pressed French by this seemingly inexhaustible flood of gleaming youth in its first maturity of health and vigour ...."[140] Allied to this was the role of the Imperial troops from around the world, whose performance throughout the entire war solidified Churchill's romantic faith in the British Empire bound by the "invisible ties of interest, sentiment and tradition which ... proved more effective than the most binding formal guarantees ...."[141] Most importantly, there was the government role in the centralized direction of the different countries, a key aspect of policy recognized as early as 1915 by Churchill in a memorandum complaining about the "lack of any real co-ordination in the exertions and plans of the allies."[142]

The issue of overall centralized government direction, Churchill believed, was the key problem that had emerged from the new relationship between the elements of the Clausewitzian trinity in total war. To begin with, there was the decision-making process. In peacetime, under a popular and democratic form of government, he acknowledged, that process could be decentralized to some extent with compromise being "very often not merely necessary but actually beneficial ...."[143] But in war, particularly total war, decision-making had to be centralized. There could be no prevarication on the part of political leaders, Churchill believed, such as that which he had witnessed by Arthur James Balfour at the Supreme Council of the Allies at Versailles during the war. Balfour spoke for ten minutes; and when he finished, Clemenceau abruptly inquired of him: "Pour ou contre?"[144] Looking back on those experiences, Churchill concluded that the decision-making process in total war was and must be entirely different from that in peacetime.

> There is no place for compromise in War. That invaluable process only means that soldiers are shot because their leaders in Council and camp are unable to resolve. In War the clouds never blow over, they gather unceasingly and fall in thunderbolts. Things do not get better by being let alone. Unless they are adjusted, they explode with shattering detonation. Clear leadership, violent action, rigid decisions one way or the other, form the only path not only of victory, but of safety and even of mercy. The State cannot afford division or hesitation at the executive centre.[145]

Policy was the result of decisions at the "executive centre," and as Churchill had learned in the war, policy must determine strategy.

When there was a complete reversal of policy and strategy, as in the case of the Second German Empire during World War I, the result was unmitigated disaster. Reflecting after the war, Churchill pointed to three cardinal mistakes, all stemming from military ascendancy over political decision-making, that caused the defeat of Germany. "The invasion of Belgium and the unlimited U-boat war," Churchill wrote, citing two of the mistakes, "were both resorted to on expert dictation as the only means of victory. They proved the direct cause of ruin."[146] For Churchill, the involvement of Hindenburg and Ludendorff in the U-boat decision was typical of what occurred when the narrow military framework of strategy, overly dependent "upon a purely mechanical device," dominated the broader implications that policy must consider. "They looked too little," he concluded, "to the tremendous psychological reactions upon the Allies, upon the whole world, above all upon their own people ...."[147] It was that disregard of the people that led to the Ludendorff offensive, the third of the great German mistakes, with its negative implosive effect on the Home Front, which in turn destroyed what had been an excellent possibility for Germany of a negotiated peace.

Germany, however, was an extreme example. A more subtle problem, as Churchill well knew, lay in the British decision-making process of World War I. To begin with, there was no tight executive core, ensuring that policy evolved from the equivalent of what in Marlborough's time was "the eye and brain and soul of a single man, which from hour to hour are making subconsciously all the unweighable adjustments, no doubt with many errors, but with ultimate accuracy."[148] Nor was there any government mechanism to ensure that the policy of "the frocks" dominated the strategy of "the brass hats," particularly when the latter could appeal on the grounds of technical expertise to the last element of the Clausewitzian trinity, the people.

But that "expertise," as Churchill had begun to realize in the days of Buller's incomprehensible procrastinations on the Tugela, resulted in a strategy of "obstinate offensives" that, in the case of World War I, was "pursued regardless of loss of life until ... the spirit of the British army... was nearly quenched under the mud of Flanders and the fire of German machine-guns."[149] Nevertheless, even the redoubtable Lloyd George was never able to establish executive machinery to ensure what Churchill came to realize was the *sine qua non* for meeting the complexities of total war: policy domination of strategy. This was demonstrated during the manpower shortage of 1918 when Churchill urged that all available men be sent to the front while forbidding absolutely any offensive resumptions. "The Prime Minister however," Churchill recalled, "did not feel that, if the troops were once in France, he would be strong enough to resist those military pressures for an offensive which had so overborne the wiser judgment of Statesmen."[150]

The Great Game

> "If you are a great general, said Pompaedius Silo
> to Marius, "come down and fight."
> "If you are a great general," was the famous
> answer, "make me fight against my will."
>
> Churchill, *The World Crisis 1915*, p. 21

After the First World War, Churchill continued to be fascinated by the cloak and dagger aspect of the "Great Game," particularly when it was directed against his *bête noire*, the new Soviet State. As a consequence, he was captivated by such spies as Sidney Reilly and, in particular, Boris Savinkov, a veteran anarchist who had also impressed Bruce Lockhart and Somerset Maugham and who was, Churchill was convinced, a good terrorist − "a Terrorist for moderate aims." That positive assessment was bolstered in the Russo-Polish War of 1920 when Savinkov formed two corps of 30,000 men and proposed "to push forward into Soviet territory collecting a huge snowball of Anti-Bolshies." The Foreign Office, however, was less romantically inclined, and support for the free-wheeling anti-Red leader was terminated, much to Churchill's bitter disgust.[151]

That same year, because of Red scares and labor turmoil, there was considerable pressure in Whitehall for revelations of Soviet subversion connected with the Soviet trade mission in London, even if such revelations had to be based on the publication of decyphered codes. Those decrypts were the product of the Government Code and Cypher School (GC&CS), established in 1919 by the War Cabinet to maintain the work of Room 40 in a peacetime cryptographic unit. The publicly announced function of the new organization was "to advise as to the security of codes and cyphers used by all Government departments." There was also, however, a secret directive "to study the methods of cypher communications used by foreign powers."[152] Churchill had always been wary of any action that might compromise Sigint and would continue to be so in the future. But in 1920, he was "convinced that the danger to the state which has been wrought by the intrigues of these revolutionaries and the disastrous effect which will be produced on their plans by the exposure of their methods outweighs all other considerations."[153] Despite his intercession, however, the Cabinet decided against the release of all but a few of the cables, probably for fear of compromising GC&CS and because a good enough case could be made for Soviet subversion without publishing sources.

Before the decade was over, another Red scare involved Churchill once again in the subject of Sigint. As a result of the furore over the Zinoviev letter affair, there was a tightening of security procedures by the incoming Conservative administration − so much so that Churchill, the new Chancellor of the Exchequer, was denied access to Soviet intercepts.

In his protest to Austen Chamberlain, the new foreign secretary, Churchill revealed not only his indignation, but an abiding faith in the efficacy of Sigint that he was never to lose.

> ... I have studied this information [the intercepts] over a longer period and more attentively than probably any other minister has done. All the years I have been in office since it began (in Room 40) in the autumn of 1914 I have read every one of these flimsies and I attach more importance to them as a means of forming a true judgment of public policy in these spheres than to any other source of knowledge at the disposal of the state.[154]

During his years in the wilderness after he left office in 1929, Churchill continued to have access to state intelligence due to one man, Desmond Morton, a severely wounded gunnery officer, whom Churchill had met during World War I on General Haig's staff, and with whom he had formed an enduring friendship. In 1931, Morton was appointed to head the Industrial Intelligence Centre (IIC) with a remit "to discover and report the plans for manufacture of armaments and war stores in foreign countries."[155] In that capacity and as a long-time friend, Morton was a natural source of intelligence for Churchill. Early on in the first National Government, Morton consulted with Ramsay MacDonald on the matter. "Tell him whatever he wants to know, keep him informed," was the reply of the Prime Minister who quickly followed this up with written permission.[156] That policy was maintained by MacDonald's successors, Stanley Baldwin and Neville Chamberlain. Thus, as Christopher Andrew has pointed out, the astonishing fact was that Churchill was "supplied on the instructions of three successive prime ministers with secret intelligence which he was to use as the basis of public attacks on their defence policies and of his own campaign for rearmament."[157]

Churchill's continued interest in the "Great Game" also stemmed from his research on Marlborough during that period. Through his studies of his illustrious ancestor, he could appreciate how operational intelligence bridged the gap between the romantic risk-taker and the rational calculator. That was particularly apparent during the 1704 campaign as Marlborough's "Scarlet Caterpillar" crawled across Europe from the North Sea to southern Germany. During the march, between Coblenz and Mainz, at Neustadt, the British leader was provided with information by an agent in Celle on the entire French campaign plan. The plan had been taken from the cabinet of the War Minister in Paris, deciphered in Celle, and sent to Marlborough's Secret Service at his Neustadt camp by long and circuitous routes through France and Germany. For Marlborough, Churchill pointed out, the plan "only confirmed what his occult common sense had divined. But it must have been nonetheless very reassuring."[158] So must have been the continual flow of information on his French opponent, Marshal Tallard, provided by his elaborate Secret Service, on which the normally stingy British commander consistently lavished funds. "Even more remarkable was Marlborough's own Intelligence," Churchill added in describing the Blenheim campaign, "for on July 3 he already knew almost exactly the number of battalions and squadrons which the King had so secretly assigned to Tallard only ten days before at Versailles. A message could hardly have covered the distance quicker."[159]

The attritive combat of World War I also played a role in Churchill's return to the "Great Game." A renewed focus and greater emphasis on strategems and deception, he believed, would be necessary to avoid future bloodbaths. "The liberties of men are no longer to be guarded by their natural qualities, but by their dodges," he wrote somewhat bitterly; "and superior virtue and valour may fall an easy prey to the latest diabolical trick."[160] Once again he found reinforcement for his thoughts in his research on Marlborough in the Blenheim campaign. In August and September of 1932, Churchill toured his ancestor's battlefields on the Continent, and was struck by the success of the overall deception operation that governed the Grand Alliance march into Bavaria. On 25 September, he wrote his cousin, the ninth Duke of Marlborough, about the first Duke's departure from Coblenz on the march that would end at Blenheim, emphasizing that:

> none of the hostile watching armies ready to spring, not even our army, was sure where it was going to. They still thought it was a campaign in Alsace; but no, a fortnight later the long scarlet columns swing off to the Danube .... This marvellous march was distinguished ... for its absolute secrecy and mystery – no one knew, not the Queen, not Sarah, not the English government, except Eugene ....[161]

Eugene was, of course, Prince Eugene of Savoy, Britain's great ally who was to play a major role in Marlborough's deception plan at Blenheim. Prior to the battle, Eugene gave Tallard the impression by numerous spies and deserters that he was moving back to his old position on the Lines of Stollhofen, thinly held against the French General Villeroy by the corps of the Prince of Anhalt. He then marched his forces ostentatiously north in the direction of the Lines. On 27 July, he reached Tuebingen, then vanished from the French view among the desolate hills of Swabia. Villeroy was convinced that Eugene was still close to the lines and showed no sign of movement toward Bavaria. As a consequence, Churchill concluded, "Villeroy, gaping at the half-vacant lines of Stollhofen, need no longer be considered as a factor in the fateful decisions impending upon the Danube."[162]

Marlborough coordinated every aspect of that deception. There was thus no sudden surprising arrival of Eugene to rescue the coalition commander at Blenheim in the nick of time, as had sometimes been reported until Churchill set the record straight in his biography. In fact, as Churchill convincingly demonstrated, Marlborough had a superabundance of information from his own Secret Service and confirmed it where necessary by Eugene's field reports. "The accuracy of his information about the enemy," he wrote, "and also the speed with which it reached him is remarkable. He knew ... exactly what had happened ... and where Tallard was baking his bread and would march."[163] The key to all that was Eugene, moving secretly with his forces to join those of Marlborough. "Eugene knew that, whatever might miscarry behind him," Churchill concluded, "... he must arrive on the Danube somewhere between Ulm and Donauwoerth at the same time that Tallard joined the Elector. Marlborough in all his conduct counted on him to do this, and his own arrangements made the juncture sure and certain."[164]

With all the coalition forces gathered together, Marlborough engaged in another deception operation on 12 August by planting four deserters in the French camp. As Churchill described it, each deserter told the same story: Marlborough had arrived with his troops; but the entire allied army was going to retire under a bold display toward Noerdlingen on the morning of 13 August. That information appeared to be confirmed by reports from the French cavalry scouts, who had watched the dust clouds above the allied baggage columns which Marlborough had sent off on a false march, and by planted rumors that came in from the countryside. Marshal Tallard and his staff agreed as a result that they should not attack so strong an army, but more important, that the allies themselves would not attack. At 7 a.m. on 13 August, just prior to Marlborough's attack on the French forces, Tallard wrote a letter to Louis XIV, describing how the enemy forces had begun to assemble before daybreak at 2 a.m. and were now drawn up at the end of their camp. "Rumour in the countryside," he concluded confidently, "expects them at Noerdlingen."[165]

Surprise, then, was a key outcome of the "Great Game" which could counter the attritive tendencies of modern war. And as Churchill knew first-hand, a major part of that element of surprise could be achieved by science and technology. The problem for him in the first decade after the war, however, was the nagging realization that technological surprise was a two-way street and that with "the march of Science unfolding ever more appalling possibilities," a type of reverse Social Darwinism could ensue which might obviate the heroic traits of Victorian England forever. In previous times, he pointed out in a pessimistic 1924 article entitled "Shall We All Commit Suicide?", war meant that "in the hard evolution of mankind the best and fittest stocks came to the fore." But a scientific or technological breakthrough, he continued, could allow "a base, degenerate, immoral race" to conquer "an enemy far above them in quality ...." Such a breakthrough, he conjectured with his ever active imagination, could come from a panoply of weapons that might include:

electric rays which could paralyse the engines of a motor-car, could claw down aeroplanes from the sky, and conceivably be made destructive of human life or human vision. Then there are Explosives. Have we reached the end? Has Science turned its last page on them? May there not be methods of using explosive energy incomparably more intense than anything heretofore discovered? Might not a bomb no bigger than an orange be found to possess a secret power to destroy a whole block of buildings – nay, to... blast a township at a stroke? Could not explosives ... be guided automatically in flying machines by wireless or other rays, without a human pilot, in ceaseless procession upon a hostile city, arsenal, camp, or dockyard?[166]

It was a pessimism that could not exist for long without a counterweight in Churchill's Victorian nature. By the 1930s, in an upbeat article entitled "50 Years Hence," he could concentrate on what science could do for man in the future, whether it be television or peaceful nuclear energy. Science had been a key element in the progress of the previous century, he pointed out; it was important to regain that faith in science. That, in turn, would find Britain realistically ready to deal with friendly or enemy technological innovations in warfare. It was a faith that returned Churchill to Tennyson and the poems of his youth as a link to the uncertain present. "The dawn of the Victorian era opened the new period of man," Churchill concluded about Tennyson; "and the genius of the poet pierced the veil of the future." That future was described in "all the wonder that would be" of "Locksley Hall," a couplet of which Churchill could even see in his rejuvenated faith as presaging the League of Nations.

Till the way-drum throbb'd no longer, and the
    battle flags were furl'd
In the Parliament of man, the Federation of the world.[167]

Churchill was aided in his pessimistic 1924 article on science and technology by a noted scientist, Professor F.A. Lindemann, later Viscount Cherwell, and known simply to Churchill as "The Prof." The two men had met in 1921. Churchill, who valued eating, drinking and smoking, took to the non-smoking, abstemious vegetarian primarily because of the value he put on what he described as Lindemann's "beautiful brain," and on the ability of the Prof. to explain even the most complicated and arcane scientific issues in clear, concise, understandable terms. Sarah Churchill recounted, in this regard, how one day at lunch her father asked the Prof. to explain in five minutes in words of one syllable the quantum theory. That was, she recalled, "quite a tall order: however without any hesitation, like quicksilver, he explained the principle and held us all spell-bound. When he had finished we all spontaneously burst into applause."[168] That type of close, unofficial scientific tutelage was to continue throughout their long relationship, even under the most adverse conditions, such as the time in December 1931 when Churchill was struck by a car on Fifth Avenue while visiting New York City. Upon learning the details of the accident from Churchill, who was convalescing in a New York hospital, Lindemann immediately wired his friend from England: "Collision equivalent falling thirty feet on to pavement .... Equivalent stopping ten pound brick dropped six hundred feet or two charges buckshot point-blank range."[169]

Both Lindemann and Churchill were vitally interested in the subject of air defense, particularly after the Nazi Luftwaffe expansion began in the mid-1930s. The pace and organization of the British bureaucratic effort, however, were not designed to please either man. "If a really scientific Committee had been set to work and funds provided," Churchill told the Commons in June 1935, "twenty important experiments would be under way by now, any one of which might yield results decisive on the whole of our air defence problems."[170] As a result of that speech, an Air Defence Research sub-committee (ADR) was formed by the cabinet. On 25 July 1935, Churchill attended his first meeting of the ADR, beginning a frustrating relationship that was to last until 1939. It was another, unprecedented access to intelligence that complemented the information Morton was already providing on the German Air Force with governmental approval.

By 1936, Churchill was clearly displeased with the workings of the ADR. "Accustomed as I was to see how things were done in the war," he noted in May of that year, "and how orders can be given for large scale experiment and supply, I have been deeply pained by the dilettante futility which has marked our action."[171] That frustration was compounded by problems with the noted scientist, Sir Henry Tizzard, who had formed a separate body under the ADR. At Churchill's suggestion, Lindemann was made a member of that organization. There was, however, almost instantaneous friction between the two men, because of Lindemann's incessant pressure for speedier action and Tizzard's open skepticism toward many of Lindemann's projects, among which were aerial bombs that were to be dropped in the path of enemy aircraft and infra-red detection of night flying aircraft.

That friction soon spread to the subject of radar. For Churchill, deeply immersed in Marlborough's life at the time, there were clear lessons in the past that pointed the way for dealing with the new device and the subject of technological surprise. The flintlock, for instance, had vastly improved the destructiveness of the infantry at the time of his great ancestor; but it was only slowly adopted. Added to this was the ring bayonet, which transformed the basic infantry soldier of the period into both a pikeman and a musketeer, which in turn transformed infantry tactics. That overall change had not been perceived with the exception of Marlborough, who "saw it and applied it" with great success. "In nearly every great war," Churchill concluded, "there is some new mechanical feature introduced the early understanding of which confers important advantages. Military opinion is naturally rigid. Men held in the grip of discipline, moving perilously from fact to fact and staking their lives at every step, are nearly always opposed to new ideas."[172]

It was thus up to the political leaders working with scientists to provide innovations to the armed forces which, in many cases, "do not know what it is they want done for them."[173] And the key innovation was radar, invented by Robert Watson-Watt, who by June 1936 was already complaining "that the Ministry wished to avoid setting up emergency machinery in place of the accelerated normal machinery. Even after acceleration, this normal machinery has held down my rate of advance." That same day, he enlisted Churchill's aid in speeding up the research process for radar; and in a follow-up letter thanked Churchill for his "generous interest," emphasizing that "urgent action" was needed immediately in terms of the new device, which had never been tested "in conditions at all comparable to war conditions."[174] But for Churchill, in constant receipt of Morton's figures concerning the growth of the German Air Force, there seemed to be no sense of urgency by the Air Ministry on radar or any other aspect of air defense. At the end of July 1936, in a deputation that met with the Prime Minister, he stated that the practical results of the ADR were "almost entirely negative," to include those concerned with radar, which would not be operational until the end of the decade. "I have been most disappointed in the rate of progress," he concluded, "and the reluctance to have large-scale experiments in rapid succession."[175]

For Churchill, as the decade drew to a close, the Air Defence Research subcommittee typified why science and technology could not be part of the "Great Game" unless there were top-down political prioritization and encouragement. By 1938, Lindemann was no longer involved with any part of the ADR; and in June of that year, Churchill was still referring to the "slow-motion picture which the work of this committee has presented," concluding that so far "as the ADR ... is concerned, there seems to br a complete lack of driving power." Typically, for his years in the wilderness, Churchill only received for his efforts a stinging personal *ad hominum* reply from Tizzard. "Contrast the developments of the last few years," the scientist wrote, "with the state of affairs when Mr. Churchill was First Lord of the Admiralty before the war. As a result of his total lack of real scientific imagination and foresight we entered the war without any defence whatsoever against submarines ...." Nevertheless, Churchill returned to the subject with increasing urgency in the fatal spring of 1939. "We go buzzing along with a host of ideas and experiments which may produce results in '41,' '42' and '43,' " he wrote the ADR chairman. "Where will you find anything that can operate in ... 1939?"[176] There was no dearth of answers to similar questions in Berlin.

4

THE SECOND WORLD WAR AND THE REMARKABLE TRINITY

> He is a man who leads forlorn hopes, and when the hopes of England become forlorn, he will once again be summoned to leadership.
>
> Harold Nicolson, 1931
>
> War had made him powerful and popular; with war, all that was brightest in his life was associated; for war, his talents were particularly fitted.
>
> Thomas Macaulay, *Essays on the Earl of Chatham*, p. 23

Walter Bagehot pointed out at the beginning of the American Civil War that in an emergency or a crisis, the advantage of the British constitution over that of the United States was that the British people could choose a leader for the occasion. "It is quite possible," Bagehot wrote in terms that presaged the arrival of Churchill in 1940,

> and even likely that he would not be ruler before the occasion. The great qualities, the imperious will, the rapid energy, the eager nature fit for a great crisis are not required – are impediments in common times .... But by the structure of the world we often want, at the sudden occurrence of a grave tempest, to change the helmsman – to replace the pilot of the calm by the pilot of the storm.[1]

When the new helmsman kissed hands in May 1940, however, he was operating from a very weak base. George VI and the majority of the Conservative Party considered Lord Halifax to be the better man; and it was widely noted that when Churchill entered the Commons for the first time as Prime Minister, the Labor benches rose more readily for him than the Conservatives, who reserved their principal applause for Neville Chamberlain. Outside Westminster, the new British leader was no better off. He had no broad territorial connections and no support by a squirearchy or by trade union blocks. Moreover, his hot-headed conduct as First Lord of the Admiralty in the fiasco of the Norwegian campaign the previous month had fueled further questions as to the stability and accuracy of his judgment in terms of strategic and operational matters as well as basic organization. And yet by the winter of 1940, Churchill had attained a greater ascendancy than any other Prime Minister in history over the government, the people and the armed forces, the basic elements of Clausewitz's "remarkable trinity" as well as the fundamental sinews of total war.[2]

THE LEGACY OF THE PAST

I believe that there was in his time no nation of men, no city, nay, no single individual with whom Alexander's name had not become a familiar word. I therefore hold that such a man, who was like no ordinary mortal, was not born into the world without some special providence.

Arrian, *History of Alexander the Great*

A major reason for Churchill's ascendancy was the sense of history that he had formed before the turn of the century. He came to office in the spring of 1940 not only with memories of the late Victorian conflicts and the First World War in which he had personally participated, but also with an impassioned knowledge of the entire panorama of European military history since Roman times. For him, Hitler was one of a series of actors on the German stage that had included Frederick the Great and Wilhelm II; and Stalin just part of a panoply of leaders that led from Peter the Great through Alexander I to Nicholas II. Above all, France was a country that transcended Pétain in a lineage passing back through Clemenceau and Napoleon to Louis XIV and beyond. This sense of history, of playing for a vast constituency in the past as well as those yet unborn in the future, enriched Churchill's strategic thinking and stood him in good stead as Axis victory piled upon victory. A statesman with a less developed sense of history might have faltered with the fall of France and the initial Nazi success in Russia. But Churchill appreciated the value of the ring formed by the encircling alliance, particularly after the United States entered the war. Such an alliance, as he well knew, had never failed ultimately to triumph in the previous 300 years of European history.[3]

It was this rich, multicolored historical imagination which dominated Churchill's moral and intellectual universe, and which allowed him to proceed with what appeared to many an obstinate irrationality against overwhelming forces in the darkest days of the war. But he knew with an absolute certainty that it had been done before, not the least successfully by the first Duke of Marlborough. "If anyone in 1672 computed the relative forces of France and England," he had written between the wars,

he could only feel that no contest was possible .... No dreamer, however romantic, however remote his dreams from reason, could

85

have foreseen a surely approaching day when, by ... the struggles of a generation, the noble colossus of France would lie prostrate in the dust while the small island ... would emerge victorious, mistress of the Mediterranean, the Narrow Seas and the oceans.[4]

Churchill's historical certainty was reflected in his wartime speeches, in which there were no intricate details, only larger than life patterns like those in an epic poem or in a drama containing persons and situations as timeless symbols and embodiments of eternal, shining principles. All this was either suffused with bright light or cast in deep shadows – all primary colors; hardly a nuance, no half-tones – responding directly and simply to the immediate demands of history. "The ideas set forth," he wrote in 1940 concerning a Foreign Office draft, "appear to me to err in trying to be too clever, and to enter into refinements of policy unsuited to the tragic simplicity and grandeur of the times and the issues at stake."[5]

History, then, provided a constant anchor for Churchill in World War II. Even his great ancestor's rise to power presaged his own. "By the time he arrived at the highest command he was passing the prime of life," he had written of Marlborough, "and older than many of the leading generals of the day. The early success and repeated advancement ... were followed by lengthy intervals of stagnation."[6] This type of connection was never far from Churchill's daily thoughts throughout the war. In his meeting with Stalin in August 1942, for instance, he referred to Marlborough as a man who in his time had "put an end to a menace to Europe's freedom, a menace as great as Hitler."[7] And during the Quebec Conference in August 1943, Churchill passed the ramparts of the Citadel each afternoon "brooding over ... all the tales of Wolfe and Quebec."[8]

There were moments, of course, when Clio provided neither relief nor reinforcement. "Anzio was my worst moment," Churchill told Lord Moran in this regard, "I had most to do with it. I didn't want two Suvla Bays in one lifetime."[9] Generally, however, history was a source of optimism for him as it had been in Victorian days. "Yesterday was a bad day," Lord Hankey wrote his wife on 19 September 1939, "what with the Courageous and the Russian defection. But ... Winston has reminded me how, about 25 years ago almost to the day we lost the *Abonkir*, *Cressy* and *Hogue*, sunk by German submarines. And this is not the first time Russia has 'defected'."[10]

Such historical signposts became even more important sources of sustenance after Churchill became Prime Minister. When faced with immediate disaster, for instance, the distant past could form the basis for psychological preparation. "Here in this strong City of Refuge," Churchill broadcast from London on 14 July 1940 as England braced itself for the first onslaught of German bombers, "which enshrines the title-deeds of

86

human progress and is of deep consequence to Christian civilization... we await undismayed the impending assault."[11] And when that assault came and even worse disasters occurred as Britain took the first faltering steps to recover in the coming years, it was his abiding Victorian historical faith in ultimate deliverance that continued to sustain him. "We must just KBO," Churchill said on 11 December 1941, the day after the sinking of the *Prince of Wales* and the *Repulse*. KBO, he explained, meant "Keep Buggering On."[12]

But if history could direct and guide, it could also divert and deceive. In World War I, as an example, Churchill, in collaboration with Lord Fisher, had been deeply committed to naval penetration of the Baltic. As First Lord again 25 years later, Churchill initiated preparation of Operation Catherine, the hopelessly impractical plan for the same type of naval excursion into the Baltic. In a similar manner, his romantic view of the French caused him to value the quantitative over the qualitative just as the Germans were emphasizing the latter and to view the French Army, as he described it a year before the war, as "the most perfectly trained and faithful mobile force in Europe."[13]

Finally, Churchill's view of history taught him nothing about the Far East, and he was almost as ignorant of the realities in that region as Hitler was in terms of the United States. This was graphically illustrated by his failure to grasp the deficiencies in defense arrangements for Singapore until disaster struck and by his various proposals throughout the war for invasions of Java and Sumatra. Moreover, despite an abstract love of Empire, the fact that he never understood the Far East as well as other areas meant that his feelings for New Zealand and Australia were not so deep as for other Imperial members. It was all very well, for instance, to take the broad view in 1942 that it did not matter what the Japanese did since their actions had brought the United States into the war. But that view was of small consolation to the Australians.[14]

Churchill's perception of history also strengthened his deep sense of humanity and generosity of spirit by reinforcing his belief in great states and civilizations. Germany, for instance, was never an object of his enmity. For him, the Germans were a great historic race and Germany an historically hallowed state. It was the Prussians in World War I and the Nazis in World War II who had undermined all this. Consequently, the British leader was appalled by the Nuremberg war crime trials. He was at Chartwell after the war when the results of those trials were published. "It shows," Churchill remarked to his Chief of Staff, General Ismay, "that if you get into a war, it is supremely important to win it. You and I would be in a pretty pickle if we had lost."[15]

The Egocentric

> Personally, I am always ready to learn, although I do not always like being taught.
>
> Churchill's speech in the House, 4 November 1952

Churchill remained the egocentric, self-absorbed man of destiny throughout the Second World War. These characteristics fostered, in turn, a remoteness in the Prime Minister that aided him in the necessary but ruthless decisions that often had to be made concerning matters ranging from life and death to the relief of military commanders. It was an indispensable insensitivity for a great leader, as Lord Moran, observing Churchill in the daily application of power, realized. "If it should happen that a man of action, exercising supreme power, is also an artist," he scribbled in the margin of his diary, "then God help him. He will have to change his nature to survive."[16]

That remoteness could also be hard on subordinates. For example, Churchill had promised Alanbrooke the position of Supreme Commander for Overlord, informally in mid-June 1943 and formally on 7 July. Nevertheless, he approached President Roosevelt and offered to accept General Marshall as overall commander for the invasion of Europe. If this was a rational acceptance of what was inevitable given increasing American predominance in overall strategy, it also illustrated a ruthless, not to mention devious, streak in Churchill who, in his own self-absorption, apparently assumed that his C.I.G.S. also realized the inevitability of the situation and would not require a modicum of tea and sympathy. "He bore the great disappointment with soldierly dignity," the Prime Minister wrote of Alanbrooke in his memoirs.[17] The general's reaction, however, showed a somewhat different perception. "Not for one moment did he realize what this meant to me," he wrote. "He offered no sympathy, no regrets at having had to change his mind, and dealt with the matter as if it were of minor importance."[18]

Part of the explanation for this type of insensitivity lay in the great pressures under which Churchill worked from the time he assumed office. On 26 May 1940, for instance, Churchill made the pragmatic decision to abandon the besieged British garrison at Calais in order to focus all military effort on the massive problem of holding Dunkirk as long as possible. "Government has ... decided that you must continue to fight," Churchill telegraphed the garrison commander. "Have greatest admiration for your splendid stand."[19] But it was hard to find the romance of a Victorian last stand in the decisions of total war, and Churchill clearly showed the strain, recalling later that he felt "physically sick" over the decision.[20] "He has quoted these words in his memoirs," General Ismay added, "but he does not mention how sad he looked as he uttered them."[21]

The pressures continued to mount on Churchill during the summer of 1940, causing his war aims momentarily to focus narrowly on the near term. "What will be your general strategy now, after the fall of France?" the Russian Ambassador asked him in July. "My general strategy at present," Churchill replied with a smile while drawing on his cigar, "is to last out the next three months."[22] The future, however, was not always so easy for the British leader to shrug off. Moran recalled how he had found Churchill in the map-room as the German submarine war pressed in. "He was standing with his back to me," the physician noted in his diary, "staring at the huge chart with the little black beetles representing German submarines. 'Terrible,' he muttered. I was about to retreat when he whipped around and brushed past me with his head down. I am not sure he saw me."[23]

The strain also showed in Churchill's direct dealings with his subordinates, as it had indirectly with Alanbrooke. At one point, one of his Private Secretaries noted in his diary that "the PM does not help the Government machine to run smoothly and his inconsiderate treatment of the Service Departments would cause trouble were it not for the great personal loyalty of the Service Ministers to himself."[24] Mrs. Churchill also noted the effect that stress was having on her husband after the British evacuation of the continent and wrote a letter to him, which she then tore up. Four days later, she pieced it together and gave it to Churchill. "My Darling Winston –," she wrote. "I must confess that I noticed a deterioration in your manner; & you are not so kind as you used to be. It is for you to give the Orders and if they are bungled ... you can sack anyone & everyone. Therefore with this terrific power you must combine urbanity, kindness & if possible Olympic calm .... Besides you won't get the best results by irascibility & rudeness. They will breed either dislike or a slave mentality ...."[25]

To the mental strain was added the physical stress throughout the war on a man in the last half of his seventh decade. As he had throughout his life, Churchill constantly fought against the limitations imposed by his physical condition, now augmented by advancing age. His most notable effort in this regard concerned his wartime travels, which included three trips to Washington, three to Canada, two to Moscow via Cairo and Tehran, and many others to North Africa, the Middle East, Italy, Greece and Central Europe. Much of this travel was in the standard aircraft of the time, not noted for either comfort or quiet. At one juncture in the summer of 1942, the 68-year-old Prime Minister was driven at midnight to a laboratory where he was tested for high altitude flying by being taken up the equivalent of 15,000 feet and kept for 15 minutes while his wife watched anxiously through a porthole.[26] And in January 1943, Moran recounted how he woke up on a leaky aircraft to find Churchill on his knees trying to keep out a draught by putting his blanket against the side of the plane.

He was shivering: we were flying at 7,000 feet in an unheated bomber in mid-winter. I got up, and we struggled, not with much success, to cut off the blast. An hour or two later he woke me and we returned to the attack. The P.M. is at a disadvantage in this kind of travel, since he never wears anything at night but a silk vest. On his hands and knees, he cut a quaint figure with his big, bare, white bottom. [27]

Churchill's favorite song from Gilbert and Sullivan was the opening from *The Mikado* which beings: "A wandering minstrel I ...." [28] Nevertheless, and despite his thousands of miles of flight, he never lost his fear of flying, which he kept typically in check if not in control. "Do you realize," he abruptly asked Moran while on a flight in 1942 from Bermuda to England, "we are fifteen hundred miles from anywhere?" [29] It was a heroic effort, not unnoticed by his Russian counterpart. During Churchill's October 1944 visit to Moscow when someone referred to the Big Three as the "Holy Trinity," Stalin commented: "If that is so, Churchill must be the Holy Ghost. He flies around so much." [30] And at least one American appreciated the great distances and concomitant dangers faced by the British leader on his travels. "If disposal of all the Allied decorations were today placed by Providence in my hands," Douglas MacArthur commented after hearing of his distant cousin's summer travels to Egypt and Russia in 1942, "my first act would be to award the Victoria Cross to Winston Churchill. No one of those who wear it deserves it more than he. A flight of 10,000 miles through hostile and foreign skies may be the duty of young pilots, but for a statesman burdened with the world's cares, it is an act of inspiring gallantry and valour." [31]

Despite the mental and physical strains, Churchill was able to bring to the job of wartime leader his tremendous powers of concentration and inexhaustible mental agility, guided by the overarching goal of victory and by his own personal sense of destiny. That sense was intuitive in him, based on his long experience, his conception of history, and his own political sensitivity. "The statesman ... must behold himself," Hans Morganthau wrote in this regard, "not as the infallible arbiter of the destiny of men, but the handmaiden of something which he may use but cannot control." [32] And so it was with Churchill, who believed that he was the servant of an historical entity called England, and that he was destined to maintain that entity and its Empire on the upward path that reached back to Alfred the Great. It was that belief, that inner certainty, that could inspire the masses in general, and his civilian and military subordinates in particular. One scientist described the effect whenever he met Churchill during the war as "the feeling of being recharged by contact with a source of living power." [33] And there was the Permanent Under-Secretary of War in 1940 who urged the Prime Minister to meet with a general about to leave on an urgent arms purchase mission to the United States, "in order that he may have the glow of Mount Sinai still on him when he reaches Washington."[34]

The Combatant

> I am certainly not one of those who need to be prodded. In fact, if anything, I am the prod.
>
> Churchill's speech in the House, 11 November 1942

Churchill's combativeness, as Anthony Storr has demonstrated, was connected to the fact that as an emotionally deprived child who later became prey to depression, he had difficulty in disposing of his hostility. One way, of course, was to seek opponents in the external world, to seek relief by finding enemies on whom it was justifiable to lavish wrath.[35] This was why there was an absolute quality to his combativeness. General Smuts, for instance, who was on General Botha's staff during the Boer War, described Churchill after his capture in the armored train as "a scrubby, squat figure of a man, unshaved. He was furious, venomous, just like a viper."[36] And when the King of Sweden wrote to George VI on 1 August 1940 to propose a conference to examine "the possibilities of making peace," Churchill would have no part of it, pointing out to the Foreign Office "that the intrusion of the ignominious King of Sweden as a peace-maker, after his desertion of Finland and Norway, and while he is absolutely in the German grip, though not without its encouraging aspects, is singularly distasteful."[37]

Churchill's aversion to the Swedish peace offer also demonstrated how closely intermingled the Victorian concepts of honor and heroism were with his will to fight, to persevere. In *Savrola* he had described the President of Laurania as he considered capitulation: "And then the alternative presented itself: flight, abdication, a squalid existence in some foreign country, despised, insulted, suspected ...."[38] It was this perspective and his basic combative nature that governed Churchill's outlook throughout the war, and he was always surprised when it was not matched by others around him. In mid-May 1940, for instance, he arrived in Paris for the first meeting of the Supreme War Council. After being briefed on the catastrophic French situation by General Gamelin, Churchill slapped the French commander on the shoulder and asked in French: "Now, my General, when and where are you going to counter-attack − from the north or from the south?"[39] In a few minutes, Gamelin's defeatist reply, with its litany of French inferiority, made it clear to the British leader that there would be no counterattack.

This type of combativeness was as natural as breathing to Churchill, often governed by his visceral reaction of the moment. On 10 June 1940, as an example, in another one of the increasingly dismal Anglo-French meetings, French Premier Reynaud asked the Prime Minister what would happen if France capitulated and all of German strength were concentrated upon invading England. Churchill replied instantly that he had not thought out his response in detail, but that basically he would drown as many as possible of the invaders on their way over to England, leaving it only to *"frapper sur la tête"* anyone who managed to crawl ashore.[40] At the end of that meeting, the increasingly emotional British leader once again reassured his French counterpart that Britain "would fight on and on, *toujours*, all the time, everywhere, *par tout, pas de grace*, no mercy. *Puis la victoire!*"[41] That such emotions were also governed by his Victorian concept of the heroic last stand was illustrated in a conversation Churchill had with President Roosevelt's Special Envoy, Averell Harriman, while sailing to the United States on the *Queen Mary* in spring 1943. When that conversation turned to the U-boat menace, the Prime Minister informed Harriman that he had arranged for a machine gun to be added to his own lifeboat, should it be necessary to abandon ship. "I won't be captured," he concluded. "The finest way to die is in the excitement of fighting the enemy."[42]

Churchill also brought his combativeness to the conference table throughout the war. "All I want is compliance with my wishes," he once remarked only half-humorously, "after reasonable discussion."[43] In meetings, he had an essentially rhetorical approach, and this combined with the normal fixity with which he adhered to a point, did not bode well for dialogue. His comment "might be short," General Eisenhower observed in this regard, "but still you felt like it was an oration."[44] Nevertheless, Churchill expected his advisers to stand up to him when they felt he was wrong. But it could be an excruciating experience, even for the most articulate subordinates, when they encountered the bedrock obstinacy that had marked the Prime Minister's character since childhood. At the highest level, that obstinacy meant unbreakable courage and resolution in adversity. On a lower level, however, in the day-to-day encounters with the Prime Minister, it could mean a sense of deep frustration. No one knew that better than General Alanbrooke.

> He is like a child that has set its mind on some forbidden toy. It is no good explaining that it will cut his fingers or burn him. The more you explain, the more fixed he becomes in his idea. Very often he seems to be quite immovable on some impossible project, but often that only means that he will not give way at that particular moment. Then, suddenly after some days, he will come round, and he will say something to show that it is all right, and that all the personal abuse has been forgotten.[45]

But it was in Hitler that Churchill found the perfect outlet for his combative nature. When he was finally confronted by an enemy who he believed to be totally evil, as he did the Nazi leader, it was a release that provided him enormous vitality. "For here, at last," Anthony Storr concluded, "was an opportunity to employ the full force of his enormous aggressiveness. Here was a monstrous tyranny, presided over by an arch-demon who deserved no mercy, and whom he could attack with an unsullied conscience."[46] Thus, there was Churchill touring the south coast of England in July 1940 indulging in what he described as "a real Hun hate" with one of his generals. "I never hated the Huns in the last war," he remarked later, "but now I hate them like an earwig."[47] That hatred extended to the entire Axis, to which the normal attributes of Victorian combat could never apply. In October 1940, for example, Admiral Cunningham sent a message to the Admiralty paying tribute to the gallantry displayed by Italian destroyers in a recent engagement in the Mediterranean. "This kind of kid glove stuff," Churchill replied, referring to the ongoing Battle of Britain, "infuriates the people who are going through their present ordeal at home ...."[48]

The threat had not always appeared so great to Churchill. In 1935 in his initial fascination with the romantic and conservative aspects of Fascism, he had written a mixed analysis of Hitler which, while hardly complimentary to the German system of government, referred to "the courage, the perseverance, and the vital force" of the Nazi leader.[49] By 1939, however, he was referring to Hitler as a "monstrous apparition," one that could fit his description of Marlborough's arch enemy, Louis XIV: "No worse enemy of human freedom has ever appeared in the trappings of polite civilization," he wrote of the Sun King-cum-Hitler. "Insatiable appetite, cold, calculating ruthlessness, monumental conceit, presented themselves armed with fire and sword."[50] But historical comparisons paled by 1940 before the glow of profound intuition about Hitler that formed the core of his convictions. At that time, C.P. Snow pointed out, "Churchill did not use judgment but one of his deep insights. This was absolute danger, there was no easy way round."[51] The British leader referred to the threat's unprecedented nature when he introduced the third edition of Pitt's speeches in October 1940. "No historical analogies can be exact," he wrote, "and in one respect our situation is very different from what it was in Pitt's day. A Nazi victory would be an immeasurably worse disaster for us and for all mankind than Napoleon's victory could ever have been."[52]

It was also a threat on which Churchill could lavish all his contempt. On 19 July 1940, three days after he had issued the Sea Lion Directive to prepare for the invasion of England, Hitler offered Britain, in a Reichstag address that mocked Churchill, the choice between peace with Germany, or "unending suffering and misery." When asked if he wished to respond to the speech, Churchill replied: " I do not propose to say anything to Herr Hitler's speech, not being on speaking terms with him."[53] Nevertheless, he delighted in bringing to bear against the threat the full brunt of his command of the English language. When, for instance, he spoke of the "Na--sies," the very lengthening of the vowel carried a stunning message of his contempt. Moreover, there were always the visual images invoked by his vivid descriptions of the enemy. Von Ribbentrop was "that prodigious contortionist" and Mussolini was a "whipped jackal, frisking at the side of the German tiger — this absurd imposter." And when Barbarossa was unleashed on Russia, he brought the event, which Hitler considered would cause the world to hold its breath, down to its basic level. "Now this bloodthirsty guttersnipe," Churchill announced, "must launch his mechanized armies upon new fields of slaughter."[54]

The Man of Action

> In the field, in spite of the newly-dug graves and hurrying ambulances, there was not the same sense of tragedy as hung around our windows in Whitehall.
>
> Churchill, *The World Crisis 1911–1914*, p. 303

Despite the realities of a newer, even more complete total war, Churchill remained enthralled with the concept of the heroic man of action in World War II. The RAF, in particular, excited his admiration, arousing in him, a Private Secretary recalled, "a latent schoolboy instinct of hero-worship" for what he considered "the cavalry of modern war."[55] It was a type of emotion that had led him throughout his civilian and military careers to seek out the recipients of Britain's highest award for valor. "You can generally tell what he finds attractive in his friends," a close friend commented late in Churchill's life; "a V.C. is in his good graces before he begins."[56]

The Victoria Cross was not always the best criterion for finding advisers, the case of Admiral Roger Keyes being perhaps the most flagrant example. Keyes was Churchill's closest naval confidant in the 1930s. He was an energetic man of action, an extraordinarily brave man, as Stephen Roskill has pointed out, "with something of the sixteenth century buccaneer in his character" who, in addition to his aggressive attitude throughout the Dardanelles naval attacks in 1915, had endeared himself to Churchill with his leadership of the spectacular, though unsuccessful, April 1918 raid on Zeebrugge for which he won the V.C.[57] But a man of action, as Churchill himself demonstrated, was not always easy to work with, and the Admiral became an increasing embarrassment after his appointment as Director of Combined Operations because of his inability to coordinate and compromise. The final result was Churchill's relief of Keyes, but only after his C.I.G.S. had advised him that "you can't win World War II with World War I heroes."[58]

Closely allied to Churchill's ingrained hero worship was his Victorian sense of honor. How honorably men conducted themselves in crisis was all important to him. The Czechoslovak legionaries after World War I, for instance, "forsook the stage of history" in their dishonorable treatment of the White Russian leader, Admiral Kolchak. In World War II, Pétain was a similar example. Admiral Darlan, on the other hand, redeemed himself in Churchill's eyes with the 1942 scuttling of the French Fleet at Toulon.[59] It was a conception that penetrated the natural, ruthless remoteness he felt and needed in order to send mass heroes to their deaths in total war. The German sinking of the *Royal Oak* in Scapa Flow in October 1939, for instance, triggered his overactive imagination concerning the 800 "heroes" who had lost their lives. "Poor fellows, poor fellows," he muttered with tears in his eyes after receiving the news, "trapped in those black depths ...."[60] And in the later stages of the war, General Eisenhower witnessed a meeting at Chequers when a logistics briefer struck a nerve in the normally imperturbable Prime Minister by using the phrase "so many thousand bodies" in referring to British reinforcements. "Sir," Churchill broke in with great indignation, "you will not refer to the personnel of His Majesty's Forces in such terms as 'bodies'. They're not corpses. They are live men, that's what they are."[61]

This sensitivity to the mass heroic man of action in total war was also demonstrated in Churchill's incredibly detailed preoccupation with such symbols as unit names and code-words. "I don't think much of the name 'Local Defence Volunteers' for very large new forces," he wrote the Secretary of State for War in 1940. "The word 'local' is uninspiring .... I think 'Home Guard' would be better."[62] And to Ismay, Churchill directed similar concerns about code words in August 1943.

> ... Operations in which large numbers of men may lose their lives ought not to be described by code-words which imply a boastful and over-confident sentiment, such as 'Triumphant', or, conversely, which are calculated to invest the plan with an air of despondency, such as 'Woebetide', 'Massacre', 'Jumble', 'Trouble', 'Fidget', 'Flimsy', 'Pathetic', and 'Jaundice'. They ought not to be names of a frivolous character, such as 'Bunnyhug', 'Billingsgate', 'Aperitif', and 'Ballyhoo' .... After all, the world is wide, and intelligent thought will readily supply an unlimited number of well-sounding names which do not suggest the character of the operation or disparage it in any way and do not enable some widow or mother to say that her son was killed in an operation called 'Bunnyhug' or 'Ballyhoo'.[63]

There was, of course, the ambivalence about conflict that had dogged Churchill since the era of total war began. "War is a game played with a smiling face," he told his daughter Sarah at Tehran in 1943, "but do you think there is laughter in my heart?"[64] And yet he was still fascinated by it. Captured German combat films, for instance, often marked the evening's entertainment. He also loved newsreels of the war and took particular delight if he was featured, often shouting to General Ismay: "Look Pug, there we are."[65] And, finally, there was his pride in *Desert Victory*, the film history of the Eighth Army, which he viewed over and over again, even sending a copy to Stalin.

J.F.C. Fuller touched upon a major reason for Churchill's ambivalence in a description that he eventually excised from his classic *The Conduct of War*. "The truth would appear to be," he wrote of Churchill, "that throughout his turbulent life he never quite grew up, and like a boy, loved big bangs and playing at soldiers."[66] Certainly, Churchill felt more intense exhilaration in battle than most professional soldiers. At one point early in World War II, enemy bombing commenced as he was being conducted around anti-aircraft sites in Richmond Park. Only after great difficulty and many protests, could the commander persuade the Prime Minister to take cover. "This exhilarates me," Churchill gleefully explained. "The sound of these cannon gives me a tremendous feeling."[67]

It was a pattern that was to be repeated many times in the war. Only George VI's intervention, for instance, kept Churchill from sailing with the assault forces on D-Day. "There is nothing I would like better than to go to sea," the King wrote his Prime Minister, "but I have agreed to stay at home; is it fair that you should then do exactly what I should have liked to do myself?"[68] Such restraint could only last a short time. A week later, Churchill crossed the Channel and had, as he wrote Roosevelt, "a jolly day ... on the beaches and inland."[69] In another example, Churchill described in his memoirs how he had gone to view a railroad bridge over the Rhine in March 1945 and how incoming artillery rounds had forced him and his party, escorted by the American General Simpson, to move off the bridge. Alanbrooke also described the scene, detailing how urgently Simpson had requested that Churchill evacuate the bridge. "The look on Winston's face was just like that of a small boy being called away from his sand-castles on the beach by his nurse!" he wrote. "He put both his arms around one of the twisted girders on the bridge and looked over his shoulder at Simpson with pouting mouth and angry eyes.... It was a sad wrench for him; he was enjoying himself immensely."[70]

Churchill's enjoyment and exhilaration in these incidents were closely tied to a schoolboy's perception of the danger and the drama involved. "A German came over," General Montgomery recalled of an air raid while Churchill was visiting the front lines in 1944. "There was an air battle. Eveyone was rather alarmed. Winston was rather pleased."[71] In a similar manner, Churchill loved the thrill of sailing through the submarine-infested waters of the Atlantic to a dramatic meeting place. But the drama, as he knew full well, was only a momentary escape from the business of total war. In the last spring of what he knew would be his last war, as he stood on a hillside watching British troops methodically cross the Rhine, he returned to the dramatic days of earlier wars. "I should have liked," he said wistfully, "to have deployed my men in red coats on the plain down there and ordered them to charge."[72]

Churchill's presence at the Rhine crossings demonstrated a key advantage offered him by the British constitution which ideally suited his temperament and views on leadership as a man of action. Unlike Roosevelt, constrained because of his special position as President, or Hitler who elected to isolate himself increasingly in command posts, the British Prime Minister traveled freely within the war zones. This allowed him to solve major military issues by face-to-face contact with his operational commanders. Moreover, the fact that his constitutional role did not prevent him from visiting the front lines, meant that he could fulfill his romantic conception of a war leader at the scene of action. Wherever he went, whether in the fighter control rooms of 1940, in the Egyptian desert, at the triumphal victory parade in Tripoli, on the beaches at Normandy, or at the Rhine crossings, Churchill's visible, inspirational presence in the most outrageous of *ad hoc* uniforms was a key factor that contributed not only to the prosecution of the war, but to the genuine affection in which he was held by the officers and men throughout the services.[73]

Such visits also renewed Churchill, allowing him to escape from the pressures of his office and exercise the degree of personal leadership that he associated with the great men of action from previous eras. Writing to his wife in August 1942 from Egypt, he recounted his visit to the front lines where he "was everywhere greeted with rapture by the troops," the same words he had used in his Marlborough biography to describe the great commander in 1705 after the battle of Elixem.[74] And on 3 February 1943, Churchill flew to forces just outside of Tripoli. In a small natural amphitheater, he told the assembled soldiers and airmen that "after the war when a man is asked what he did it will be quite sufficient for him to say, 'I marched and fought with the Desert Army'." The next day, he drove in an armored car into Tripoli, moving past the assembled forces, amazed to see the Prime Minister among them, but recovering sufficiently to remove their helmets and give three cheers. A short time later in Tripoli's main square, surrounded by veterans of the Eighth Army, Churchill took the marchpast of one of the Desert divisions, the tears streaming down his face.

For Churchill, this need to be at the center of action also involved the need to create that action. Once again, there was the romantic impetus. It was in his nature to demand the great marches and sweeping advances that would result in the capture of key cities whose names he could proudly proclaim in Parliament. After the 1943 seizure of Sicily, for instance, Churchill began immediately to press for bold action to bring about the fall of Italy. In a note to the Chiefs of Staff, he emphasized accordingly that Allied forces should not "crawl up the leg of Italy like a harvest bug, but strike boldly at the knee," which was Rome.[75] Moreover, for him to have allowed British policy to lapse into a purely defensive attitude would have nullified the effects of his refusal to seek a compromise with Hitler which had left him victory as the only alternative to defeat. "Wars cannot be won by sitting still and doing nothing," he remarked during the 1940 Norwegian campaign.[76] And despite the unfortunate outcome of doing something in that case, Churchill continued to press for new initiatives throughout the war.

There was at the same time a more rational, pragmatic basis for Churchill's call to action, a basis that he had foreseen in his study of Marlborough. "If the Allies were to rid themselves of the peril of being attacked in detail," he wrote, "they must wrest the initiative from Louis XIV, and by dominant action at one point or another rivet the attention of the central mass."[77] That dominant action for Britain in World War II initially involved strategic bombing and the offensives in the Middle East. The former was "not decisive, but better than doing nothing," particularly with public opinion and morale to consider.[78] In a similar manner, the campaigns in the Middle East were something the British Home Front could not ignore. More importantly, neither could the Nazi leader. For Hitler, as Churchill recounted it, those campaigns by the British were similar to the story of the horse with a raw hind leg who kicked anybody attempting to nurse it, until a veterinarian put a twitch in his nose, which in turn allowed the doctor to rub the leg with disinfectant. "That illustrates the initiative," Churchill concluded. " .... Once you grab the enemy by the nose, he will be able to think of nothing else."[79]

To define goals for action, however, as Churchill discovered in his dealings with his major military subordinates, did not necessarily ensure agreement on concepts to implement the action. On the one hand there was the impulsive, intuitive Prime Minister, who in Ismay's judgment, could be "relied on to make a century in a test match, but ... is no good at all at village cricket."[80] From this perspective, Churchill was an amateur. A gifted amateur, but an amateur all the same, who could not be allowed to indulge his impulses. "His military plans and ideas," Alanbrooke wrote of Churchill, "varied from the most brilliant concepts at the one end to the wildest and most dangerous ideas at the other. To wean him away from these wilder plans required superhuman efforts and was never entirely successful insofar as he tended to return to these again and again."[81]

Alanbrooke's assessment ignored, however, that middle ground between impulsive, intuitive feelings and rational calculation, where risk and audacity might be the best, if not the only means, to achieve a larger strategic goal. This was the ground frequented, as Churchill knew, by Marlborough whose "extraordinary quality of using audacity and circumspection as if they were tools to be picked up or laid down according to the job is the explanation of his never being entrapped in ten years of war." [82] And it was this ground that Churchill found again and again in the war in order to maintain the offensive spirit so necessary for final victory. The decision in 1940, for example, to risk the security of the British Isles in order to reinforce the Middle East, was taken by the Prime Minister against the advice of most of his military advisers. "In both these cases," one of his severest critics acknowledged, "we were endeavouring to base our action on a reasoned appreciation of what the Germans might do. Churchill seemed to move by impulse and by intuition, and we therefore regarded him as a gambler. In each case it must be admitted that the gamble would have come off." [83]

THE GOVERNMENT

> In total war it is quite impossible to draw any precise line between military and non-military problems.
>
> Churchill, *The Second World War*, Vol. II, p. 18

Political leaders of nations in total war normally tend to dominate government, no matter what the form of that government. In a dictatorship, as in Hitler's case, this type of war can reinforce an already pervasive totalitarian control. On the other hand, in a parliamentary government like England fighting for its survival, there can be a very fine line between authoritarianism and dictatorship. That Churchill walked that line successfully throughout the war was due in part to what C.P. Snow described as "the small size, the tightness, the extreme homogeneity, of the English official world." [84] The British leader was at home with both the civil and military elements of that essentially patrician world and would not go ultimately beyond what those elements allowed in his decisions as war lord. In many respects, Churchill conducted the war in this environment as though it were a very small family business. How informal the government could be, not to mention the security precautions, is illustrated in an account by General Pile, the anti-aircraft commander in Britain. At 4:30 a.m. after a night of examining Ack-Ack sites in the autumn of 1940, Pile and Churchill returned to 10 Downing Street almost unnoticed. "The Prime Minister," Pile recalled, "had a walking-stick with him with which he rapped the door sharply: When the butler opened it the Prime Minister said: 'Goering and Goebbels coming to report', and added, 'I am not Goebbels'. And so we went in." [85]

In the end, however, it was Churchill's unique blend of romanticism and pragmatism that allowed him to direct his nation in total war without subverting the beliefs and institutions for which Britain stood. For example, his dominance of the government's day-to-day machinery represented his rational and pragmatic tendencies at their best. At the same time, his romantic notions of key government institutions translated into maintenance of their traditional forms no matter what the exigencies of total war might be. Both tendencies were directly linked to the government's successful dealings throughout the war with the other elements of the "remarkable trinity," the people and the military. And finally, it was the successful confluence of those tendencies that allowed Churchill to form the "Grand Alliance," the ultimate key to victory.

The Machinery

> The pursuit of power with the capacity and the desire to exercise it worthily is among the noblest of human occupations.
>
> *Marlborough*, Vol. IV, p. 171

> Those who are charged with the direction of supreme affairs must sit on the mountain-tops of control ....
>
> *Thoughts and Adventures*, p. 7

Churchill took immediate action to consolidate his power in May 1940. To begin with, in creating his War Cabinet, he deliberately excluded service ministers, limiting the Cabinet members to five, including himself. The Secretary to the Cabinet was Sir Edward Bridges who was the link for Churchill to the principal civil and military departments of State. Churchill's direction of civil affairs, however, was not always clear-cut. Normally, his ministers and committees were left fairly much up to their own devices with the War Cabinet acting only as an occasional court of last appeal before his own final arbitration. In terms of foreign policy, on the other hand, the Prime Minister's domination was clear and complete, primarily due to his personal relationship with Anthony Eden, his Foreign Secretary for most of the war, and partly because he tended to go his own way regardless of Foreign Office opinion.

As for political competition, possible rivals were not tolerated near the seat of power. Halifax, the only possible alternative as Prime Minister, for instance, was dispatched to Washington as ambassador, and Stafford Cripps, a possible Labor alternative, was similarly relegated to obscurity. Another aspect of total war, however, was that because all else was subordinated to winning the conflict, and because political divisions therefore became less important, Churchill could afford to appoint non-political figures with special qualifications to certain ministerial offices. In the end, men accustomed to obey one master such as non-party specialists and former civil servants became the most successful ministers under Churchill.[86]

Churchill's most important step in centralizing power, however, was his assumption, with the King's blessing but without parliamentary mandate, of the post of Minister of Defence, a position unknown during World War I. Churchill was careful not to define the powers of the new post too precisely. But it was in this combined capacity as Minister of Defence and Prime Minister that the British leader was able to supervise the war effort, both as the ultimate political authority and as the specific war lord directing defense policy. "Henceforth," General Ismay commented in this regard, "the Prime Minister himself with all the powers and authority which attach to that office, exercised a personal, direct, ubiquitous and continuous supervision, not only over the formulation of military policy, but also over the general conduct of military operations."[87] This centralization of power would mean a crushing burden for Churchill, particularly in 1942; but as Roosevelt, Stalin and Hitler fully realized, power in total war is centripetal. Moreover, there was also the pragmatic recognition by Churchill that while it was all very well for emotion to provide an impetus for action, there had to be practical ways for implementing that action.

From first to last, Churchill's organization was rational and efficient, creating, as he rightly claimed, "a stream of coherent thought capable of being translated with great rapidity into coherent action."[88] The major problems in World War I, he continued to believe, had been the dominance of policy by strategy on the part of the Central Powers and the gaps in Britain between the central political direction and the service directorate. Above all, there was his experience at the Dardanelles, a principal lesson of which was that daring ventures could not be conducted by those holding subordinate offices, or indeed by those in the highest offices who did not have supreme power.[89] Churchill eliminated all this by creating under the War Cabinet the Defence Committee (Operations) consisting of the Deputy Prime Minister, the three Service Ministers and, later, the Foreign Minister. The Chiefs always attended meetings of this committee as did other ministers when required; and it was this organization, as well as Churchill himself, that became the focal point at which the political-military elements of power were brought together. In addition, there was the Defence Committee (Supplies), also normally chaired by the Prime Minister, which separated the many detailed logistics issues from policy and operations, while ensuring that the important link was not ignored.[90]

Directly under the Defence Committee (Operations) was the Chiefs of Staff Committee, presided over in many instances by the Prime Minister. It was through this committee that the Chiefs operated as a joint headquarters, using two principal subordinate structures, the Joint Planning Board and the Joint Intelligence Sub-Committee. Both committees not only emphasized inter-Service cooperation, but had either statutory

CHURCHILL, THE GREAT GAME AND TOTAL WAR

members or liaison officers as well from such key civilian ministries as War Transport, Home Security and Economic Warfare. It was, in short, a unified command with clear lines of responsibility that allowed Churchill to form an intimate relationship with the Chiefs that never emerged with the Germans or the Americans. Under this arrangement, the responsibility of the Chairman was confined to taking the chair at meetings, acting as spokesman for the Chiefs in terms of reporting to the Defence Committee or Cabinet, and advising on matters concerning only his own Service. Thus, there was no independent principal strategic adviser, which suited the temperament of Churchill, who always believed in dealing directly with the men who both knew the details and bore the responsibility. There were undoubtedly disadvantages to such a relationship in terms of what the military sometimes perceived as operational interference; but there was also a unique political-military bond that had a synergistic effect on all involved in the direction of war.[91]

To operate this organization, Churchill relied on what he termed his handling machine, General Sir Hastings (Pug) Ismay. Ismay brought to his job years of invaluable experience on the Committee of Imperial Defence. He was a hard worker of unchallenged reliability, a consummate bureaucrat who could elicit decisions and compromises without antagonizing – a staff officer, in the words of one of the Prime Minister's Private Secretaries, "to whom Churchill owed more and admitted that he owed more than to anybody else, military or civilian in the whole of the war."[92] That debt evolved, in part, from Ismay's extremely complex job. He served on the Chiefs of Staff Committee as Churchill's "Chief Staff Officer" and as his personal representative – roles that allowed him full membership without the right to sign the Committee reports. Ismay kept the Prime Minister informed of the routine meetings of the Committee, often submitting reports and plans to him for approval. At times this approval would be immediately forthcoming; on other occasions, Churchill would summon the Chiefs to discuss their proposed action or some associated issue on which political guidance was required.

In addition, Ismay's duties, carried out through the small but efficient Defence Secretariat, included keeping Churchill in touch with all organizations concerned with defense; conveying his instructions to those responsible for action with the appropriate follow-up, and coordinating actions whenever more than one department was involved in a defense decision.[93] Finally, the debt to Ismay included the general's resistance to the attempts by Churchill to fill the Office of the Minister of Defence with such well known court favorites as Professor Lindemann and Desmond Morton. Such power in defense matters without responsibility could have been disastrous. In the end, by sitting on the Prime Minister's memorandum concerning the matter, Ismay was able to discourage those "friends and adherents of Churchill who were at first like bees around a honey-pot."[94]

This did not mean, of course, that those men did not play a part in Churchill's decision-making process as the war proceeded. Lindemann, in particular, demonstrated how important access by an adviser could be. Churchill established the Prof. at 11 Downing Street with a door leading directly into the adjacent Prime Minister's residence – an example, as one expert on decision-making has described it, of "almost medieval or Renaissance propinquity" between ruler and adviser.[95] It was a propitious combination for the Prime Minister of intimacy and frequency of contact. In his seven varied ministerial positions since early in the century, Churchill had always absorbed an immense amount of detail, some of it, as in the case of the Admiralty, extremely technical. As Prime Minister, he maintained those habits, bringing everything he saw under intense scrutiny, then following up with comment and exhortation. Time was therefore limited; and it was precisely the value of this commodity to Churchill that made his intimate relations with Lindemann such an asset. For Lindemann had a special way of stripping a document to its base components and providing synthesized results that permitted rapid and easy understanding – particularly important in the case of statistics, which were always difficult for Churchill to understand.[96]

Access to any decision-maker is also dependent on the number of advisers. At the beginning of his tenure, Churchill often called full meetings of either the Defence Committee or the War Cabinet to address the myriad political-military issues associated with total war. Both organizations, however, fell increasingly into disuse as the war continued. The War Cabinet was content to leave the strategic questions as well as the day-to-day conduct of the war to the Minister of Defence and the Chiefs. At the same time, Churchill tended to rely more and more on meetings just with the Chiefs and those Ministers whose jurisdiction concerned a particular problem or issue, rather than convening the formal Defence Committee. Despite those changes, the system continued to function well in the conduct of total war. In particular, the advantages of combining the posts of Prime Minister and Minister of Defence were never more clearly demonstrated than in Churchill's dealings with the manpower budget, in which he exercised his authority over the entire panoply of government activities. In that process, military and civilian requirements were always in conflict, and it required an overarching concept of war direction to allocate manpower for the military forces, for the production of key war supplies, and for essential civilian needs.[97]

In addition to the permanent machinery of government, Churchill made a practice of establishing *ad hoc* committees over which he presided whenever he wanted to focus dramatically on a particular aspect of the war effort. It was the best combination of the emotional romantic and the rational pragmatist, as the Prime Minister's actions against the growing U-boat menace in 1941 demonstrated. On the one hand, there was the inspirational response to that menace, described by Churchill after he had heard the latest figures from Admiral Pound concerning Allied sinkings in the Atlantic.

> I said to Pound, "We have got to lift this business to the highest plane over everything else. I am going to proclaim, 'the Battle of the Atlantic.'" This, like featuring the "Battle of Britain" nine months earlier, was a signal intended to concentrate all minds and all departments concerned upon the U-boat war.[98]

On the other hand, there was the hard-headed, top down organization coupled with coordinated decentralization and supervision to back up the Prime Minister's abstract battle cry. On 6 March 1941, Churchill published his campaign directive which outlined civil and military responsibilities for the many agencies concerned. The efforts of those agencies were to be directed at the highest level by means of the newly created Battle of the Atlantic Committee. There were weekly meetings of this committee, initially chaired by Churchill, often of at least two hours' duration, and composed of the War Cabinet, Naval and Air Chiefs, scientists, and in Churchill's words, any other "high functionaries concerned." By 22 October 1941, the date of its last meeting, the committee had succeeded in the major political and military tasks outlined in Churchill's campaign plan.[99]

In other somewhat similar organizational efforts, Churchill demonstrated a pragmatic flexibility as he groped to find the most efficient ways to direct total war. In July 1940, for example, he established a standing ministerial committee on the Middle East. The committee, chaired by Eden, rarely met and caused a great duplication of effort. The mistake, as it had been with the ill-fated Dardanelles Committee in 1915, was not to co-locate policy representatives from the Middle East Committee with those charged with implementing strategy in the field. In 1941, Churchill attempted another organizational innovation for the Middle East by establishing the position of Minister of State in that region with the task of presiding over the entire war effort as the representative of the War Cabinet, to include providing the local Commanders-in-Chief with "that political guidance which has not hitherto been available" and to relieve them of "extraneous policies."[100] When the original incumbent of that position returned to fill another post in London later in the war, the Commanders-in-Chief in the Middle East urged an immediate replacement, emphasizing the indispensability of the political field direction. It was a development that would have been inconceivable in the "frocks-brass hats" atmosphere of the previous conflict. By the end of the war, Churchill's experiment had been repeated in all theaters of war.

In the end, Britain's organizational machinery for prosecuting the war achieved an important balance. On the one hand, it allowed Churchill to bring the full forces of his personality and eloquence to bear in decision-making sessions with his advisers. At one meeting of the Defence Committee in 1941, for instance, after unsuccessful attempts to cajole the participants into accepting his views, the Prime Minister adjourned the organization for a few hours. When the participants returned, he provided each with a Havana cigar, an extremely rare luxury at the time, which he had received from the President of Cuba. "It may well be that these each contain some deadly poison," Churchill joked as he made the presentations. "We lit up," one committee member recalled. "We sailed into the Cabinet room. In half an hour we had settled all we had argued about for hours."[101] On the other hand, the Defence Committee represented the type of restraints that could be imposed on the Prime Minister from a variety of military and civilian resources – "one of the reasons," a member of the Defence Secretariat later told Martin Gilbert, "why we won the war."[102] The fact that those restraints worked, however, was also due in large part to Churchill's respect for the system when his own forces of persuasion or intimidation failed to win the day. "I cannot recollect a single minister, serving officer or civil servant," Lord Bridges recalled in this regard, "who was removed from office because he stood up to Churchill."[103]

The Institutions

> The Parliamentary debates on the Combined General Staff and
> the higher direction of the war have fizzled out .... In the end
> Winston has been left supreme, and stronger than before, and
> it has been demonstrated again that all the other politicians are
> pigmies compared with him ....
>
> Kennedy, *The Business of War*, p. 233

Churchill's reverence for traditional liberties and political institutions allowed him to avoid the nemesis of his romanticism that was inherent in the dictatorships he opposed. "Though I have to strive with dictators," he wrote on his second anniversary as Prime Minister, "I am not, I am glad to say, a dictator myself."[104] Churchill had, of course, a passion for authority and order. But this was overshadowed by his extraordinary love of life that rebelled at any attempts to impose rigid disciplines upon the variety of human relations. To this was added an instinctive sense, which he demonstrated throughout his life, for those institutions that could either promote or retard and distort human growth and vitality. Preeminent for him among the former were the British Monarchy and Parliament. "He was only a subject under a monarchy and patriciate and the House of Commons," Churchill wrote of Marlborough. "He could never be more ...."[105]

The British Crown was a source of strength for Churchill as the leader of the government. To begin with, it provided a visible sign of continuity to the British people throughout the war. Equally important, by remaining in London to endure the hardships of the Blitz, the Royal Family reinforced the defiant spirit Churchill invoked in the British people. The Prime Minister's relations also improved dramatically with George VI, a personal development of great importance for the morale of a man whose romantic reverence for the Monarchy was deep and abiding. "It is needless for me to assure Your Majesty," Churchill wrote to the King after the victory at Alamein in November 1942, "of my devotion to Yourself and Family and to our ancient and cherished Monarchy – the true bulwark of British freedom against tyrannies of every kind ...."[106]

That romantic vision did not include the King's brother, whom Churchill had championed only a few years earlier. In the summer of 1940 as Britain prepared for possible invasion, the Prime Minister's approach to the Duke of Windsor was distinctly rational, ruthless and pragmatic in his efforts to remove the former King from the continent to the Bahamas as Governor. The change was apparent in the firm but polite letters in which Churchill resisted sending two servants of military age to the Duke and forbade his traveling in the United States. Most importantly, there was the matter of Windsor's own view of Britain's enemy. "The freedom of conversation ... is not possible in any direct representative of the Crown," he wrote the Duke on 27 July. "Many sharp and unfriendly ears will be pricked up to catch any suggestion that your Royal Highness takes a view about the war, or about the Germans, or about Hitlerism, which is different from that adopted by the British nation and Parliament."[107]

Churchill's linkage of the British nation and Parliament in his letter to the Duke of Windsor was significant. For him, despite the advent of radio, Parliament was his conduit to the people; and it was no accident that many of his radio addresses to the nation were barely reworked Parliamentary speeches. In his first speech after taking office, Churchill addressed this issue and clearly indicated that both Houses of Parliament had important roles to play in the supreme test of the national will. He never deviated from this policy. Throughout World War II, he continued to consult with Parliament and keep its members up-to-date on the progress of that conflict. At one such session, an MP who had entered the House of Commons in 1891, thanked Churchill for his treatment of members "as responsible individuals and not as irresponsible nobodies" and then went on to praise the Prime Minister's leadership as "incomparably the most brilliant that I can remember since perhaps that of Mr. Gladstone."[108]

Both Houses of Parliament continued to meet in London throughout the war. With his romantic reverence for the institution, Churchill's rejection of an evacuation plan for Parliament was a foregone conclusion, with alternative accommodations established instead in London. Within those romantic parameters, however, there was an element of rational prudence. In a September 1940 secret session of the Commons, he outlined plans to keep the dates of Parliamentary sessions as secret as possible in order to prevent both Houses from becoming targets for the German bombers. "We ought not to flatter ourselves," he concluded, "by imagining that we are irreplaceable, but at the same time it cannot be denied that two or three hundred by-elections would be a quite needless complication of our affairs at this particular juncture."[109] Such elections were not necessary when the empty Parliament buildings were bombed in the spring of 1941. On the morning of 11 May, Churchill wandered in the still smoking ruins of the House of Commons, savagely poking the end of his walking stick into the cinders that had once been the doors leading from behind the Speaker's Chair. Tears ran unchecked down his cheeks. Brushing the sleeve of his coat across his eyes in the manner of a schoolboy ashamed of his tears, the Prime Minister turned abruptly on an official and with a voice controlled only with effort, said with quiet ferociousness: "This Chamber must be rebuilt − just as it was! Meanwhile, we shall not miss a single day's debate through this!"[110]

During the early dark years of the conflict, Churchill never lost his romantic faith in Parliament, even when there were indications that many of its members and their constituencies were questioning his conduct of the war. In the spring of 1941, the fall of Greece and the loss of Cyrenaica led to an increase of criticism in the House of Commons which culminated on 7 May in a vote of confidence of 447 to three − a clear victory for Churchill who had accepted ultimate responsibility as head of the government. "It follows therefore," he had stated prior to the Division in which the government had received the vote of confidence, "when all is said and done, that I am the one whose head should be cut off if we do not win the war."[111] And that seemed a distinct possibility by the end of the year. For six months, from the December 1941 Arcadia Conference until Rommel was halted in the first battle of Alamein, there was a constant series of British disasters in the Far East, in Africa, in the Atlantic and even in the Channel, which undermined Churchill's domestic power.

In January 1942, mindful of mounting press and political criticism, Churchill insisted on a vote of confidence from the Commons and won handily by a 464 to one vote. But as he and his wife pushed through the congratulatory crowd as they left Parliament, the ticker tape was bringing news of German claims to have entered Benghazi and Japanese claims to have reached Singapore. By the end of February, Singapore had been captured, General Auchinleck had been pushed back to Gazala, and the Channel had been traversed with humiliating ease by the *Scharnhorst* and *Gneisenau*. On 25 June 1942, after Auchinleck's defeat, Churchill faced a motion in the Commons that "this House, while paying tribute to the heroism and endurance of the Armed Forces of the Crown ... has no confidence in the central direction of the war."[112] On 1 July, the debate began on the Vote of Censure, the thrust of which was to eliminate Churchill's position of Minister of Defence. That same day, German forces reached El Alamein, 130 miles inside Egypt, 80 miles from Cairo, and in the Crimea captured Sebastopol.

Churchill would not turn away from the institution he revered. At the same time, however, harkening back to World War I and his experiences thus far in the current conflict, he would not approach leadership in total war without possession of the means necessary to prosecute that type of conflict. "I am your servant," he told the Commons on 2 July, "and you have the right to dismiss me when you please. What you have no right to do is to ask me to bear responsibilities without the power of effective action ...."[113] At the conclusion of the debate, only 25 members supported the vote, a consoling figure to the historically-minded Prime Minister in more than one way, since it duplicated the number of votes against the conduct by Pitt of the war in 1799. Equally important, there was a message from across the Atlantic. "Good for you," Roosevelt telegraphed. "Action of House of Commons today delighted me."[114]

After July 1942, Churchill could devote all his energies to the war without worrying about party politics. The Conservatives retained their vast majority, and he was supported by loyal colleagues from all parties. There was some question as to whether a truly national leader should be a party leader at all, but Churchill remembered the final days of Asquith's Government in World War I and had no doubt on the subject. Most importantly, the Prime Minister's parliamentary position enhanced his dealings with the other two-thirds of Clausewitz' "remarkable trinity." So great was his confidence in his standing with Parliament as the war continued, that on 30 March 1944, after the government's defeat by a single vote on an Education Bill, Churchill announced that the Bill would be debated on the following day and if the government did not secure an adequate majority, it would "entail the usual constitutional consequences."[115]

The threat of Churchill's fall was too much. On 31 March, the government received a majority of over 400. "I was sure you would be interested in the House of Commons racket," Churchill wrote his son on 4 April 1944. "I am the child of the H. of C., and when I was molested by a number of cheeky boys I ran for succour to the old Mother of Parliaments and she certainly chased them out of the back yard with her mop."[116]

In the end, Parliament, like the Monarchy, fulfilled Churchill's romantic Whig perception of an institution for all ages − an institution which, because it had evolved slowly by trial and error in an ever-progressive path, was flexible enough to respond to the needs of total war. It was a source of strength to him throughout the war as a visible manifestation that he was representing not only the British people in their ultimate time of trial, but that vast once and future constituency to whom he was equally devoted.

At the conclusion of his address to parliament on VE Day, Churchill put his manuscript aside and spoke of his "deep gratitude" to the Commons which had proved itself "the strongest foundation of waging war that has ever been seen in the whole of our day. We have all of us made our mistakes," he added, "but the strength of the Parliamentary institution has been shown to enable it at the same time to preserve all the title-deeds of democracy while waging war in the most stern and protracted form."[117]

The Grand Alliance

> The Grand Alliance quivered at this moment in every part of its vast fragile organization. Marlborough saw that without some enormous new upholding force it must come clattering down.
>
> *Marlborough*, Vol. III, p. 290

> The history of all coalitions is a tale of the reciprocal complaints of allies ....
>
> *Marlborough*, Vol. V, p. 246

Churchill had long recognized the value of gaining and preserving a victorious combination of allies in total war. His government's achievement of such a combination in World War II was one of its major, if not most decisive, accomplishments and was due in large part to the favorable confluence of the romantic and practical streaks in the Prime Minister's character. Churchill's romantic concept of the Grand Alliance was inspired by his studies of Marlborough and was so successful that it continued to live on in many history books after the war as a definition of the tripartite relationship between the wartime allies. There were actually, however, three distinct bilateral relationships. Two of them, the Anglo-American and the Anglo-Soviet, were consistently functioning political associations. The third, that between the Soviet Union and the United States, was significantly less developed, depending as it did on the emphasis attached to it by Roosevelt, who only asserted himself at the 1942 Second Front negotiations and at the Teheran and Yalta conferences. That divided framework provided more than enough room for Churchill in the early years of the war to seize the initiative and indulge his compulsive activism.[118]

When Churchill assumed office on 10 May 1940, he had an idiosyncratic, emotional and romanticized view of Anglo-American relations that tended to an over-reliance on constitutional themes and historical presuppositions. That view reinforced the new Prime Minister's primary, pragmatic insight into the potentially decisive character of United States power and his conviction that America could be harnessed to further Britain's wartime interests. On the morning of 18 May 1940, Randolph Churchill asked his father if he really believed that defeat could be avoided and after receiving an affirmative reply, persisted in asking exactly how this would be accomplished. Churchill, who was shaving at the time, turned from the mirror to his son and replied with great intensity: "I shall drag the United States in."[119] That, in turn, required negotiations in the coming months, normally conducted by the British leader from a position of weakness. Nevertheless, he managed to manipulate the fragile lines of communications across the Atlantic in a manner that was, in Ronald Lewin's assessment, "feline, adroit, and far-sighted."[120]

All these characteristics were brought to play on 15 May 1940 in the first of the Churchill letters to Roosevelt signed "Former Naval Person," designed to further a chivalric link between the two-time First Lord of the Admiralty and a President who loved the sea and who looked back nostalgically to his tenure as Assistant Secretary of the Navy in the First World War.[121] Despite the pragmatic motivation for this effort, Churchill never lost his genuine romantic perception of the evolving "special relationship" that formed the basis for the chivalric link. For him, brotherhood in war between allied chieftains was as natural at the strategic level as at the tactical. Had not Marlborough on the night after Ramillies invited Goslinga, the Dutch field deputy, to share his cloak spread on the ground for a few hours sleep?[122] And there was the ultimate example of Marlborough and Eugene throughout the wars against Louis XIV. "Then at once began that glorious brotherhood in arms," Churchill wrote of the first meeting between the two men in June 1704, "which neither victory nor misunderstanding could disturb, before which jealousy and misunderstanding were powerless and of which the war furnishes no equal example."[123]

So it was with Churchill and Roosevelt. Both men were imaginative, but whereas Roosevelt was steeped in the idea of social progress, Churchill was steeped in history which fostered his belief in institutions and the permanent character of races, classes and types of individuals. It was a more serious, more intently concentrated and preoccupied outlook, which caused the British leader to believe that external differences could make the new, freer and richer order envisioned by his American counterpart very difficult to attain. Their methods of operation also contrasted sharply. Roosevelt believed in flexibility and improvisation while practicing a highly personal form of government. As a consequence, his own office was not tightly organized and his bureaucracy was often chaotic, perhaps by design. Churchill, on the other hand, organized his government on clear principles and operated his private office in a highly disciplined manner. Moreover, his habits, although unusual, were normally regular.

Despite these differences, each man perceived the other in a romantic light, above the battles of allies and subordinates, much like royal cousins. In this regard, Churchill described in his memoirs an evening ritual with the President at the White House. "I wheeled him in the chair from the drawing room to the lift as a mark of respect," he recalled, "and thinking also of Sir Walter Raleigh spreading his cloak before Queen Elizabeth."[124] Both were proud of this relationship, a pride tempered by a sometimes amused, but never ironical, perception of the other's peculiar qualities. It was this mutual romantic perception that made their meetings and correspondence occasions to which both consciously rose.[125]

Churchill played this romantic link to great effect. There was, for instance, his first wartime meeting with Roosevelt in August 1941 on board the *Prince of Wales* at Placentia Bay in Newfoundland. For the moving church service on the windswept deck of the ship that would be sunk within a few months, Churchill personally selected the hymns and arranged for each of the hundreds of British sailors, many soon to perish with their ship, to share his hymnsheet with an American counterpart.[126] And there was his vision of an external union of the English-speaking peoples, an inexorable fusion of the two democracies which, as he told the Commons, like "the Mississippi, it just keeps rolling along."[127] In a speech to Harvard at the height of the war, in this regard, the British leader referred to a common conception of what was "right and decent" and of a common "regard for fair play," which along with the "priceless inheritance" of a common tongue might someday become the basis for a common citizenship. "I like to think," Churchill concluded, "of British and Americans moving about freely over each other's wide estates with hardly a sense of being foreigners to one another."[128] It was this vision that brought the American Congress to its feet a few weeks after Pearl Harbor, when Churchill referred to the Japanese attack in a speech before a joint session of that body and asked: "What sort of people do they think we are?"[129]

Throughout the war, the personal link between the two leaders continued to govern the Anglo-American coalition. There were, of course, as Churchill ruefully acknowledged, increasing strains in that coalition as the enormous power of the United States began to dominate the partnership. "In working with Allies," he reported to the Commons, "it sometimes happens that they develop opinions of their own." Since 1776, he added, "we have not been in the position of being able to decide the policy of the United States."[130] Still, the romance of the relationship never failed to sustain the British leader, even in the acrimonious final year of the war. "Our personal friendship," he telegraphed Roosevelt two days before the invasion of France, "is my greatest stand-by amid the ever increasing complications of this exacting war."[131] And when that relationship ended, it was as if Eugene had been struck down at Marlborough's side in the final heat of victorious battle. After a memorial service in St. Paul's Cathedral for President Roosevelt on 17 April 1945, the American Ambassador escorted a tearful Churchill to the door. Outside, one participant about to drive away, turned back toward the

Cathedral and "saw Winston standing bare-headed, framed between two columns of the portico, and he was sobbing as the shaft of sunlight fell on his face ...."[132]

But all that was relatively far in the future in the summer of 1940 when Churchill pleaded for the immediate dispatch of 50 or 60 of America's oldest destroyers. "Mr. President," he wrote on 31 July 1940, "with great respect I must tell you that in the long history of the world this is a thing to do *now*."[133] It was an impassioned request that had to wait, however, the course of more realistic events. The first event had already occurred in June with the German subjugation of France, which focused American attention on the key issues of British survival and German European hegemony. But this revelation alone was not enough. There would be no American intervention in a lost cause, which was why the second event, the Battle of Britain in the autumn of 1940, was so important. For it was that battle that gave substance to Britain's determination to resist, as proclaimed by Churchill in his continuing dialogue with his nation. Finally, the reelection of Roosevelt in November 1940 opened the way for the full practical support that formed the real beginning of the Anglo-American alliance.[134]

There was, however, one more personal obstacle for Churchill to surmount. On 9 January 1941, Harry Hopkins arrived as Roosevelt's personal emissary to assess not only the British war effort, but the British Prime Minister as well. The two men had never met. Churchill knew nothing of the visiting American and had to be specifically briefed. Hopkins, on the other hand, knew enough of Churchill to entertain large reservations about him. These reservations were soon dispelled, as Churchill launched an all-out effort to win him over, which included propelling the fragile Hopkins on a whirlwind tour of military installations and units throughout England. The American visitor would often attempt to hide in the Prime Minister's entourage on those occasions, but to no avail. "Harry, Harry, where are you?" was Churchill's remorseless cry as he brought the President's personal representative up to the front to be displayed.[135]

By the end of the trip, Hopkins was converted. To the President, he wrote: "*Churchill* is the gov't in every sense of the word – he controls the grand strategy and often the details .... I cannot emphasize too strongly that he is the one and only person over here with whom you need to have a full meeting of minds."[136] To the Prime Minister, Hopkins was equally direct, while displaying, as Lord Moran reported, a newly formed sense of romantic communion.

> I suppose you wish to know what I am going to say to President Roosevelt on my return. Well, I'm going to quote you one verse from that Book of Books ...: "Whither thou goest, I will go; and where

thou lodgest, I will lodge: thy people shall be my people, and thy God my God." Then he added very quietly: "Even to the end."

"I was surprised to find the P.M. in tears," Moran added. "He knew what it meant. Even to us the words seemed like a rope thrown to a drowning man."[137] The conversion of Hopkins was a significant achievement. In the short term, he returned to the United States to become the driving force behind Lend Lease and to confirm and support Roosevelt's policy inclinations toward Great Britain. In the long term, it provided Churchill, through his correspondence with Hopkins, which started at that time, a means to raise issues of a more realistic, pragmatic nature than he felt able to raise in the "Former Naval Person" exchanges.[138]

The immediate result of all those events was Roosevelt's Lend Lease program, described by Churchill as "the most unsordid act in the history of any nation," but more accurately by Ronald Lewin as "perhaps the most enlightened act of self-interest." For if the "special relationship" was no fiction, it was certainly less idealistic and romantic than Churchill presented it. American commercial self-interest was a dominant theme throughout the war, and interspersed among the many acts of generosity and forbearance by the Roosevelt administration, were the attempts by the United States to use military aid as commercial leverage against Great Britain. And yet once again, it was the rational pragmatist making the best of reality with romantic gloss. Britain, in fact, was bankrupt at the time, and Churchill was bargaining for survival means in any way he could. By the following spring, Britain's reserves of gold and cash did not exceed 12 million dollars. If it is true, as some have written, that during the war Churchill sacrificed Britain's tomorrow for the nation's today, it seems equally certain that there would have been no tomorrow for Britain if he had not grasped at his only realistic option for survival.[139]

Churchill's relationship with the other third of the Grand Alliance was equally realistic, but without any attempt to cloak it in romance. In fact, Britain had much more in common with each of the other two stronger allies than they had with each other. Both Britain and the Soviet Union, for example, lived on the edge of the threat and both could look back on long term involvement as well as rivalry in terms of Europe, the Eastern Mediterranean and the Near East. Most importantly, the two countries were used to operating in the style of European diplomacy that, among other things, included the habit of unembarrassed *Realpolitik* discussions on such topics as spheres of influence and balance of power. As a consequence, Stalin was generally more receptive in the early years of the Grand Alliance to Churchill and his attempts to develop a strong working relationship than to Roosevelt.[140]

At the beginning of the war, of course, the situation was different. Churchill was able to indulge his distaste for the Soviet regime in a series of schemes at that time that might have brought on war between Britain and Russia had not each scheme been overcome by events. For instance, he actively promoted Anglo-French plans to reduce Soviet ore shipments to Germany by bombing the Caspian city of Baku and by dispatching submarines to the Black Sea. In addition, there were his enthusiastic plans to provide military aid to Finland during the Russo-Finnish War; and there was his call for action in Norway to prevent iron ore shipments to Germany, which might also have brought Britain into direct confrontation with the Soviet Union. Churchill returned to a more levelheaded, pragmatic approach after the German invasion of France, and made several approaches to Stalin. There was no response, even when the British leader warned Stalin of the impending German invasion. Churchill did not persist in the warning. "Now is the time for sombre restraint on our part, and let them do the worrying."[141]

At no time during the war was the value of the rational, pragmatic side of Churchill's nature more clearly demonstrated than his immediate decision to join Russia as an ally after Barbarossa, leaving no time for mistrust or for doubts and misgivings to fester. On 21 June 1941, the day the German attack on Russia began, Churchill went on the air to declare that "we shall give whatever help we can to Russia .... The Russian danger is therefore our danger ...." Much of the Prime Minister's broadcast was addressed to those who remembered his long record of virulent anti-Bolshevism. "No one has been a more consistent opponent of Communism than I have .... But that all fades away before the spectacle which is now unfolding ...." And for those who dwelt upon Russia's collusion with Germany and her indifference to Britain's survival, there was "but one aim and one single, irrevocable purpose. We are resolved to destroy Hitler and every vestige of the Nazi regime."[142]

More than any other lesson from his first encounter with total war, Churchill had learned the value of policy's domination of strategy. That lesson was clearly apparent in the decisions that the British leader made regarding the Soviet Union in the last half of 1941. To begin with, there were the northern sea convoys, carrying weapons and equipment from Britain's meager supplies in the face of opposition from the Chiefs of Staff for whom invasion was still a very real possibility. That flow to the north, as General Ismay later recalled, "was like having all one's eye-teeth drawn at the same time."[143] On 28 August, the Chiefs sent a memorandum to Churchill concerning the issue of Hurricanes for Russia. "These aircraft," they wrote, "would pay a better dividend if sent to the Far East and to the Middle East .... On the other hand, the Chiefs of Staff realize that political considerations may be overriding."[144]

And so they were. In the final analysis, as Churchill well knew, he had to take calculated military risks to keep the Russian colossus, with whom Britain's survival was now linked, in the fight as a politically and militarily viable entity. And this was by no means certain in 1941 as German forces sliced through Western Russia. Moreover, there was always the possibility of another rapprochement between Stalin and Hitler, when German forces stalled before Moscow the following winter. By that time, neither Roosevelt nor Churchill could ignore the precedent of the 1939 Non-Aggression Pact, particularly since there could be no immediate response to Stalin's imperious demands for a Second Front. It was in this sense, then, that Churchill used the political-military strands of his dual positions as Prime Minister and Minister of Defence to weave ever-tightening links, totally devoid of any romantic notions, with the Soviet Union.

The process was not an easy one. In the spring and summer of 1942, for instance, Churchill was faced with a key political-military dilemma by his new allies in the Grand Alliance. During this period, Hitler tightened the pressure on the Murmansk convoys by increasing the number of U-boats, surface vessels and aircraft along the northern approaches to Russia. At the same time, the spring thaws released the German forces on every front in the East, causing mounting pressure on the British leader from both his allies to increase the number of convoys to the Soviet Union. In April and May there was a tense exchange of messages between Churchill and Roosevelt concerning "the log jam," and a final attempt at delay on 2 May. "I beg you not to press us beyond our judgment in the operation," Churchill cabled the President on that day.[145] But the pressure was unremitting, supporting an already existing conviction on the part of the Prime Minister that an undefeated Russia was worth almost any risk. "We are resolved," he cabled Stalin on 9 May, "to fight through to you with the maximum amount of war materials."[146] The implementation of this decision included overruling objections by the Chiefs in mid-May. "The operation is justified," Churchill responded to his military leaders, "if a half get through. Failure on our part to make the attempt would weaken our influence with both our major allies."[147]

It was not, however, such an easy matter. Misgivings concerning northern resupply were borne out in late May by a massive German air attack on two convoys and the disaster to convoy PQ17 in July. PQ17 sailed from Ireland to Archangel on 27 June 1942. It consisted of 34 merchant ships and 21 escort vessels, the first Anglo-American escort. Of the 34 merchant vessels, 23 were sunk, 14 of them American. Churchill now had to contend with the inevitable wave of public indignation; and geopolitical risk assessments were subordinated to a different, equally pragmatic realism that took into account the domestic pressure of total war. On 17 July 1942, acting on the recommendations of the Chiefs, the Prime Minister suspended further convoys until the perpetual daylight of summer on the northern routes had ended. At the same time he provided a detailed rationale to Stalin who replied that his "naval experts consider the reasons put forward ... wholly unconvincing."[148]

A month later, Churchill had to deal with similar reactions in his first visit to the Soviet Union, the "sullen sinister Bolshevik State I had once tried so hard to strangle at its birth ...." Not only did the British leader have to confirm his convoy decision, but he had to inform Stalin that there would be no Second Front in Europe for 1942, a mission, Churchill pointed out, "like carrying a large lump of ice to the North Pole."[149] It was a price Churchill was willing to pay as the middle link to the other two desperately needed elements of the Grand Alliance. Nevertheless, he could take only so much of the Soviet leader's insults. At one point, Churchill lashed back at a deprecating remark by Stalin concerning the British war effort, growing more and more heated until he overwhelmed the interpreter who was so enthralled by the Prime Minister's speech that he put his pencil down. "Did you tell him this? Did you tell him this?" Churchill repeatedly queried the interpreter who was attempting to impart his words to the Russian leader. Stalin began to laugh. "Your words are not important," he said, "what is vital is the spirit."[150]

That spirit would continue to animate the Grand Alliance. By 1943, however, both Stalin and Roosevelt were operating from a position of increasing power and influence, while that of Churchill was in decline. That vulnerability was suddenly and humiliatingly exposed at the November 1943 Teheran conference, in which the American President actively sided both publicly and privately with the Soviet leader against Churchill on several key strategic issues. It was a turning point in the tripartite alliance. But the fact remained that it was a victorious alliance and one that would never have come into existence without the sustained, inspired efforts of the British leader. To the United States, Churchill had called forth from his heritage and character the right blend of romance and pragmatism. To the Soviet Union, he had subordinated his deepest political hostility in a coalition that would always be for him one of pragmatic necessity rather than sentiment. All in all, it was a stupendous accomplishment calling for skills similar to those demonstrated by the first Duke of Marlborough in forming an equally unlikely coalition against an earlier European despot.

THE PEOPLE

The human element – in defiance of experience and probability – may produce a wholly irrational result, and a starving outmanoeuvred army win food, safety and honour by their bravery.

Churchill, *The River War*, p. 318.

These are the actions of the Duke of Marlborough, performed in the compass of a few years; sufficient to adorn the annals of ages .... The sense which the British Nation had of his transcendent merit was expressed in the most solemn, most effectual, most durable manner. The Acts of Parliament inscribed on this pillar shall stand as long as the British name and language last — illustrious monuments of Marlborough's glory and of Britain's gratitude.

From the inscription on the Column of Victory
at Blenheim Palace

At the beginning of the First World War, the British people had no real notion of what total war was like. They were not used to rationing, and the myriad regulations that came to govern their daily lives were intensely unpopular, the all encompassing DORA, the Defence of the Realm Act, being the most egregious example. The Russian Revolution only fueled this discontent, and there was increased industrial unrest in Britain toward the end of the conflict that sometimes took on an anti-war character. Nor could the people grasp the totality of defeat in modern war, the majority imagining that submission to Germany would require a gold indemnity, much like the one that the French had provided to Germany in 1871. In the Second World War, there were no such delusions. Defeat would mean slavery and the destruction embodied in the German bombings and, later in the conflict, the V-weapons. In this regard, Churchill emphasized in an unpublished note originally intended for his memoirs, "everyone realized how near death and ruin we stood. Not only individual death, which is the universal experience, stood near, but, incomparably more commanding, the life of Britain, her message and her glory."[151]

Part of that realization was due to Churchill and his concept of total war. For him, the people were the basis for that concept, whether serving in the military or on the Home Front. That there would be no such distinction was made clear in an early speech that left no effort in the totality of war unaddressed. "Come then: let us to the task, to the battle, to the toil — each to our part, each to our station," he exhorted in January 1940. "Fill the armies, rule the air, pour out the munitions, strangle the U-boats, sweep the mines, plough the land, build the ships, guard the streets, succour the wounded, uplift the downcast, and honour the dead."[152]

It was a war cry to an entire nation that retained the romance of earlier wars in previous centuries because of its combative focus on the people. In a radio broadcast that summer, Churchill reconfirmed that focus when he placed the coming struggle in the context of a total war which, however impersonal and technical in nature, still depended on the anonymous individual citizen and his faith in Britain. "This is no war of chieftains or of princes, of dynasties or national ambition," he said; "it is a war of peoples and of causes .... This is a war of the Unknown Warrior; but let all strive without failing in faith or in duty, and the dark curse of Hitler will be lifted from our age." The effect of such an appeal was

117

immediate. "But really he has got guts that man," Harold Nicolson wrote his wife after the speech, reflecting the national impression. " ... I felt a great army of men and women of resolution watching for the fight. And I felt that all the silly people were but black-beetles scurrying into holes."[153]

Nicolson's reaction demonstrated how important a sense of participation in total war was to members of the Home Front and how perceptively Churchill had gauged that need. The Blitz, of course, more than satisfied that need for the people of London and other major cities that bore the brunt of German air attacks. Nevertheless, Churchill pointed out in October 1940, the air attacks were a manifestation of total war "which would suit the English people once they got used to it. They would prefer all to be ... taking part in the battle of London than to look on hopelessly at mass slaughters like Passchendaele."[154] His experiences with the British people throughout the war only reinforced this impression. In June 1945 while presiding over a meeting of the Crossbow Committee to discuss the V-1 menace, the Prime Minister talked of the Home Front in terms of a flying bomb that had killed more than 60 people the day before, many of them serving officers, during a service at the Guards Chapel. "He was at his best," one participant noted in his diary, "and said the matter had to be put robustly to the populace, that their tribulations were part of the battle in France, and that they should be very glad to share in the soldiers' danger."[155] A few days later in a letter to Stalin, Churchill reconfirmed his faith in those who manned the Home Front. "You may safely disregard all the German rubbish about the results of their flying bomb," he wrote, "... The people are proud to share in a small way the perils of our own soldiers ...."[156]

Churchill also realized, however, that there were limits to mass patience and forbearance. In 1943, he warned the American Congress in this regard that "it is in the dragging-out of the war at enormous expense, until the democracies are tired or bored or split, that the main hopes of Germany and Japan must now reside."[157] One answer, the British leader believed, was to demonstrate concern, appreciation and common sense in dealing with the deprivations of the population in total war. In this regard, he understood that general rationing was not in itself harmful to morale. But smallmindedness was. "Try to cut out petty annoyances," Churchill wrote the Minister of Food,

> whether in hotels, the little shops or the private lives of ordinary people. Nothing should be done for spite's sake. The great work of rationing in this country, which has given so much confidence and absence of class feeling, should not be prejudiced by little trumpery regulations which when enforced make hard cases.[158]

As the war progressed, other schemes emerged on a personal *ad hoc* basis that demonstrated the Prime Minister's constant concern about the British people. After a visit in August 1940 to the badly bombed coastal town of Ramsgate, for instance, Churchill initiated immediate action on financial compensation to all citizens whose homes had been destroyed. And a few months later, he wrote to the Minister of Transport suggesting a scheme to shorten bus queues and thereby improve public morale. "Get 20,000 unused motor cars," he wrote, "to ply in the rush-hours and ... organize them into a regular corps." Thousands of men and women, the Prime Minister added, "would be enchanted to come in and carry off this painful accumulation of hard-working folk."[159] But it was in his attempts to minimize the rationing of foodstuffs that Churchill devoted his most consistent, pragmatic efforts. "The way to lose the war," he wrote in this regard, "is to try to force the British public into a diet of milk, oatmeal, potatoes, etc., washed down on gala occasions with a little lime juice."[160]

Ultimately, as Churchill also realized, the maintenance of public morale was to a large extent dependent on his frankness and openness with the people, particularly in his radio broadcasts. Censorship aided him in those broadcasts, because the public was starved for news and information. Moreover, censorship always left the lingering suspicion that what news remained might be altered for policy purposes. But with Churchill, the public felt that he would give them the facts straight, that he would not try to disguise bad news. Furthermore, there was always the hope that he might give more information than planned, since he was one of the few men in England who could not be censored, and particularly since he revised his texts right up to broadcast time. As a consequence, Churchill had a ready-made and sympathetic national audience with enormous confidence in him.[161]

The public confidence was also a result of Churchill's sensitivity throughout the war to what the people were thinking and what they wanted. If times were tense, he gave them a moment's relief. Early in the war, for instance, when German forces were bombing and machine-gunning merchant vessels and fishing boats, Churchill's broadcast concluded: "I am glad to tell you that the heat of their fury has so far exceeded the accuracy of their aim."[162] But he also believed that the people should not be caught unawares by events, that they would respond positively no matter how grim the event if they were properly prepared, as they were for the Blitz. On 26 June 1940, Churchill emphasized that air raids should be treated "in a cool way," while pointing out that most people were "not at all affected" by any single air raid. "The people must learn," he added, "to take air raids as if they were no more than thunderstorms."[163] And when he learned in 1941 of Hitler's plans to drive into the Balkans with all that the invasion entailed, public support was uppermost on Churchill's mind. "He knows this will be a blow to British prestige," Harry Hopkins reported, "and is obviously considering ways and means of preparing the British public for it."[164]

In a similar manner, the proclamation of good news also had to be handled carefully. On 23 October 1942 the final battle of Alamein began and by 6 November, General Alexander was able to proclaim victory in a message to Churchill that began: "Ring out the bells!" But Churchill was reluctant to raise the expectations of the British people precipitously. He recalled how in 1917 the first substantial armored action at Cambrai had fired the enthusiasm of the population, only to be followed swiftly by the news that German divisions had recovered all the ground gained by British forces. As a consequence, he waited until the Torch landings occurred two days later before making a full announcement of the Alamein victory.[165]

Churchill's sensitivity to news from the battlefield was understandable. There was, of course, the immediate upward surge of public morale after a great victory as he had noted of Marlborough's time when "Blenheim ... aroused the spirit of the English to a degree of warlike enthusiasm scarcely ever equalled in our records."[166] The problem for Churchill in the Second World War was that there was very little such news in the first two years of his leadership, leaving only the fairly constant flow of information concerning war-related disasters that had to be carefully managed. On 17 June 1940, for instance, the *Lancastria* was bombed during an evacuation of 5,000 soldiers from St. Nazaire. Almost 3,000 soldiers were killed. "When the news came to me in the great Cabinet Room during the afternoon," Churchill recorded in his memoirs, "I forbade its publication saying: 'The newspapers have got quite enough disaster for today at least.' "[167] Churchill carefully monitored the press reaction to such disasters. At midnight every night, he received the next day's newspapers by special courier from Fleet Street and would often read them before going to bed. The next morning, if he were not too busy, he would read them again. From all that would come a flood of questions for not only his ministers, but the newspaper proprietors as well.[168]

This type of concern formed the backdrop for much of the pressure that Churchill applied to his military field commanders. "Feeling here has risen very high," he wrote General Auchinleck on 16 October 1941, urging him to launch his "Crusader" offensive in North Africa, "against what is thought to be our supine incapacity for action ...." Two days later, the Prime Minister was more urgent. "It is impossible to explain to Parliament and the nation," he concluded to Auchinleck, "how it is our Middle East Armies had to stand for 4½ months without engaging the enemy while all the time Russia is being battered to pieces."[169] Allied to this was Churchill's appreciation of the fact that the people needed action – needed to perceive that Britain was striking back. It was for that reason in the summer of 1940 that he requested assurance from Bomber Command that

Britain could conduct extensive bombing raids over German cities if London were attacked in force. In a similar manner, he initiated a successful scheme in October 1940 to confuse enemy pilots by the firing of blank charges in anti-aircraft guns. Most importantly, he added, the blanks would also help "to avoid discouraging silence for the population."[170]

Again and again in that fateful year of 1940, it was the British people that preoccupied Churchill as he prepared them for total war. He was aided in that endeavor by the fact that the dialogue he established with the people was based on a common acceptance of the vastly simplified, often manufactured Whig picture of the past. The British people of all classes in 1940 were more historically oriented than most nations. Their national symbols were all around them, reminders of a continuous, progressive past that had resulted in liberty and power. It was an historical heritage which, unlike that of Germany, did not emphasize fragmentation, and unlike that of France and Russia, did not bring revolution to mind. It was, instead, a heritage of positive continuity which Churchill shared with his nation and which allowed him constantly to invoke the past in order to fortify the present for himself and the British people.[171]

That continuity was reinforced in the closing months of the Chamberlain government by the vindication of Churchill's longtime opposition to appeasement as well as his warnings concerning the danger inherent in the weakening of Britain's role in the world. All of that was to him a denial of England's historical destiny, and thus bound to end in disaster. That is why the British people rallied to him in 1940, why David Low's cartoon of a grim Churchill rolling up his sleeves to get on with the wartime work was so apt. For behind the new Prime Minister, in addition to clearly recognizable members of the Cabinet in the drawing, were row upon row of the anonymous public, all looking equally determined, over the caption which read: "All behind you, Winston."

It was the strength of history to which Churchill continued to turn as the war progressed, for he understood that he was leading a nation, as J.H. Plumb has pointed out, "more deeply conscious of, and committed to, its sense of the past than any the world has known since Imperial China."[172] As a consequence, the British leader could move back and forth with ease, as he talked to the nation on radio, from the *annus mirabilis* of 1940 to earlier crises in England's glorious Whig past. For example, in a broadcast to the people on 11 September 1940 as the island prepared for invasion, Churchill pointed out that the coming period:

> ranks with the days when the Spanish Armada was approaching the Channel, and Drake was finishing his game of bowls; or when Nelson stood between us and Napoleon's Grand Army at Boulogne. We have read all about this in the history books; but what is happening now is on a far greater scale and of far more consequence to the life and

future of the world and its civilization than those brave old days of the past.[173]

Such historical continuity had always engendered in Churchill high expectations for the British people. "I hope that if evil days should come upon our country," he wrote after contemplating the thousands of Dervish dead at Omdurman, "and the last army which a collapsing Empire could interpose between London and the invader was dissolving in rout and ruin, that there would be some ... who would not care to accustom themselves to the new order of things and tamely survive the disaster."[174] And so it was in 1940 when he molded the people's aspirations to fit his by recognizing no other mood in them than what he felt. During the Blitz, while walking with Churchill in the garden at Chequers one evening after dinner, Ismay remarked how the Prime Minister's speeches had inspired the nation. "Not at all," was the almost angry retort from Churchill who could see the glow of London burning in the distance. "It was given to me to express what was in the hearts of the British people. If I had said anything else, they would have hurled me from office."[175]

That was the essence of Churchill's power. If his fellow citizens were not initially with him in their hour of danger, that soon changed. Because he idealized them with such fevered intensity, in the end they approached his ideal and began to view themselves as he saw them with their "buoyant and imperturbable temper." It was the intense eloquence in his speeches that caught the British people in his spell until it seemed to them that he was indeed expressing what was in their hearts and minds. As a consequence, Churchill created in 1940 a heroic mood in which the British people conceived a new image of themselves as acting in a larger litany of great deeds ranging from Thermopylae to the Spanish Main. He imposed those responses through his speeches and through his expectations of the people, which in turn caused the British people to impose upon the present, however momentary, the simple virtues they believed had prevailed in the past. The combination of his personality and powerful imagery focused through the medium of radio invested the squalid and fearful circumstances of those days with overtones of glory.[176]

In the end, Churchill accomplished all that, not by catching the mood of his country, which in Isaiah Berlin's estimate was "somewhat confused; stout-hearted but unorganized," but by being obstinately impervious to it, as he had always been to the details, to the passing shades and tones of ordinary life. For him, the Battle of Britain was "a time when it was equally good to live or die."[177] His busy imagination, imposed on his countrymen, lifted them to abnormal heights in their nation's supreme crisis and allowed Churchill to enjoy a Periclean reign. But it could only last a short time. It was a climate in which people normally do not want to live, demanding as it did a violent tension which, if not soon ended, destroys normal perspectives, overdramatizes personal relationships and distorts normal values to an intolerable extent. But for a time in the 1940s, by dramatizing their lives and making them seem to themselves and to each other as acting appropriately for a great historic moment, Churchill transformed the British people into a collective, romantic and heroic whole – a supreme optimization for total war of that key element of the "remarkable trinity," no matter how irrational. C.P. Snow recalled, in that regard:

> Oddly enough, most of us were very happy in those days. There was a kind of collective euphoria over the whole country .... In one's realistic moments, it was difficult to see what chance we had. But I doubt if most of us had many realistic moments, or thought much at all. We were working like mad.[178]

It was natural, then, that at the moment of victory, Churchill should turn again to the people whose faith, which he had unconsciously brought forth, had done so much to sustain him. "This is your victory!" he told the vast VE Day crowds assembled before where he stood on the Ministry of Health balcony overlooking Whitehall. The crowd immediately roared back: "No – it is yours." Later that night, Churchill addressed another crowd stretching far up Whitehall to Parliament Square. "My dear friends, this is your hour .... It is a victory of the great British nation as a whole. We were the first ... to draw the sword against tyranny .... There we stood alone. Did anyone want to give in?" "No," the crowd shouted. "Were we downhearted?" "No."[179]

THE MILITARY

War is a business of terrible pressures and persons who take part in it must fail if they are not strong enough to withstand them.

Churchill, *The World Crisis 1915*

In 1940, Churchill was at the zenith of his political authority with a Parliamentary support never even granted to Pitt and a moral support granted to him not only by Britain and the Commonwealth, but by the world at large. Nevertheless, as Prime Minister, his impulsive nature was held in check because he had to work within the limitations of a well-ordered government, the constitutional principles of which he venerated. It was with a conscious mixture of pride and humility as the war progressed that he bowed to the Commons, using all his Parliamentary skills to maintain his coalition and turn back the occasional votes of no confidence. As Minister of Defence, however, working purposely without specific constitutional guidelines and often in secrecy and high speed with the

Chiefs of Staff and the Commanders-in-Chief (CINCs) in the field, Churchill could give more rein to his impulsive and autocratic instincts. But the Chiefs and the CINCs were not just extensions of his will, a fact of which he was rationally aware, but against which his powerful, often irrational, emotions were in frequent rebellion.

In many instances during World War II, Churchill showed the same romantic impetuousness and failure to calculate that he had demonstrated in World War I. But there was also a pragmatic hesitation in insisting on many of his more prescient views due to his own experiences in that earlier war; and he was never so dominant, nor dared to be, as popular opinion imagined or his military advisers apprehensively believed. "The reader must not forget," Churchill wrote, "that I never wielded autocratic powers, and always had to move with and focus political and professional opinions."[180] Nevertheless, he managed to keep his finger on the vast political-military pulse of the British effort at total war. The constant surveillance often stretched even his enormous capabilities, but its benefits far outweighed the inconveniences of childish, petulant, or ill-considered queries and exhortations. In a similar manner, the stimulus he provided miltiary advisers and subordinates more than counterbalanced his frequent injustices and intemperate browbeating.[181]

The Decision-Maker

> Could he but have said to the generals who argued everything beforehand and criticized everything after: who had to be convinced, persuaded, wheedled or even hoodwinked into every march or manoeuvre, 'Obey, or I will have you shot! Silence, or I will deprive you of your command!' ... It was for him to invent and urge, for them to cavil and oppose.
>
> *Marlborough*, Vol. IV, p. 218

Churchill's relations with his military subordinates reflected an inextricable linkage of professional and personal judgment. Without a personal relationship with the Prime Minister, no senior military officer, whether at the Chiefs of Staff or Theater level, could have a viable professional relationship with him. That did not mean that the British leader was seeking abject pandering to his opinions. On the contrary, problems usually arose when the military leaders failed to provide, in General Ismay's words, "the one thing that was necessary, and indeed that Winston preferred — someone to stand up to him."[182] But such resistance required an oral fluency and articulateness. "The Prime Minister is a woman," Ismay advised General Auchinleck at one point, " — you've got to woo him."[183] That was as much beyond Auchinleck's capability, however, as it was beyond General Wavell's interest; and the personal rapport never did develop as it did between Churchill and the articulate General Alexander. At the Chiefs' level it was equally important, as demonstrated by Air Marshal Portal's recollection of a late night meeting with the Prime Minister:

I had to disagree very forcibly with some proposal of his and used language which would have been much more polite if I had had more time to choose my words. During my tirade he fixed me with a glassy stare and at the end when I said I was sorry if I had seemed rude, a broad smile appeared across his face and he said: "You know in war you don't have to be nice, you only have to be right."[184]

That type of adversarial approach to decision-making could be exhausting, particularly with Churchill who thrived on the combative give-and-take of spirited argument. At one point in June 1940, for instance, as Churchill was questioning Alanbrooke by telephone concerning the situation in France, he insisted that the general comply with his wishes for troop dispositions. For almost half an hour, Alanbrooke resisted the arguments in an increasingly heated manner. "At last," he noted in his diary, "when I was in an exhausted condition, he said: 'All right, I agree with you.' "[185] In a similar manner, Churchill's work routine, which played a key role in the decision-making process, also placed a heavy strain on the Chiefs of Staff. His normal hour for meeting with them, for instance, was 9:30 p.m., and these meetings often lasted until early in the morning. Churchill usually spent the following morning working in bed and normally managed a nap in the afternoon. The Chiefs, on the other hand, had to respond throughout the day to a constant flood of paperwork and were thus harassed by a system which allowed the Prime Minister to remain fresh.[186]

Churchill brought to the decision-making process an absolute conviction that policy must dominate strategy, augmented by memories of past military incompetence from the Tulaga to Passchendaele. At the same time, he had a genuine love for the military profession, an outstanding flair for soldiering, and an informal understanding of the working of the military mind. To this was added a personal and continuous interest in all the Services, which coupled with his reservoir of wartime experience and knowledge as well as his organization for defense, contributed positively to his leadership in World War II and helped prevent a recurrence of the political-military schism that had divided the "frocks" and the "brass hats" in the preceding war.[187]

The paradox was that while Churchill was comfortable in the environment of total war with vast armies, fleets and air forces, and had a clear understanding of the nature and refinements of global combat, his vision and attitudes were still limited by the military ethos formed in his earliest campaign at the end of the Victorian era. "I do not think ... he ever understood the administrative side of war," Wavell wrote of Churchill; "he always accused commanders of organizing 'all tail and no teeth' .... In fact I found that Winston's tactical ideas had to some extent crystallized at the South African War ...."[188] This was at least partially true of armored warfare despite the fact that he had been instrumental in the development of the tank. In terms of armored doctrine, Churchill had been in regular communication during the interwar years with Liddell Hart and other experts in the field. Nevertheless, as he admitted when the German Blitzkrieg smashed through the Allied lines in May 1940, "the idea of the line being broken, even on a broad front, did not convey to my mind the appalling consequences that now flowed from it."[189]

There were also times when Churchill actually appeared to consider the tank as he would a horse. He did not understand, for instance, why Crusaders and Shermans could not be disembarked at Suez and thrown directly into desert combat. Nor did he fully grasp the extent to which mechanization had complicated logistics arrangement and revolutionized the concept of time and space. "When I was a soldier," he would say, "infantry used to walk and cavalry used to ride. But now the infantry require motor-cars, and even the tanks have to have horse boxes to take them to battle."[190] Immediate action was the key for Churchill, particularly in terms of armor; and the business of adjusting tank mechanisms to the special desert environment and training tank commanders to assimilate new tactics and to navigate in featureless terrain were only perceived as obstacles.

It was in this context that Churchill evaluated Wavell's assessment in June 1941 of why the British offensive, Battleaxe, had failed.

> Main trouble was that 7th Armoured Division hastily re-equipped was not fit for battle tactically or technically. Infantry tank without transporter is definitely not weapon for desert warfare. Tank crews were not sufficiently trained, hence shooting not good and too many mechanical breakdowns.[191]

Churchill continued to focus on the problem of supplies and equipment throughout the war. In 1942, he was incensed about the large number of vehicles being shipped to the Middle East. "Will the War Office never cease adding to the interminable tail?" he asked. Ismay, who had committed parts of the Prime Minister's earlier books to memory, quoted in a reply, which went unheeded, a striking metaphor used by Churchill before the turn of the century in *The River War*: "Victory is the beautiful bright-coloured flower: transport is the stem without which it would never have blossomed."[192] That notwithstanding, the British leader continued his pressure to reduce the amount of support equipment, even expressing his concern to General Montgomery on the eve of the invasion of France about the proportion of administrative vehicles included in the first wave of that invasion.[193] "He does not seem to realize," one subordinate commented in exasperation, "that men without proper equipment ... do not count in modern war — after all, we are not living in the age of Omdurman."[194]

Churchill reserved his strongest "tooth to tail" criticism for military personnel, a holdover from his first encounter with total war. In a May 1916 address to the Commons, he had referred to a distinction between "the trench and the non-trench population," explaining that "the trench population lives almost continuously under the fire of the enemy ... while all the time the non-trench population scarcely suffers at all and has good food and good wages ...."[195] It was a typical reaction of a front-line man of action to the denizens of the rear area, and one he never completely lost. "I feel I have a right to ask you," Churchill wrote Wavell in January 1941, "to make sure that the rearward services do not trench too largely upon the effective fighting strength ...."[196] And in the spring of the following year, it was Alanbrooke's turn. "Pray explain C.I.G.S.," the Prime Minister demanded in a Cabinet meeting, "how is it that in the Middle East 750,000 men always turn up for their pay and rations, but when it comes to fighting only 100,000 turn up. Explain to us exactly how the remaining 650,000 are occupied."[197] The technical answers to such questions, however rational and scientific, could never fully satisfy Churchill whose Victorian units, to a man, had participated in the front-line combat from India to the Sudan. As late as 21 May 1944, as D-Day drew near, he was still complaining to Alanbrooke about "the comparatively small number of troops that will be landed" and the "smallness of the infantry component of the fighting troops."[198]

The military ethos of the Victorian era intruded upon the political-military decisionmaking process in other ways. At times, for instance, Churchill tended to think in terms of "sabres and bayonets," the terms used in the past to measure the strength of opposing forces. As a consequence, Singapore and Tobruk were for him old-fashioned fortifications in which thousands of defenders, because they possessed rifles and small arms, or could be provided with them, were capable of selling their lives dearly in a protracted heroic manner, if necessary in hand-to-hand fighting. The fall of Tobruk was particularly hard since the news was received in Roosevelt's presence. "Defeat is one thing," he wrote; "disgrace is another."[199] And later he confided to Moran: "I cannot understand why Tobruk gave in. More than 30,000 of our men put their hands up."[200]

During the Boer War, Churchill pointed out that "the hoisting of a white flag in token of surrender is an act which can be justified only by clear proof that there is no prospect of gaining the slightest military advantage by going on fighting ...."[201] Thus, in the case of Singapore in the winter of 1942, the Prime Minister could exhort commanders and senior officers to "die with their troops," because with "the Russians fighting as they are and the Americans so stubborn at Luzon, the whole reputation of our country and our race is involved ...."[202] On 14 February, when resistance had degenerated to street fighting, Churchill instructed Wavell to use his own judgment concerning surrender. Still, the final denouement was incomprehensible to him. "How come 100,000 men (half of them of our own race) hold up their hands to inferior numbers of Japanese?" was his plaintive query to Moran.[203] And to Violet Asquith, he also confided his pained confusion. "We have so many men − they should have done better."[204]

In a similar manner, Churchill tended to attribute a power to the great ships of the line that they no longer possessed. The *Bismarck*, of course, did prey upon relatively unprotected British convoys in the Atlantic. But conditions in World War II could be vastly different when there was no vital enemy supply line to be threatened or, more importantly, when enemy air power could be deployed either from land or carriers. It was Churchill's emotional attachment to the technology of those ships that led him to dispatch the *Prince of Wales* and *Repulse* to the Far East "to exercise that kind of vague menace which capital ships of the highest quality whose whereabouts is unknown can impose upon all hostile naval calculations ...."[205] And if deterrence should fail, Churchill envisaged the great, grey hulks vanishing "into the immense [eastern] archipelago," looming like "rogue elephants" in that vast space as a menace to the Imperial Japanese Navy.[206]

The Chiefs

> The Chiefs of Staff complain that I have led them up the garden path. But at every turning I have provided them with delicious fruits and wholesome vegetables. Poor Chiefs of Staff.
> Churchill, in Colville, *The Churchillians*, p. 146

> To cope with the situation adequately, it would almost have been worthwhile to have two staffs: one to deal with the Prime Minister, the other with the war.
> Kennedy, *The Business of War*, p. 173

Churchill's relationship with his Chiefs of Staff, as we have seen, was heavily dependent on personality factors and remained strongly adversarial in nature throughout the war. How much resistance to the Prime Minister was the *modus operandi* of the First Sea Lord, Admiral Pound, is still debated.[207] What is apparent, however, is that Pound was congenial personally and therefore professionally to Churchill. "Pound," the British leader told the editor of the *Times*, "is necessary to me. His slow, unimpressive look is deceptive."[208] Years later, he noted of Pound that as the war progressed, "we became ever truer comrades and friends."[209] And when Pound died, the only one of the original Chiefs not relieved by Churchill, the Prime Minister never established the same rapport with the new First Sea Lord, Sir Andrew Browne Cunningham, known as ABC. Again, it was a combination of personality and articulateness. Cunningham often failed to make his point in discussion and generally expressed himself badly.[210]

It was left to General Dill to have the most severe problems with Churchill. Shortly after assuming the post of CIGS on 27 May 1940, he took the measure of his new boss. "I'm not sure that Winston isn't the greatest menace," he wrote his former commander, Lord Gort. "No one seems able to control him. He is full of ideas, many brilliant, but most of them impracticable. He has such drive and personality that no one seems able to stand up to him ...."[211] Least of all, Dill, who while recognizing Churchill's enjoyment of the thrust and counterthrust of verbal argument as well as his susceptibility to the articulate, found the process of aggressive debate futile, sickening and exhausting. As a consequence, the CIGS confined his major arguments to paper, the least likely method of gaining the approval of Churchill, who only rarely found lengthy exposition convincing. Equally important, Dill's style did not take into account the need to enthrall the Prime Minister who, in Wavell's words, was "always expecting rabbits to come out of empty hats."[212]

As a result, Churchill's antipathy to Dill, whom he nicknamed Dilly-dally, continued to grow. To this was added a disagreement on the allocation of scarce resources. "A successful invasion alone spells our final defeat," Dill wrote the Prime Minister in a lengthy memorandum on 6 May 1941. "It is the United Kingdom therefore and not Egypt that is vital, and the defence of the United Kingdom must take first place. Egypt is not even second in order of priority, for it has been an accepted principle in our strategy that in the last resort the security of Singapore comes before that of Egypt." Churchill was "astonished" to receive Dill's memorandum. "I gather you would be prepared to face the loss of Egypt and the Nile Valley," he wrote on 13 May, "together with the surrender or ruin of the Army of half a million we have concentrated there, rather than lose Singapore. I do not take that view."[213] For the Prime Minister, it was just another example of caution carried to extremes; of pessimism beginning to merge into defeatism; of "the dead hand of inanition," as he once accused Dill in front of the War Cabinet.[214] Dill stood up to Churchill in words that could only pain a romantic Victorian, whose earlier war experience was being used against him.

> I am sure that you, better than anyone else, must realize how difficult it is for a soldier to advise against a bold offensive plan. One lays oneself open to charges of defeatism, of inertia, or even of 'cold feet.' Human nature being what it is, there is a natural tendency to acquiesce to an offensive plan of doubtful merit rather than to face such charges. It takes a lot of moral courage not to be afraid of being thought afraid.[215]

It was not enough. The following December, Churchill used the excuse of Dill's 60th birthday to replace him with Alanbrooke. But by then Dill had led the way into the uncharted waters that defined the unprecedented relationship between the tri-Service Chiefs of Staff Committee and Churchill as Prime Minister and Minister of Defence. Ismay's role, of course, was important with "its unique brand of lubrication."[216] But it was Dill who structured the draining but constructive adversarial relationship between the Chiefs and the many-faceted Prime Minister on which Alanbrooke so successfully built.[217]

Equally important, it was Dill during his tenure in Washington from January 1942 until his death in November 1944, who established the basis for the similarly unprecedented relationship with the Combined Chiefs of Staff (CCS). The key to this establishment was Dill's enormous influence, based partly on his three inseparable roles as Head of the British Joint Staff Mission, as senior British member of the CCS, and as personal representative of Churchill in his capacity as Minister of Defence. But it was also the strong relationship that the British general established with the Washington hierarchy, particularly General Marshall, that was so important. To the American Chief of Staff, Dill was the guarantee against what he perceived as Churchill's imperial pretensions and strategic prejudices. The value of his military representative's efforts in moving through the uncharted waters of combined global strategy and operations was never fully appreciated by Churchill — a fact recognized by Marshall. "To be very frank and personal," he admonished the Prime Minister after Dill's death, "I doubt if you or your Cabinet associates fully realize the loss you have suffered."[218]

With the ascendancy of General Alanbrooke as CIGS in the late autumn of 1941, Churchill had found, as R.W. Thompson has pointed out, "his 'Katherine Parr.' No more heads would fall on that level."[219] The Prime Minister admired Alanbrooke's intelligence, his ruthlessness in dealing with unsuccessful commanders and his strategic sense. Moreover, the new CIGS was also quick, decisive, methodical and not afraid to decentralize. In addition, there was an underlying vein of pessimism and uncertainty in Alanbrooke that was an invaluable complement to Churchill's constant self-confidence and occasional euphoria. It was the difference between Churchill's ebullient acceptance of his office in May 1940 and Alanbrooke's reaction to his appointment as CIGS. "I had never hoped or aspired to reach those dizzy heights," the general noted in his diary that day, "and now that I am stepping up on to the plateau land of my military career the landscape looks cold, bleak and lonely, with a ghastly responsibility hanging as a black thundercloud over me."[220] Those emotions remained a permanent fixture. "I have felt that every day of this war," Alanbrooke confided to Moran in July 1945, "was taking off a month of my life."[221]

Part of Alanbrooke's outburst was certainly due to the constant efforts by the Chiefs throughout the war to dissuade Churchill from his penchant for tangential enterprises that led him to dissipate the energies of his staff and commanders, and even the strength of his forces, on secondary or wholly irrelevant objectives. In part, that stemmed from his combative nature, from a desire to attack in an environment, at least in the early stages of the war, in which there were few real opportunities. In July 1940, for instance, Churchill listened to a general provide a reasoned and cautious approach to the Italian air and submarine base at Massawa. When he was through, the Prime Minister rolled up his map of the Mediterranean port and muttered in frustration: "You soldiers are all alike, you have no imagination."[222] And after the invasion of Russia, Churchill was even more anxious to undertake some action to help his new ally. On 23 June, with German forces still crossing the frontier, he ordered the Chiefs to examine the viability of a raid on the Pas de Calais. "I have in mind something of the scale of 25 to 30 thousand men ...."[223]

Similar projects would also appear to tax the Chiefs when there was a lull in the action. Ronald Lewin has pointed out, in this regard, that "it was precisely at times when the heat was off, when his imagination could roam freely, unshackled by the practical needs of the insistent present, that he was most prone to indulge his weakness for the tangential, the idiotic, the unattainable."[224] Such was the case with Operation Workshop, the plan for the invasion of the island of Pantellaria between Sicily and Tunisia which Churchill pressed on the Chiefs in early December 1940. On 5 December, the Defence Committee unanimously rejected the operation. Night after night over the next two months, the Prime Minister brought the military advisers together to convince them of the efficacy of "Workshop." On 21 January 1941, he finally gave up at a Defence Committee meeting in which the Chiefs opposed the Pantellaria operation as too risky, a conclusion that, Churchill observed, "seemed to lead to the minimum of aggressive action."[225]

In a similar manner in the fall of 1941, Churchill's enthusiasm returned for what Ismay once termed "an Artic Gallipoli." On 3 October, the Prime Minister directed Alanbrooke to prepare immediate plans for an attack on Trondheim. In the following week, the Chiefs provided him with a pessimistic appreciation of the proposed action, primarily based on the lack of air support. On 12 October, Churchill confronted his military advisers in a lengthy meeting in which he cross-examined Alanbrooke on every conceivable detail concerned with the Norwegian enterprise. The Chiefs held firm, however, and the Trondheim expedition was cancelled. "A very unpleasant gruelling to stand up to in a full room," Alanbrooke noted, "but excellent training for what I had to stand up to on many occasions in later years."[226]

The Chiefs maintained this solid front against efforts by Churchill in the next two years to launch a Norwegian expedition (Operation Jupiter). "Why he wanted to go back and what he was going to do there ... we never found out," Alanbrooke commented in 1942, "The only reason he ever gave was that Hitler had unrolled the map of Europe starting with

Norway ....Heaven knows what we should have done in Norway had we landed there."[227] At one point in his impetuous enthusiasm for the project, Churchill even made firm commitments to Stalin concerning a Norwegian landing. And as late as 24 August 1943, the British leader managed to keep the project alive in a paragraph of the Quebec Conference Final Report that ended: "In case circumstances render the execution of OVERLORD impossible, it may be necessary to consider JUPITER as an alternative."[228]

The system worked because Churchill would not ultimately go against the unanimous advice of his military advisers. But when that advice was faulty, the results could be militarily disastrous, as they were in Greece in early 1941. The British expedition to that country is often portrayed as an impulsive, emotional move by an incurable romantic. In fact, it was just the opposite. Churchill's decision to support Greece was made only after he dispatched Anthony Eden and General Dill for extended on-the-spot consultations with theater commanders as well as Greek authorities, and only after he had extensive consultations with the Cabinet, the Chiefs and the leaders of New Zealand and Australia. In the end, the move into Greece was based on a rational and reasonable prospect of success held out by Churchill's military and political advisers in the field who had been specifically directed by the Prime Minister to reject the venture if they doubted its military viability. On that basis, General Wavell began the expedition without protest.[229]

There were, of course, other occasions when Churchill was able to bring at least some of his military advisers around to his side, often with mixed results. In the fall of 1941, for instance, Admiral Pound proposed to dispatch four old battleships to Ceylon as reinforcements for the Eastern Fleet. But Churchill was focused on at least a two battleship deterrent force operating in the great Simonstown–Aden–Singapore triangle. At the 14 October meeting of the Defence Committee, the British leader argued for the dispatch of this deterrent force, buttressed by a scathing attack on the Admiralty's reluctance for such a venture. The Vice Chief of Naval Staff represented Pound at the meeting and subsequently sent a memorandum of the proceedings to the First Sea Lord. "The First Lord and I defended the position as well as we could," he wrote, "but the Prime Minister led the other members of the Defence Committee to the conclusion that it was desirable to send the *Prince of Wales* to join the *Repulse* and go to Singapore as soon as possible. The Admiralty expressed their dissent."[230] The end result was a far cry from the hidden deterrent menace envisaged by Churchill. At the first sign of the Japanese landings in Malaya, the commanding officer launched his two battleships into action without air cover, and on 10 December both were sunk by a force of enemy high-level and torpedo bombers in a little over two hours.[231]

On the other hand, there were equally propitious examples of

Churchill's ability to sway the Chiefs of Staff. In the summer of 1940, no one was yet aware how inept the Italians would prove to be in their use of their dominant air and sea power in the Mediterranean. "So formidable did the situation appear at the end of June," Churchill recalled, "that Admiralty first thoughts contemplated the abandonment of the Eastern Mediterranean and concentration at Gibraltar."[232] It was thus an enormous act of romantic faith for him to veto the Admiralty on this issue, and to swing to his side all the Chiefs, who on 3 July 1940 informed theater commanders that the fleet was to remain in the Eastern Mediterranean. Once that decision was reached, a more pragmatic side to Churchill's willingness to take calculated risks was his approval at the height of the Blitz and invasion scares of a proposal to send 154 tanks as well as assorted field artillery and anti-tank weapons to Egypt. It was as momentous a decision of grand strategy as the one he had made as First Lord on 28 July 1914 to move the Battle Fleet to Scapa Flow.[233]

The element of calculated risk was also inherent in the Prime Minister's evaluation of the occasional need for surface resupply to British Mideast forces directly through the Mediterranean as opposed to the route around the Cape of Good Hope. "From time to time," he wrote in the summer of 1940, "and for sufficient object this risk will have to be faced. Warships are meant to go under fire."[234] Such was the philosophy concerning the "Tiger" convoy the following spring. On 20 April 1941, Churchill learned from Wavell that British tanks were reaching a dangerously low level in Egypt and that a new German armored division had been spotted arriving at Tripoli. The British leader immediately proposed Operation "Tiger," the dispatch of tanks directly through the Mediterranean to Egypt. "The risks of losing the vehicles," he minuted Ismay, "or part of them must be expected. Even if half get through, the situation would be restored."[235] There was some hesitation on the part of the Chiefs. But by noon of the following day, they agreed to Churchill's plan. Later that night, Churchill telegraphed to Wavell: "I have been working hard for you in the last few days ...."[236]

On 9 May, Operation Tiger began from Gibraltar, and within 24 hours the tanks had reached Alexander with the loss of one out of five ships to a minefield off Malta. "The poor tiger has already lost one claw and another is damaged," Churchill commented; "but still I would close on what is left."[237] In mid-May, however, the Admiralty resisted a repeat of Tiger; and Churchill, despite his determination to reinforce Wavell quickly, deferred, as he ultimately would throughout the war, to the military judgment of his Chiefs. "Tiger No. 2" sailed around the Cape, reaching Egypt in July.

In no issue was Churchill's relationship with the British Chiefs of Staff more important than that of the cross-Channel invasion of northwest Europe. The British leader, as we have seen, had often pressed the Chiefs to undertake offensive operations on the Continent, his most consistent project being Norway. Despite his weakness for such ventures, or perhaps because of the concomitant discussions with the unyielding Chiefs who since Dunkirk had been examining the means to effect a continental landing, Churchill was well aware of the practical difficulties. Nevertheless, he did not abandon his determination to reenter Europe, an act which he believed necessary to bring home the meaning of victory and defeat in total war to both the allied and enemy populations. But he did reject any premature attempt, and clearly, Sledgehammer, the plan for a 1942 cross-channel invasion was in that category.

The British Chiefs were no more sanguine about the possibilities of Roundup, the plan for a 1943 invasion in northwest Europe, recommending instead continued operations in the Mediterranean coupled with strategic bombing. Churchill, on the other hand, believed that it was necessary to urge a Roundup in 1943 as well as movement through Sicily or Sardinia towards Italy as the natural result of Torch, the November 1942 invasion of North Africa. Only in this way, he contended, could Washington be restrained from moving in disillusionment away from the established policy of Germany First. During the remainder of 1942, as Michael Howard has pointed out,

> Mr. Churchill urged and worried the Chiefs of Staff Committee to admit the possibility of carrying out "Roundup" in 1943 with a pertinacity which gives the lie to the belief ... that he consistently favoured a predominantly Mediterranean strategy. Paper after paper was put up by the Chiefs of Staff arguing the impossibility of "Roundup" in 1943, which the Prime Minister analysed line by line, challenged in minutest detail and reluctantly accepted; only to question their conclusions a few days later when some fresh victory spurred his unquenchable optimism, ...[238]

On 18 November 1942, Churchill stated his commitment once again to Roundup. "I cannot give this up," he told the Chiefs, "without a massive presentation of facts and figures which prove the physical impossibility."[239] The Chiefs were happy to oblige, particularly because of the upcoming summit at Casablanca. Their opinions might well have caused an Allied schism at the conference. But while Churchill went far in meeting the professional advice of his Chiefs, he also injected a note of determination into the British paper for the conference with his militancy and his powerful advocacy of a Second Front. "Its realism," Michael Howard noted of the paper, "was due solely to the Chiefs of Staff; but the positive, offensive spirit which inspired it was largely the work of the unwearying and merciless interventions of the Prime Minister himself."[240]

In the end, British acceptance of the general reference to Roundup in the Casablanca agreement was a moot issue, because Roosevelt had accepted Churchill's suggestion the preceding summer that allied operations in 1942 should be in French North Africa, the only proposal "which, either at the time or in retrospect, seemed to make strategic sense."[241] That Torch would preclude Roundup became apparent as operations in North Africa continued into 1943. That this was a fortunate byproduct of the Roosevelt–Churchill agreement in the summer of 1942, which had bypassed the American Chiefs of Staff, has also become apparent over the years. "A cross-Channel offensive in 1942," Ronald Lewin noted in this regard, "would have been a guaranteed, and in 1943 an almost certain, failure."[242]

But if the pragmatic caution and realism of Churchill and his Chiefs was an invaluable and necessary element in the early efforts at combined strategic planning, it was the stubborn perseverance of the American military leaders in the closing years of the war that ensured the ultimate implementation of the allied grand strategy. For by mid- to late 1943, Churchill's enthusiasm for an attack on northwest Europe had disappeared, and he increasingly regarded the Mediterranean not as a subsidiary theater, but a primary one where successful operations were themselves the ultimate justification for that primacy. It was in that theater that he saw the remaining possibility for enhancing British military prestige as well as for indulging in his continuing passion to direct the war. Certainly, there was also the romantic lure of the Eastern Mediterranean from the earlier war. But there were also the memories from that war of northwest Europe, the source of the attritive blood baths, which he admitted in his memoirs "were not to be blotted out by time or reflection."[243] For this and many similar reasons, the British Chiefs were essentially in agreement with their leader. In the end, like World War I, the decisive campaign had to be fought in France. And it was the dominant and consistent American pressure that made that possible.[244]

The Field Commanders

Prime Ministers need luck as well as Generals; Prime Ministers who usurp the role of Commanders-in-Chief need a double dose of it.

Kennedy, *The Business of War*, p. 239

The Prime Minister at this phase of battle resembled, to the irreverent eye of the historian, nobody so much as some loud-mouthed follower of a football team, who having poured advice, objugations, jeers and insults on his team while they were being hard pressed, now, when they show their calibre, shouts at them, "Shoot! Put it in! Give it to 'em! Sock 'em!"

Connell, *Auchinleck*, p. 655

Churchill's professional relations with his field commanders, like those with the Chiefs of Staff, were heavily dependent on personal links. Nowhere was this better illustrated than with his army commanders in the Middle East, particularly General Wavell. Wavell had not endeared himself to the new Prime Minister when after Dunkirk he had balked at transferring British battalions from Palestine back to England after appropriate replacement by Indian troops. "We are indeed the victims," Churchill angrily minuted to Eden concerning the affair, "of a feeble and weary departmentalism."[245]

A conference between the two men at Chequers the following August did not help. The meeting showed Churchill at his worst and at his best. There was his nagging over minor matters or misguided operations fueled by out-of-date ideas, lack of technical knowledge and a passion for action. At the same time Churchill, with the Chief's approval, filled a shopping list for three Middle East armored units that included Matilda tanks which no Italian weapon could penetrate just at that point when Britain was virtually denuded of effective armor and when intelligence sources still held out the very real possibility of an invasion. "The decision to give this blood-transfusion while we braced ourselves to meet a mortal danger," he wrote proudly, "was at once awful and right."[246]

Wavell's taciturnity at the August meeting played a primary role in his failure to retain the confidence of the ebullient Prime Minister. Once when asked why Churchill did not like him, the general replied: "Perhaps because I don't talk enough."[247] He was right. After that first meeting in August 1940, Churchill did not conceal his disappointment at Wavell's "cool and reticent" nature which had caused the emotional temperature to drop severely. "I do not feel in him," the British leader wrote Eden, "that sense of mental vigour and resolve to overcome obstacles, which is indispensable to successful war." And when Eden defended Wavell, Churchill persisted in his view that he was "a good average colonel," who could be a "good chairman of a Tory association."[248]

Wavell did not help his cause after returning to Cairo. In response to a message questioning the small amount of British casualties sustained during the recent evacuation of Somaliland, he replied that "a big butcher's bill was not necessarily evidence of good tactics."[249] It was a gratuitous and unnecessary insult from a general who should have known from his historical studies if not experience, that a commander in a detached and distant theater of war needed a firm political base at home. Moreover, his message, as Operation Compass was beginning in December 1940, which warned against "undue hopes being placed on this operation," was hardly designed to appeal to a man who still believed in the Victorian concept of the heroic man of action. "If, with the situation as it is," Churchill wrote to Dill, "General Wavell is only playing small, and is not hurling in his whole available forces with furious energy, he will have failed to rise to the height of circumstances," adding: "I never 'worry' about action, but only about inaction."[250]

The tragedy behind the acrimony and misunderstanding was that Wavell, like Churchill, was a romantic who loved mystery, daring, the calculated risk and above all the secret of the campaign locked in the leader's head. In the matter of poetry, at least, Churchill knew he had a kindred spirit, quoting Walt Whitman on 13 December 1940 as he urged Wavell to follow up on his victory at Sidi Barrani. A few days later, still encouraging the general to press on with the offensive, Churchill telegraphed simply: "St. Matthew, Chapter 7, Verse 7," which read: "Ask and it shall be given you; seek and ye shall find; knock, and it shall be opened unto you." The next day, Wavell replied: "St. James, Chapter 1, Verse 17," which read: "Every good gift and every perfect gift is from above ... and cometh down from the Father of lights ...."[251]

This type of poetic banter went on nicely throughout the remainder of the "Compass" campaign which terminated on 8 February 1941 with the conquest of Cyrenaica. But Churchill's gnawing doubts were only allayed by that victory and soon quickened as events in Greece, Iraq and Syria unfolded. Crete was the crowning blow. Over six months elapsed between the invasion of Greece by the Italians and the 20 May 1941 invasion of Crete by the Germans. During that period, despite Churchill's urgings, the overtaxed Mideast command failed to take the relatively simple measures that could have denied success to the German forces. "The truth is," an historian of that campaign concluded, "that Wavell could have rendered the island impregnable using the forces available, without air support, and with no addition to his heavy equipment."[252]

General Alexander, on the other hand, was an example of how personal relations with the Prime Minister could enhance the professional link. He was known for his gallantry as an Irish Guards officer in World War I. That reputation, enhanced by his cool command of the Dunkirk rearguard, appealed to Churchill. In addition, the British leader liked Alexander's direct approach and his appearance – what he termed the general's "easy smiling grace."[253] Most importantly, Alexander was neither reticent nor taciturn in his dealings with Churchill. In any event, as Lord Moran pointed out, "listening is not just a question of keeping silent; it can be a means of communication of a more subtle kind. Besides, when Alex does open his mouth he is always so reassuring, always so sure that the P.M.'s plans are right, and that there will be no difficulty at all in carrying them out."[254] Finally, there was the fact that Alexander was able to bring a touch of romance into the chill corridors of total war – a fact perceptively observed by Moran who pointed out that "Alex has been able to confirm what Winston had always felt about war."

137

... To him it was a romantic calling, the highest man could embrace, but it was a game for gentlemen, which had to be played according to the rules. What he loved in Alex was that he had justified his own feelings about war, tried them out in the field and made sense of them. Alex had redeemed what was brutal in war, touching the grim business lightly with his glove. In his hands it was still a game for people of quality. He had shown that war could still be made respectable.[255]

During 1940 and 1941, Churchill kept in daily, sometimes hourly contact, with his Mideast field commanders. Part of the reason for his consistent stream of messages was to ascertain what was happening, to keep each commander on his toes, and to make sure that all available resources were being used properly. But there was another aspect of this "interference" that had to do with Churchill's idealistic, historically focused concepts concerning soldiering and leadership. He wanted to impart to those commanders, in Macaulay's words on Pitt the Elder, his own "impetuous, adventurous and defying character." They were to feel they were always in the Prime Minister's thoughts, and that he was there to share their difficulties, fears and failures as well as their hopes and successes. He actively solicited advice from them on ways he might help them; and he constantly advised and demonstrated to them that, providing they showed the proper offensive spirit, he would back them to the limit regardless of the result. But there had to be the desire to engage the enemy, and Churchill often quoted Nelson's Trafalgar memorandum in this regard: "No captain can do very wrong if he places his ship alongside that of an enemy."[256]

The man of action, in other words, could still play a part in modern conflict. Emotions, as much as material, could still prevail in total war. "Retreat would be fatal," Churchill telegraphed Auchinleck in June 1942 as Rommel's forces drove to within 15 miles of Tobruk. "This is a business not only of armour but of will power. God bless you all."[257] Without personal leadership, "a wild cat" hurled on the shore at Anzio could become "a stranded whale."[258] It required a leader at the center of action as it had always done in his youth. "Your presence on spot," he suggested in this regard to Auchinleck as Crusader began to falter at the end of November 1941, "will be an inspiration to all."[259] And even Alexander received a heavy-handed hint in September 1943 in terms of influencing the battle of Salerno. "I hope you are watching above all," Churchill wrote, "the Battle of 'Avalanche,' which dominates everything .... The battle of Suvla Bay was lost because Ian Hamilton was advised ... to remain at a remote central point where he would know everything. Had he been on the spot he could have saved the show."[260]

Those types of messages demonstrated how Churchill's temperament and organization for total war impelled him into a civilian direction of war not seen since the days of Pitt. When informed, in this regard, that Hitler constantly interfered with his generals, the British leader replied: "I do the same."[261] There were no details, no statistics concerning the war effort that were too minor for him. In the summer of 1943, for instance, Churchill telephoned Major-General Kennedy, the Director of Military Operations, for information on British casualties in Sicily. Kennedy provided the details, but when he read off the total casualty figure, the Prime Minister informed him correctly that he was a thousand off.[262] In an earlier and equally revealing incident, the commanding general of III Corps in Britain was invited to Chequers for dinner in the summer of 1940 and queried about the state of readiness of his corps. The general replied that equipping his force was far from complete. Years later, he recounted the British leader's reaction:

> Churchill looked at me incredulously and drew a sheaf of papers from the pocket of his dinner-jacket. "Which are your two Divisions?" he demanded. "The 53rd (Welsh) and the 2nd London" I replied. He pushed a podgy finger on the graph tables in front of him and said: "There you are; 100 percent complete in personnel, rifles and mortars; 50 percent in field artillery, anti-tank rifles and machine-guns." "I beg your pardon, Sir," I replied: "That state may refer to the weapons which the ordinance depots are preparing to issue to my units, but they have not yet reached the troops in anything like those quantities."
>
> The P.M.'s brow contracted; almost speechless with rage, he hurled the graphs across the dinner-table to Dill, saying: "CIGS, have those papers checked and returned to me tomorrow."[263]

Churchill's love of details combined with his early soldiering experience continued to pull him down to the operational and even the tactical level throughout the war. Maps, for instance, were a lifelong passion. Once, as General Kennedy was briefing him on current force dispositions in the desert, he remarked that Kennedy's map was much better than his and asked for a copy.[264] And when he ventured abroad, Churchill always arranged for a map room, as well as members of the map room staff under Captain Pim to accompany him. During the voyage on the *Queen Mary* to the August 1943 Quebec Conference, Churchill began his day by visiting the map room. "It was always a source of pleasure to the Prime Minister," Pim reported, "to mark in china-graph pencil in very considerable detail advances made by the various Divisions and Brigades ...."[265] It was information that was always at his finger tips. In early September 1942 as the battle of Alamein was beginning to develop, for example, Churchill described the terrain of the battlefield at length, based on his recent visit to Egypt, adding such details as the number of tanks on both sides and the dates operational reserves might arrive on the line.[266]

The result of this type of preoccupation on Churchill's part was a constant stream of messages to the field commanders, many concerning issues at the lowest level of war-fighting. After their meeting in August 1940, for instance, the British leader sent Wavell a general directive containing detailed tactical instructions down to the dispositions of battalions.[267] And to Auchinleck in September 1941, his message began: "I have studied attentively your field status and was relieved to see that your sixty infantry battalions average 880 ...."[268] General Eisenhower, of course, was a first hand observer of this tendency throughout the latter part of the war. "Churchill was so interested in every detail, he would frequently send telegrams to soldiers in the field and want to know about a particular regiment or brigade or division and what it was doing, and so on. General Marshall," Eisenhower concluded, "never asked a thing like that in the whole time I was in the field."[269]

"When British generals of modern times," Churchill wrote concerning his ancestor, "feel themselves embarrassed by the political situation at home, let them draw from the example of Marlborough new resources of endurance ... without losing his faculty of 'venturing all.'"[270] But Marlborough, unlike Wavell and Auchinleck, did not have to contend with direct political control from London, certainly not with anything approaching the endless streams of messages that flowed from the Prime Minister in World War II. In that same study, Churchill seemed to recognize the dangers inherent in a leader's involvement in details at a lower level on the hierarchical scale. At Ramillies, as he described it, the French cavalry were driving in on the Dutch and were about to fall upon the left flank of the allied infantry. Marlborough arrived on the scene at that moment and after sending for 21 squadrons of cavalry from his right flank, he plunged into "the whirlpool" of the cavalry fight in order to rally the Dutch squadrons. "This lapse from the duty of a commander-in-chief," Churchill wrote, "nearly cost him his life, and might well have cost the Allies the war." It was clearly a case in which his ancestor "had wrongly descended from his high station upon an immediate local need."[271]

And yet Churchill constantly did this throughout the war with his determination to maintain day-to-day, sometimes hour-to-hour, control. Such direction often not only wore his field commanders down spiritually, but also compelled them to act in haste and fatigue. "Had he been less impulsive," John Connell wrote in this regard, "he could have had his victories at far less terrible risk and price."[272] But as Connell also admitted, that trait stemmed from the Prime Minister's ardor and single-mindedness which were necessary ingredients for survival and final victory in total war. A more cogent criticism of Churchill's tight control was that it placed the field commanders charged with war-fighting in the same moral dilemma as his professional Service advisers. "They had constantly to ask themselves,'' Connell wrote in this regard, "how far their professional judgment ... should be opposed to his impetuosity, and at what point they must face the alternatives either of resigning or of complying with instructions which they believed to be dangerous, possibly disastrous."[273]

The Chiefs and Ismay attempted to mitigate the differences. Ismay, for instance, pointed out to Auchinleck that Churchill "apparently sees no difference between harsh words spoken to a friend, and forgotten within the hour under the influence of friendly argument, and the same harsh words telegraphed to a friend thousands of miles away − with no opportunity for 'making it up.' "[274] And when Churchill directed Dill to transmit instructions to Wavell concerning the defense of Crete that included details on the number of battalions for that island's garrison, the Chiefs managed to bring him out of the operational and tactical level. The final telegram that was dispatched emphasized the importance of securing Crete while making it clear that the responsibility for determining the size of the garrison lay with the field commander.[275] In retrospect, in terms of Crete, it might have been better to let the Prime Minister have his way.

The pattern continued throughout the war. On 23 September 1942, for instance, Churchill discussed with the CIGS a message urging Alexander to begin the attack at El Alamein. "I ... told him that he was only letting Alex see that he was losing confidence in him, which was a most disconcerting thing before a battle," Alanbrooke noted in his diary. "He then started all his worst arguments about generals only thinking about themselves and their reputations and never attacking until matters were a certainty; of never being prepared to take any risks, etc .... However, I succeeded in getting a very definite tempering down of the message."[276] In another incident later in the war, Churchill was "completely startled" when Eisenhower informed him that a cable the Prime Minister was planning to send to Alexander would cause Eisenhower to resign if he received it from his American commanders. The message, Eisenhower explained, "looks as though you, who are three thousand miles away ... feel that you are more competent to judge on the readiness of this army to attack, its morale, its equipment, its strength, its positions, training and everything, than is General Alexander. This I don't think is possible." Churchill's reply was almost plaintive. "As a military man and as the Chief Minister of His Majesty," he queried, "don't I have the right to ask questions?"[277]

In the end, the Chiefs approved the relief of both Wavell and Auchinleck. And if they could never bring themselves to condone Churchill's "interference" with the field commanders, they did come to understand it. When Auchinleck assumed command in June 1941, Dill wrote him that he would be subjected to pressure that "often comes from very broad political considerations ... sometimes so powerful as to make it necessary to take risks which, from the purely military point of view may seem inadvisable."[278] Those pressures came almost immediately. From July until November 1941 when Crusader began, Churchill constantly urged Auchinleck to attack. The result was a premature battle fought by the newly manned Eighth Army which had only been brought together at the last minute and lacked unity, training and cohesion.

And yet, as the Chiefs came to realize, Churchill was also under extreme strategic pressures. German forces were slicing daily through the Soviet heartland during that period. The Butt Report had revealed that Bomber Command was blind, weak and inaccurate, and that as a consequence, there was no strategic offensive in the offing which might help Britain or relieve the intolerable pressure on Russia. Moreover, during that summer and early fall, it became increasingly clear to Churchill that intervention in Norway or sizable cross-Channel expeditions would not be possible. Finally, the threat of invasion of Britain was once again after September considered serious, as was the possible threat to Gibraltar and the mouth of the Mediterranean. At the same time, at the operational level, there was the urgent need to capture the airfields in Cyrenaica from which the supply convoys to the desperately stranded Malta garrison could be protected. All these considerations, as they did so many times in the war, explain, at least in part, Churchill's intense preoccupation with the operational campaign and his impatience with the field commander directing that campaign.[279]

5

THE GREAT GAME IN THE SECOND WORLD WAR

It's a great huge game of chess that's being played — all over the world — if this is the world you know.

Lewis Carroll, *Through the Looking Glass*

In war and policy one should always try to put oneself in the position of what Bismarck called "the other man." The more fully and sympathetically a Minister can do this, the better are his chances of being right. The more knowledge he possesses of the opposite point of view, the less puzzling it is to know what to do. But imagination without deep and full knowledge is a snare ....

Churchill, *The Second World War*, Vol. III, p. 581

Churchill carried to great advantage the Victorian tension between romanticism and pragmatism in his extension of the "Great Game" into World War II. His fertile imagination and enthusiasm for scientific gadgetry contributed not only to Allied technological surprise during that conflict, but to the protection against such surprise on the part of the enemy as well. Moreover, his schoolboy's delight in tricking the other side, in knowing something that others did not, ensured his constant and unswerving interest in all facets of intelligence throughout the war. In addition, there was his lifelong fascination with cloak and dagger operations ranging from sabotage to espionage. Even the secrecy surrounding his wartime movements delighted him. He was enthralled by the fact that Germany would sacrifice almost anything to kill or — better — capture him. And when he had to leave the country in 1941 for his first meeting with Roosevelt, he gloried in the various security measures, particularly the special photograph of himself outside No. 10, purchasing a flag from a beaming woman, which was used a week later on the actual flag day.[1]

There were also, of course, less romantic sources for Churchill's continued interest as Prime Minister in the "Great Game." To begin with, there was his acute awareness of Britain's overall weakness. In 1940, with Britain's back to the wall, there was a feeling that all possible courses of action must be explored. "Remember it isn't only the good boys who help win wars," Churchill reminded General Dill in this regard. "It is the sneaks and the stinkers as well."[2] Moreover, the indecisive, incredibly attritive combat of the Great War led the British leader to look for more effective methods of combat. Finally, there were the new technologies that affected the ability of the military to shoot, move and communicate – all of which created new intelligence opportunities ranging from Sigint to deception. It was at that time that the Prime Minister's ruthless pragmatism was a continuing inspiration to the intelligence community. "When England's fate hung in the balance," Michael Handel has pointed out, "Churchill was ready and eager to open other gentlemen's mail."[3]

ORGANIZATION AND POLITICS

> There has been disseminated ... from time to time the theory that John Bull ... is a simple sentimentalist, without care or forethought, and a ready dupe of continental craft and machinations. This too perhaps had its utility.
>
> *Thoughts and Adventures*, p. 59

As has been demonstrated, Churchill was not a unitary actor in the British political-military decision-making process. Unlike Hitler, for instance, he was buffered by myriad intelligence organizations and military staffs. Thus, while the British could focus their intelligence operations on the Nazi leader whose quirks and goals were well known, German intelligence operations did not just have Churchill to deceive. On the other hand, the British leader was deeply involved in many aspects of intelligence during the war, ranging from security considerations and organizations to policy concerning how new information should be used. His temperament and policy inclinations had to be taken, therefore, into serious consideration throughout the war by the many actors and agencies in the British intelligence community.

Organizations

> Obtain a most careful report today from the Joint Intelligence Staff of any further indication of enemy preparations for raid or invasion. Let me have this tonight.
>
> Prime Minister to Colonel Jacob, 6 July 1940.
> *The Second World War*, Vol. II, p. 643

> In the higher ranges of Secret Service work the actual facts in many cases were in every respect equal to the most fantastic inventions of romance or melodrama. Tangle within tangle, plot and counter-plot, ruse and treachery, cross and double-cross, true agent, false agent, double agent, gold and steel ... a texture so intricate as to be incredible and yet true.
>
> *Thoughts and Adventures*, pp. 58–59

Churchill approached the problems of intelligence organizations with the same pragmatic and rational flair and energy that he used in other aspects of the war. As Secretary of State for War in 1920, he had vainly made the revolutionary suggestion that all British intelligence branches be combined in a single secret service. He repeated this proposal to the Chiefs of Staff after becoming Prime Minister only to be met by similar institutional resistance. Despite this rebuff, Churchill directed the Chiefs to review the system for relating intelligence to the government's procedure for making operational decisions. The result was a considerably strengthened Joint Intelligence Committee (JIC), and the creation of the Joint Intelligence Staff (JIS), a subcommittee of the JIC charged with coordinating, assessing and disseminating strategic intelligence.[4]

As a result of those changes, the JIC was confirmed by 1941 as the key organization for producing intelligence estimates and for bringing those estimates to the attention of the operational authorities. In addition to the Directors of Intelligence from the three Services, the refurbished JIC also brought under its control MI-5, the Security Service, and incorporated representatives from the Foreign Office; the Ministry of Economic Warfare with its expertise in industrial intelligence and blockade matters; the Inter-Services Topographical Department at Oxford; and the Inter-Services Security Board (ISSB). The ISSB was particularly important, since it controlled security in all offensive operations throughout the war, administered the creation and assignments of operational code-words, and through its London Coordinating Section (LCS) conducted deception and counterpropaganda operations. Finally, the JIC and its JIS were authorized to issue at any time of the day or night urgent papers on any strategic development to Churchill, the War Cabinet and the Chiefs of Staff.[5]

Churchill interacted constantly with the Joint Intelligence Staff throughout the war. On one occasion in 1943, Captain Drake, the Director of Naval Intelligence's senior representative to the JIS, was duty officer when he received a call late at night from Brigadier Hollis, the Secretary to the Chiefs of Staff. Hollis informed Drake that the Prime Minister wanted an intelligence estimate of the German reinforcements in Italy as well as the potential for the political collapse of the Italian government, and that he wanted it by 10:30 that same morning. After a series of strained exchanges in which he explained the impossibility of the assignment in such a short time, Drake finally exploded. "Hollis, why don't you tell the silly old man to go to bed, and we'll get on with it as quickly as we can and probably have it ready tomorrow afternoon." Just at that moment, as Drake later recounted it, Churchill, who had been listening on the extension, boomed: "Perhaps it would help in your deliberations if the silly old man came down to help you." In 15 minutes, Churchill, dressed in his "rompers" was in the Intelligence Operations Room outlining his intelligence requirements. When he was finished, he left the room to return to bed. Just as Drake and his staff were heaving sighs of relief, the door opened and Churchill stuck his head in. "Would 3 o'clock tomorrow afternoon be satisfactory to you, Captain?" he asked. And after being assured that it was, replied, "Very well, make it so. Good night."[6]

Churchill's rational reorganization at the top permeated with mixed results down to the two major intelligence branches: the Secret Intelligence Service (SIS) or MI-6, concerned with foreign intelligence operations, and MI-5 concerned with intelligence operations in Britain, primarily against subversion and espionage. SIS was headed by Brigadier Stewart Menzies, an Old Etonian, who was to benefit as far as Churchill's patronage was concerned by the fact that his organization also had jurisdiction over the cryptoanalysis operations at Bletchley Park. Initially, however, SIS was diminished by Churchill's reorganization after the fall of France. One result of that failure in regular warfare was to focus on redemption by irregular warfare, which in turn led on 16 July to the establishment of the Special Operations Executive (SOE), independent of SIS, under the cover organization of the Ministry of Economic Warfare. The aim of the new organization, as its chief later recalled, was to coordinate subversion and sabotage efforts against the enemy overseas – "A Ministry of Ungentlemanly Warfare," as Churchill described it. But the romantic expectations of the Prime Minister were more than a little unrealistic, as demonstrated in his exhortation for SOE to "set Europe ablaze." In actuality, throughout most of the war, Europe remained "too damp to do more than smoulder."[7]

The creation of SOE led to conflicts of interest between it and SIS that Churchill resignedly termed "lamentable but perhaps inevitable."[8] Ironically, the Prime Minister's penchant for the romantic led to similar diffusion of SOE's authority. In August 1942, when Churchill stopped in at Cairo on his return from Moscow, he met a Captain Sterling of the Special Air Service (SAS), who had wangled an invitation to a reception honoring the Prime Minister in order to plead the case for his organization's continuing independence from SOE. Sterling's detachment had destroyed over 250 enemy airplanes in various raids on airfields behind enemy lines, and Churchill was delighted with the young officer. His son Randolph had been on the SAS raid against Benghazi, and that sort of luck-and-pluck endeavor appealed to the British leader above all other operations. By the end of the evening, Churchill was describing the SAS leader in the words of Byron's Don Juan as "the mildest mannered man that ever scuttled ship or cut a throat." The upshot was that the Prime Minister directed that the SAS not be placed under the SOE.[9]

Many of Hitler's early regular warfare successes, which had led to the creation of the SOE, were also mistakenly attributed to extensive Fifth Column activities. As a result, Churchill focused on MI-5 as soon as he took office. There had been several incidents since the beginning of the war which he believed reflected adversely on that organization, the most important being the 14 October 1939 sinking of the *Royal Oak* by a U-boat in Scapa Flow. In June, he fired Sir Vernon Kell who had been head of MI-5 since 1909 when it was known as M05. At the same time, the new Prime Minister formed the Security Executive under Lord Swinton to deal with "overlaps and underlaps" in the MI-5 agencies operating against subversion and espionage and to "find out whether there is a fifth column in this country and if so to eliminate it."[10]

MI-5 was spectacularly successful in fulfilling that charter with the so-called "double cross" system, the expansion of which was facilitated by Britain's virtual isolation from the Continent after June 1940. That expansion, in turn, meant that a more rational and coordinated approach to the use of the various intelligence fiefdoms was necessary. Dealing with double agents, as an example, cut across the line which confined MI-5 to Britain and SIS to foreign operations. Out of this came the Twenty Committee, so named for the Roman Numerals formed by the symbol for double cross (XX), which held its first meeting on 2 January 1941. How far the system had come by that time for coordinating the efforts of the British intelligence community was illustrated by the membership of the committee, which included representatives from SIS, the Service intelligence branches, the Home Forces Headquarters, and the Security Executive − all under the MI-5 chairmanship of J.C. Masterman.[11]

Amateurism and Security

> I, too, was proud of my prisoner − until we reached the army.
> Then it appeared that ... he was a most important individual
> in the employ of the Intelligence Department who had been
> spying in Omdurman ....
>
> Churchill, *The River War*

Churchill believed that amateurs, no matter how eccentric, had an important part to play in intelligence − a fortuitous legacy from Victorian days that had been reinforced by his Room 40 experiences in World War I. For him in this particular regard, military professionals were generally inferior to the gifted civilian amateur because the military's education and performance emphasized obedience and loyalty. The civilian amateurs, on the other hand, frequently brought with them new enthusiasm, creative imagination, informality, and a somewhat more open, detached and objective approach − all intellectual qualities highly useful for intelligence work. Moreover, they tended to resist pressures and retain, as Donald McLachlan has pointed out, "a reasonable independence of service loyalties ...."[12] As a result, there was an influx of recruits from the universities into the various organizations of the British intelligence community. The membership of the Special Operations Executive (SOE), for

147

instance, had a large contingent from Balliol College, Oxford. And Cambridge supplied many of the unorthodox and unsoldierly crew that made up the cryptoanalysis community at Bletchley Park. "I told you," Churchill was reported to have commented to the Director of that community after first addressing the Bletchley Park amateurs, "to leave no stone unturned in your recruiting. I did not expect you to take me so literally."[13]

In addition, there was a wide range of amateurs whom Churchill had come to know over the years and who were put to work after 1940 in many unorthodox positions. One early acquaintance of the Prime Minister's, for instance, was the Canadian millionaire, William "Little Bill" Stephenson. Stephenson was a former lightweight world champion, known as "Captain Machine Gun" because of his rapid-fire punches, who had also served in World War I as a fighter pilot. Churchill had asked him to do part-time intelligence work for him in the mid-thirties during business trips to Germany. In May 1940, Stephenson was appointed as Passport Control Officer in New York where the diminutive representative's clubbable personality and remarkable capacity for dry martinis soon made him, through his American contacts, an invaluable part of SIS's intelligence liaison work.[14]

There was also an amateurish side to Churchill's concern for intelligence security. This was due in part to an impulsive nature that sometimes made concealment difficult. In 1908, for example, while taking shelter from the rain in a building on the grounds of Blenheim, Churchill proposed to Clementine Hosier and was accepted. They agreed to say nothing until she had told her mother. As they were walking back toward the palace, however, Churchill saw Lord Birkenhead and impulsively ran over to his friend, threw his arms around his neck and blurted out the news.[15]

At times during the war, particularly in his long distance banter with Roosevelt, Churchill's disregard for security appeared to stem from an impatience with bureaucratic procedures. When Roosevelt selected the cover name "Admiral Q" prior to the Casablanca Conference, for instance, the British leader cabled: "However did you think of such an impenetrable disguise?"[16] And in 1942, after being warned about telephone security before making a call from Florida to the President, Churchill told Roosevelt: "I mustn't tell you on the open line how we shall be travelling, but we shall be coming by puff puff."[17] At other times, security breaches were the unintentional results of an overworked man in his sixties, operating under tremendous pressures. In May 1940, as an example, Churchill was discussing by telephone with General Gort his plans to visit the French leaders on the Continent. He began: "I am going to fly with the C.I.G.S. to ...." and got no further. On an impulse, an aide had reached out and switched off the call. "Please Sir," he said when Churchill looked up in surprise, "it is not safe to speak of these plans on the telephone."[18]

Perhaps the most egregious security lapses on the part of the British leader occurred during his many trans-Atlantic conversations with Roosevelt using a private radio telephone on which all conversation was scrambled by a device known as the Bell A-3. The Germans learned of this system and established an interception and unscrambling station on the Dutch coast near the Hague where they were able to listen to conversations between the two leaders despite the fact that the frequencies were changed often, regularly and at random. Churchill and Roosevelt were instructed, in any case, to use code words and be guarded in their speech. Nevertheless, as Ultra revealed, the Germans possessed information that could only have come from conversations between the two leaders. The leak ended in February 1944 when a new scrambler was introduced and the German interception station in Holland was destroyed by the RAF.[19]

Those types of lapses notwithstanding, Churchill was a consistent and demanding advocate of tight intelligence security. He was always conscious of that need as he pored through his daily mass of reading materials, repeatedly demanding to see circulation lists for particular telegrams and then directing cuts in those lists. "With the new year," he minuted on Christmas Day 1940, "a fresh effort must be made to restrict the circulating of secret matters in Service and other Departments. All ... papers should be reviewed with a view to striking off as many recipients as possible." By the following May, Churchill had a new, much more comprehensive security directive promulgated under his covering note that began: "An intense effort should be made to achieve greater security in matters where secrecy is of fundamental importance to the conduct of the war."[20]

Churchill was particularly sensitive throughout the war to leaks concerning future war plans and operations. On 9 November 1940, for instance, he read a message to the Dominion Prime Ministers providing details of British aid to Greece that included information on naval movements. "Who is responsible for drawing it up and sending it out?" he minuted furiously. "No one is entitled to be informed of impending movements of British ships ...."[21] The issue also demonstrated the problem of security when it came to Britain's allies. It was during that same period, as an example, that the Dominion governments expressed their belief that they should have been consulted on Operation "Menace," the expedition with the Free French against Dakar. Churchill rejected that contention, pointing out that "unity and secrecy in the command" had been required for the safety of the troops. He might also have added that the Inter-Service Security Committee had reported to him after the operation "that the leakage of information had undoubtedly taken place through French sources." While at a Liverpool restaurant, "French Officers had toasted 'Dakar.'" Moreover, the report continued, one of the principal offenders had been General de Gaulle, who "when purchasing a large quantity of tropical equipment at 'Simpsons' in Piccadilly, remarked in public that his destination was West Africa."[22]

Politics of Intelligence

> Sir Douglas Haig was not at this time well served by his advisers in the Intelligence Department of General Headquarters. The temptation to tell a Chief in a great position the things he most likes to hear is one of the commonest explanations of mistaken policy.
>
> Churchill on the battle of the Somme,
> *The World Crisis 1916–1918*, Pt. 1, p. 193

Churchill insisted on raw intelligence whenever he could have it. "I do not wish such reports as are received," he wrote Ismay in August 1940, "to be sifted and digested by the various intelligence authorities."[23] The result, of course, was a crushing load of documents. "Please look at this mass of stuff which reaches me in a single morning," he wrote a few months later to the War Cabinet Secretariat. " ... more and more people must be banking up behind these different papers, the bulk of which defeats their purpose ...."[24] Nevertheless, in discussing the advice he received from the JIC in 1941 concerning German preparations for Barbarossa, Churchill reconfirmed his preference for raw intelligence material, which, although he could not allude to it in his memoirs, primarily concerned Ultra. "I had not been content with this form of collective wisdom," he wrote in *The Grand Alliance*, "and preferred to see the originals myself."[25]

For Churchill, this intelligence meant power, not just in dealing with the enemy, but with the three elements of the "remarkable trinity." As Minister of Defence, he knew what his Chiefs did and could deal with them on equal terms. Ultra, in particular, strengthened his political-military position by providing him with inside information which he soaked into his prodigious memory and applied almost oppressively and often infuriatingly in combination with his passionate interest in the smallest details of military affairs. Nevertheless, it was not information that the British leader hoarded for his own use, as did Hitler and Stalin. Although he kept the list of Ultra recipients carefully restricted, he never attempted to play a private game with the Enigma decrypts. Such deviousness was not in Churchill's nature. The information was to be used for service to the nation, as relevant evidence in the debates that swirled about him on how best to defeat Germany. It was thus made available to the Chiefs of Staff, the JIC and the Commanders-in-Chief, to be used by all as Churchill hectored his military advisers on various issues throughout the war, but only acting in the end after he had persuaded them or they, normally after Herculean efforts, had convinced him.[26]

The Chiefs, themselves, were always on guard to make sure that while Churchill's request to get intelligence direct was honored, he should have competent advice available for evaluation. But as the Chiefs well realized, they were fighting an ingrained habit in the Prime Minister of forming his own opinion, of acting as his own intelligence officer. Nevertheless, when Churchill did act on this intelligence, he did so for the most part through the fine webbed systems of his administration, which provided numerous checks and balances.[27]

In terms of the government and the people, Churchill's possession of the latest intelligence greatly increased his central power in directing total war. At times, both as First Lord and then as Prime Minister, that meant the management of that intelligence. "He claimed the right to approach the British people in his own way," Admiral Godfrey, the Director of Naval Intelligence noted of Churchill in early 1940; "he did not hesitate if it suited his conception of the interest of a nation at war to twist the truth or to paint a rosy picture that had no connection with veracity."[28] Thus on 20 January, the First Lord broadcast over the BBC "that half the U-boats with which Germany began the war have been sunk ...."[29] The Anti-Submarine Warfare staff, under the direction of a Captain Talbot, asserted on the other hand that only 19 U-boats had been sunk, leaving 43 fit for service. The result of that challenge caused Churchill "to think it might be a good thing if Captain Talbot went to sea as soon as possible."[30]

Churchill continued to reject the submarine estimates of Naval Intelligence after he became Prime Minister, expressing his frustration in August 1940 at the Admiralty's assertion that Britain had only destroyed 25 U-boats since the beginning of the war — an assertion, he concluded, that could adversely affect public morale by "declaring futile all the efforts of our hunting craft."[31] Most importantly, Churchill had already surrounded such pessimistic estimates with great secrecy and deliberately restricted distribution. In the short run, those restrictions allowed him to bolster public morale by broadcasting his own highly optimistic, less accurate, figures. But the restrictions, which lasted until 1941, also officially denied detailed information on the growing U-boat offensive to a majority of personnel and agencies with an urgent need to know, ranging from the Plans and Operations Divisions and the Assistant Chiefs of Naval Staff to the Controller and the Fourth Sea Lord, whose job it was to build and supply the ships for the Battle of the Atlantic. It was a political distortion of intelligence that could not last. Soon U-boats began claiming victims at such a rate that there could be no illusions.[32]

In a similar manner, Churchill manipulated intelligence concerning the possible German invasion of England. By the end of October 1940, when intelligence estimates made it clear that plans for that invasion had been cancelled, the Prime Minister deliberately did not act on that information. To begin with, there were the British people who needed, Churchill believed, the stimulus of mortal danger embodied in the invasion threat to apply themselves fully to the demands of the Home Front. And there were also his efforts at that time to sharpen anxiety in the United States concerning the fate of Britain and the possibility of the British fleet in German hands. "I cannot feel that the invasion danger is past," Churchill wrote Roosevelt that month. "The gent has taken off his clothes and put on his bathing suit, but the water is getting colder and there is an autumn nip in the air." The telegram concluded: "We are maintaining the utmost vigilance."[33] It was a delicate game that succeeded. On the one hand, there was the desperate urgency that caused Harry Hopkins to tell Roosevelt in January 1941 "that any action you may take to meet the immediate needs here must be based on the assumption that invasion will come before May 1st."[34] On the other hand, there was the increasing knowledge of German deficiencies revealed by British intelligence that was added to the overpowering faith Churchill imparted to the American leader that the "hinge of fate" would turn positively for the allies in 1941.

In the end, the British intelligence agencies generally took what Michael Handel has called "the realistic approach" to intelligence politicization in dealing with Churchill. Rather than pursue a utopian goal of an independent, completely objective intelligence community, the majority of agencies placed greater emphasis on supplying the Prime Minister with the best and most useful information on issues that were of interest to him. Implicit in all this was the acceptance that Churchill would use the intelligence as he saw fit to further an overarching greater goal in total war that might not be perceptible to the intelligence producer. It was an understandable compromise, since the alternative was the so-called "idealistic approach," in which intelligence agencies, like the Admiralty in 1940, maintained their professional integrity at the cost of a sterile and self-defeating failure to influence the policy-maker.[35]

ULTRA

Then came in all the King's wise men; but they could not read the writing, nor make known to the King the interpretation. Then was King Belshazzar greatly troubled, and his countenance was changed in him, and his lords were perplexed.

The Book of Daniel

Sigint appealed to Churchill on both his romantic and pragmatic levels. The idea of plucking the enemy's most recent thoughts from the air waves was a source of excitement and enthusiasm for a man whose imagination could surround even ordinary events with romance and enchantment and whose strength as a war leader lay in large part in his ability as a myth-maker. That had been the case with the Room 40 decrypts in the First World War, and it was even more so with the British decrypts of the German Enigma machine ciphers that came to be known as Ultra.

"Where are my eggs?" Churchill would demand imperiously, referring to the box containing the latest Ultra intercepts.[36] From that box would emerge secrets with an irresistible appeal for the schoolboy who was never very far from the surface with the British leader. They were also secrets that fundamentally changed the course of the war; for with Ultra, Churchill was able to move inside the German mind as events occurred or even before they took place — to read operations orders, to monitor battlefield maneuvers, to follow the fortunes of German commanders and to learn about German weapons development. It was thus not surprising that the British leader referred to the Ultra cryptologists as "the geese who laid the golden eggs but never cackled."[37]

Those code-breakers were members of the Government Code and Cipher School (GC & CS), established as a successor to Room 40 in the 1920s, which ultimately came under SIS (MI-6), directed during the Second World War by Stewart Menzies, also known as "C." On 22 May 1940, the GC & CS cryptologists, now established at Bletchley Park, broke the Luftwaffe version of the Enigma machine cipher. A year later, they mastered the German naval Enigma followed by the breaking of the OKH Engima in spring 1942. In the beginning, the Enigma decrypts were referred to by the code word "Boniface" in order to suggest, if compromised, that they were derived from a secret agent rather than from cryptoanalysis. Churchill continued to refer to the decrypts as Boniface even after the code name was replaced by "CS," the standard two-letter symbol for a British-run secret agent in an enemy area. But by 1941, the "golden eggs" were commonly known to the staff at Bletchley Park as Ultra.[38]

That staff was not of the normal bureaucratic composition, primarily because of Churchill's Victorian belief that amateurs could excel in intelligence work. It was that belief in amateurism, shared by the Director of GC & CS and his hierarchy, that was central to the success of Bletchley Park. Without it, the organization would have been awash in the normal military discipline and civil service routines that would have made it impossible to exploit the talents of such unconventional and eccentric personalities as Alan Turing, the gifted code-breaker, who bicycled to work wearing a gas mask to guard against pollen; buried his life savings converted to silver ingots in the Bletchley Woods, only to forget the location; and listened each night to the adventures of Larry the Lamb on "Toyland," a BBC children's program. Tolerance of such eccentricity, combined with a high-spirited, quick-minded amateurish enthusiasm, led to a creative anarchy which took little account of rank and hierarchy, ignored bureaucratic demarcation lines, and thereby created with great speed, as Christopher Andrew has pointed out, "perhaps the ablest team of cryptographers and intelligence analysts in British history."[39]

No matter how able the men and women at Bletchley Park, however, it would have been extremely difficult for the Ultra organization to maintain its increased efforts in the rising tempo of the war over a six-year period without Churchill's direct and personal protection and interest. Without that support, as Harold Deutsch has pointed out, "Bletchley Park would have been almost inconceivable."[40] Churchill's support for the entire intelligence effort, of course, was widely known. But it was his interest in Enigma decrypts, combined with the high quality of product that emerged from Bletchley, that allowed Sigint to come of age. Soon Service representatives were beating a path to the Park to express their gratitude. In 1941, the First Sea Lord paid a visit after the sinking of the *Bismarck* and the initial breaking of the U-boat cipher. Admiral Cunningham also made a similar call that same year in regard to a battle in the Mediterranean that Enigma decrypts had made possible. And when the Director of Military Intelligence for both Wavell and Auchinleck returned from the Mideast in the spring of 1942, he made a special point of explaining to the men and women of Bletchley Park how invaluable Ultra had been in the battles against the *Afrika Korps*.[41]

But, above all, there was Churchill, who was in constant touch with the facility. On some occasions, it might be a direct call to a surprised officer in one of the Bletchley Huts from the Prime Minister in search of the latest news. At other times, it could be a translated Enigma decrypt returned to Bletchley with Churchill's handwritten query as to the accuracy of the translation by the overworked staff. In one such instance, the British leader's confusion with the phrase "parachute horse" was traced to the original hurried scribble at Bletchley which read "parachute losses." Finally, there were the visits, by which Churchill could express his own gratitude and maintain the morale at Bletchley. "You all look," he began a speech on one such visit to the assembled staff, "very ... innocent."[42]

How direct Churchill's top down interest in the activities at Bletchley could be was illustrated in October 1941 when four cryptoanalysts wrote a letter directly to the Prime Minister complaining of the lack of sufficient staff as well as administrative, bureaucratic problems. One of the four code-breakers, P.S. Milner-Barry, was selected to deliver the letter in person. Years later, he recalled his sense of "total incredulity" when upon arriving by train in London, he hailed a taxi and told the driver to take him to 10 Downing Street. He became more amazed as he approached the Prime Minister's residence when one uniformed policeman waved the taxi through a wooden barrier. At the door of No. 10, Milner-Barry paid off the taxi, rang the bell and was ushered into the residence, where he was told he could not see the Prime Minister personally, but that his letter would be delivered. After reading the letter the next day, Churchill immediately minuted Ismay:

ACTION THIS DAY

Make sure they have all they want on extreme priority and report to me that this has been done.

Within a month, "C" reported that the requests in the letter were well on their way to being fulfilled. But as Milner-Barry recalled, "almost from that day the rough ways began miraculously to be made smooth ... and we were able to devote ourselves uninterruptedly to the business at hand."[43]

Golden Eggs

> It will be very necessary for me to be kept fully informed during these critical days. Particularly I must have good "C" stuff.
> Churchill minute to his Private Office, 1 August 1943.
> Gilbert, VII, p. 459

Churchill's appreciation of the "Golden Eggs" from Bletchley was demonstrated in the internal methods he established to receive his daily Ultra information, in his active support of attempts to break additional cyphers, and in the intricate lengths to which he went to conceal the British possession of Ultra. The most immediate beneficiary of the "Golden Eggs" was Brigadier Menzies. Because of Ultra, Menzies was not required at any time during the war to deploy his service in conventional attempts to penetrate German security screens in order to obtain enemy secrets. Moreover, he ensured his position at the center of power by controlling the principal flow of intelligence from Bletchley not only to the Services, but most importantly to the Prime Minister.[44] At one point, Churchill instructed Menzies to send him "daily all Enigma messages," but soon came to accept that such procedure was impracticable given the ever-increasing flow of Ultra traffic.[45]

In August 1940, a direct teleprinter circuit was established between Bletchley Park and MI-6 at Broadway, only five minutes from Downing Street. Within MI-6, Menzies appointed Group Captain Winterbotham to select and forward to the Prime Minister all important Enigma decrypts, marking them, at Churchill's insistence, with a brief analysis of their significance – in Winterbotham's words, "the headlines." Before dispatch, the messages were placed in a locked buff-colored box and provided to Menzies for examination. In some cases the MI-6 Chief would deliver some Ultra decrypts by hand to Churchill, either because he had an appointment in any case with the Prime Minister, or perhaps to associate himself more fully in Churchill's mind with an incredibly successful intelligence product. In most cases, however, the messages were sent in the locked box either to No. 10 or to Storey's Gate, the British leader's underground complex of war rooms.[46]

At either of those locations, Desmond Morton, Churchill's source of much intelligence in the inter war years, took over. Morton was only one of a few in the Prime Minister's immediate entourage who were allowed into what Churchill termed the "Secret Circle." Sir Ian Jacob, for example, the Military Secretary to the War Cabinet, knew nothing about the existence of Ultra, and the same applied to Churchill's Private Secretaries as well. Like Winterbotham, Morton was crucial in the process of selecting Ultra material. Upon receiving the Ultra box, he would inventory the documents and divide them into two bundles, those Churchill should see and those he need not. Often, Morton would write a memorandum to the Prime Minister concerning a particular decrypt, attach it to the document and place it and the other documents selected for Churchill back in the box. At other times, particularly after a spate of Enigma decrypts was received, he would send similar memoranda concerning Ultra to Ismay or Lindemann, or, in some cases to selected members of the Joint Intelligence and Joint Planning Committees.[47]

From the beginning, Churchill was concerned that he receive the "Golden Eggs" even while abroad. Before leaving for his first meeting with Roosevelt in August 1941, he made arrangements for the Enigma decrypts to reach him in Newfoundland by air, "in a weighted case, so that they will sink in the sea if anything happens to the aeroplane."[48] Similar arrangements were supposed to be made for the Casablanca Conference in early 1943, and Churchill was not pleased at the apparent disregard of his instructions. "Why have you not kept me properly supplied with news?" he signaled to Menzies. "Volume should be increased at least five-fold with important messages sent textually."[49] There had been, however, no special Enigma link established for the conference. And although Churchill was able to receive Ultra through the Admiralty's most secret channel, a Special Liaison Unit (SLU) for that purpose accompanied him on all future travel abroad. Despite those arrangements, he never lost his concern that he might be severed from Ultra. "I must have good 'C' stuff," he reminded his Private Office before sailing to the Canadian port of Halifax for the August 1943 Quebec Conference. " ... Make sure that full pouches by air including 'C' stuff await me at H."[50]

Churchill's regard for and dependence on Ultra were illustrated by his attempts from the outset of the war, initially as First Lord and then as Prime Minister, to capture a German naval version of the Enigma code machine. In 1939, three wheels of the machine were taken from a German submarine, and the following year, papers found on a captured German patrol boat permitted the British to read German naval messages for six days. In March 1941, the capture of a German trawler during the raid on the Lofton Islands enabled the cryptoanalysts at Bletchley to make progress. Nevertheless, they were still unable to break the code. Later that spring, the Admiralty dispatched an expedition to capture two German weather ships. The information from that successful venture was supplemented by an even more profitable windfall, when a boarding party from the HMS *Bulldog* captured the Enigma machine on 9 May from U-110 before that submarine sank. By the end of July 1941, the breakthrough of the German naval Enigma was complete, with instructions for U-boats being read "continuously and with little or no delay."[51]

At the end of January 1942, the U-boats, which had previously used the same Enigma as other ships, acquired their own machine. U-boat signals were suddenly unreadable at Bletchley and would remain so for nearly a year. That development coincided with a sharp increase of U-boats, which together caused a large rise by the autumn of 1942 in the monthly rate of allied merchant ship losses. Those losses, Churchill believed, were not sufficient to risk compromising Ultra by another deliberate attempt to capture German naval ciphers. Instead, he exerted enormous and continuous pressure on the hierarchy at Bletchley which resulted in an initial breakthrough by December. On 19 March 1943, Menzies informed the British leader that a final impasse had been overcome, and by June the Admiralty could read not only the pattern of U-boat patrol routes, but the scale of their losses. At the end of that month, Churchill noted in a speech at the Guildhall that in May over 30 U-boats had been destroyed and that June had been the best month for British merchant shipping since the war began.[52]

It was that type of positive direct cause and effect relations that caused Churchill to take extraordinary security precautions with Ultra throughout the war. As early as October 1940, for instance, he became disturbed at the burgeoning circulation list for the Enigma decrypts. "I am astonished at the vast congregation who are invited to study these matters," he minuted Ismay. "... I have marked a number who should be struck off at once, unless after careful consideration in each individual case it is found indispensable that they should be informed."[53] He continued the review throughout the autumn. At one point he instructed that the American Military Attaché be cut out of the Enigma net, not because of any lack of confidence in the general, he explained, "but because the wild scattering of secret information must be curbed."[54] On 8 November 1940, Churchill had a list drawn up of all those on Ultra circulation. There were 31 recipients.

No matter how circumscribed the circulation of Ultra material, however, there was always the danger that use of that information in other conversations or correspondence could compromise the Enigma decrypts. How sensitive Churchill was to that aspect of the security problem during that period was illustrated by his decision to replace all references in British assessments to "Sealion" with "Smith." Bletchley Park had identified the German code word for the invasion of England, and the Prime Minister was concerned that its future use might compromise Ultra. Immediately after the decision, there was a decline in the War Office's interest concerning Ultra information on the German invasion. The reason, as it turned out, was that the War Office already had its own "Operation Smith," a code name for the movement of a minor administrative branch in the event of a German invasion. The result was that the Bletchley products were immediately sent to the alternate headquarters site in the field where, as R.V. Jones reconstructed the situation, a relatively junior officer, "no doubt impressed by the service that the War Office was providing but realizing that the material was too secret for general circulation, locked them in his safe and told nobody."[55]

Churchill's circumspection with Ultra was not initially in evidence concerning the field commands. Early in the war, he was impatient with precautions concerning operational use of Sigint, in particular the requirements of GC & CS to paraphrase decrypts before passing them to the Middle East commands and for that agency to withhold what was considered nonessential information. In April 1941, for example, he complained about the failure of GC & CS to mention that Hitler was personally interested in Rommel's operations against Tobruk, and he continued to criticize the summaries from Bletchley as not fully reflecting the flavor of the original decrypts. A few months later, the British leader insisted that the verbatim texts of the more significant decrypts be sent directly to General Auchinleck. By the fall of 1941, however, a more cautious approach had crept into Churchill's impulsive enthusiasm. "C is sending you daily our special stuff," he wrote Auchinleck during the Crusader offensive. "Feel sure you will not let any of this go into battle zone except as statements on your own authority with no trace of origin and not too close a coincidence."[56]

Those concerns grew more urgent after the landings in French North Africa in November 1942. "Pray consider whether, at this period in the operations," he minuted "C" at that time, "it would not be wise to have a general campaign to reduce to one-third the circulation of Boniface here, in the Middle East and at the *Torch* Headquarters ...."[57] There were further alarms concerning the Enigma decrypts the following spring. So much so that a week prior to the battle of Medenine, while Montgomery was preparing to defend against the attack predicted by Ultra, Churchill cautioned him to "guard our precious secret even, so far as possible, in your dispositions. Tell even your most trusted commanders only the minimum necessary."[58]

Churchill's security concerns governed his use or nonuse of the information provided by Ultra. To begin with, there was the intelligence that he could not pass on to the consumer for fear of compromise. This did not include, as has been proven, the bombing of Coventry. Even without this proof, it is almost inconceivable that the Victorian tension between the emotional romantic and the ruthless pragmatist could have been skewed to such an extent that the British leader would deliberately have allowed the destruction of Coventry to save Ultra's secret. Nevertheless, as Forrest Pogue has pointed out in this regard, it will take some time before fact catches up with fiction sufficiently to prevent the fraudulent Coventry story from "being used to keep sophomores awake in the classroom."[59]

There were occasions, however, when Churchill could be ruthless in his withholding of information. In 1944, for instance, he used Ultra to monitor SOE efforts in Yugoslavia and to see how successful Tito's partisans were in either pinning down German forces or drawing them in from other fronts. Among the SOE irregulars was his son. "Give my love to Randolph," he telegraphed Tito on 25 May 1944. "... I wish I could come myself but I am too old and heavy to jump out in a parachute."[60] That same day, German paratroopers attacked Tito's headquarters in Bosnia in a surprise raid that had been indicated earlier by Ultra. Nevertheless, even though Randolph would be in jeopardy, no alert had been sent to the British Mission because the mission cypher was not of the highest grade, the Partisan cyphers were not secure, and because action based on Ultra without proper precautions might have aroused German suspicions about the vulnerability of Enigma. In any event, the British Mission had already moved its location based on persistent German reconnaissance flights in the area. "We are told that British liaison officers are safe," Harold Macmillan telegraphed Churchill on 26 May. "This includes Randolph."[61]

There was also other more immediate information from Ultra on damage assessments that could not be used. In January 1942, for instance, the government added to the bad news from the Middle East and the Far East the public announcement of the loss of the battleship *Barham* the previous December with the loss of at least 500 lives. The sinking had been kept secret because the Admiralty knew from Ultra that the U-boat commander did not realize the fate of the *Barham*. More frustrating for the British leader was the incident a month later when two German battle cruisers, *Scharnhorst* and *Gneisenau*, and the cruiser *Prinz Eugen*, slipped out of Brest harbor and sailed up the Channel, past the Dover batteries to the North Sea. The public outcry, which almost reached the proportion of that directed against the ongoing situation in Singapore, would have been stilled if the news of the damage sustained by the three ships during the dash could have been revealed. But that news, as Churchill informed Roosevelt on 16 February, was based on Enigma decrypts and thus could not be revealed.[62]

For the most part, however, Churchill was able to use information from the Enigma decrypts, particularly at the operational and tactical level, by the use of cover stories that attributed Ultra successes to agents, captured documents and sightings. The British leader's concern with that aspect was illustrated in November 1941 when two Italian convoys bringing military supplies to Tripoli were intercepted by the Malta-based "Force-K."

Nine of the ten supply ships were sunk as were three of the four destroyer escorts – all made possible because of Enigma decrypts that provided precise details of the route and timing of the convoys. Although elated at the news, Churchill was worried that Ultra had been endangered by a signal from Malta giving details of the convoy. "C" reassured him. "The Malta signal," Menzies minuted to the Prime Minister, "was sent out as a result of an aircraft sighting which quite naturally corresponded with our Most Secret Information."[63]

Cover stories, however, did not always have such a confluence of fact and fiction. In September 1942, for instance, an Enigma decrypt showed the Germans to be aware that the Eighth Army had known the plan and date of a key German attack and highly suspicious of the information planted by the British that the plan had been extracted from an Italian prisoner. Churchill suspected that Montgomery had been too free with Ultra information precisely because of the cover story concerning the Italian prisoner, and in his rebuke to the general, pointed out that the cover was far from adequate. In a similar manner in March 1943, the British Mideast command failed to provide realistic alternate sightings as a cover rationale for the destruction of two Mediterranean convoys with cargo described by General Kesselring as "decisive for the future conduct of operations." The next day, when an Enigma decrypt outlined German suspicions of a security breach, Churchill was furious. Ultra would be withheld, he cabled immediately, unless it was "used only on great occasions or when thoroughly camouflaged."[64]

On other occasions, cover stories had to be manufactured after the fact, as was demonstrated during the battle of El Alamein in October 1942. At one point during the battle, Rommel was informed by wireless that a convoy of five Italian ships with desperately needed ammunition and fuel was on its way. The decrypted signal with this information arrived at the desk of the Ultra duty officer at about the same time the German general received it. The duty officer immediately notified Churchill at Chequers by secure voice telephone. After a moment's hesitation, the Prime Minister ordered an attack on the convoy. The subsequent destruction of the ships, however, triggered Rommel's suspicions concerning possible sources of leakage, to include the Enigma system, the security of which he had hitherto accepted without question. Only a British signal, which the Germans could read, complimenting a phantom group of Italian agents on their information, managed to divert suspicions. And even then, Ultra's usefulness was not at an end, since it allowed the British to intercept a message between German forces in Italy and Rommel's headquarters which clearly showed that the fraudulent British signal had been intercepted by the Germans who were initiating inquiries concerning the phantom Italian agents.[65]

Finally, there was the matter of Churchill's partners in the Grand

Alliance. The United States presented no immediate problem in terms of complete and open provision of Ultra intelligence. In June 1941, Churchill began to press Menzies to pass to Washington the contents of Enigma decrypts pertaining to U-boats and German policy toward US Atlantic naval units. In August, the Japanese Ambassador in Berlin reported to Tokyo a conversation in which Hitler had given assurances that Germany would immediately open hostilities with the United States in the event of a conflict between that country and Japan. By that time, the passage of Ultra information to Washington was such standard procedure that Churchill, upon seeing the decrypts of the Japanese telegram, merely asked for confirmation that Roosevelt had seen it.[66] It was not so clean cut, however, with the Soviets. Nevertheless, given the stakes, Churchill was willing to supply such intelligence even before Russia became an ally. On 3 April 1941, the Prime Minister sent information on German movements in the East in a personal message to Stalin to be hand delivered by his Ambassador to Moscow. The information was based on Ultra, and although the source was disguised, the evidence was not – a calculated risk on Churchill's part.[67]

Three days after the German invasion, Churchill instructed "C" to provide certain Ultra-based intelligence to the Soviets, "provided no risks are run."[68] And when it later became clear through Enigma decrypts that the Germans planned to initiate an all-out attack on Moscow in early October, the British leader sent nine separate warnings to Stalin within the week. At the same time, British intelligence began to supplement the information based on the Luftwaffe Enigma decrypts with a more operationally-oriented variety based on the German Army Enigma key, codenamed "Vulture." That key was used for primary secure communications between the OKH on the Eastern Front and its Army Groups and Armies. By late September 1941, "Vulture" was being broken with some regularity, and it was those decrypts that allowed the British to provide Russia with the number of German armored and motorized divisions committed to the 2 October drive on Moscow. Nevertheless, Churchill required constant assurance. "Are you warning the Russians of the developing concentration?" he queried "C" on the day the offensive began. "Show me the last five messages you have sent out to our mission on the subject."[69]

Churchill maintained the flow of Ultra-based intelligence to Stalin until the tide of war turned. At no time during that period was the thought of compromising his most valuable intelligence asset far from his mind. "I have got the following information," he prefaced one message to the Soviet leader in September 1942, "from the same source that I used to warn you of the impending attack on Russia a year and a half ago. I believe this source to be absolutely trustworthy. Pray let this be for your own eye."[70] Nevertheless, as Churchill well realized, the dénouement in the

East was well worth the risk even of Ultra, and he did not stint on his support. At one point midway through the war, for example, after reading his daily Enigma decrypts, the Prime Minister minuted to Menzies: "Has any of this been passed to Joe?"[71]

Levels of War

> Boniface shows the enemy in great anxiety and disarray ....
> Reading Boniface ... I cannot help hoping that you may find
> it possible to strike earlier than the date mentioned ....
>
> Churchill to Alexander, 27 December 1942
> Hinsley, *British Intelligence in the Second World War*,
> Vol. II, p. 456

As Minister of Defence, Churchill's proper concern was the strategic level of war. And yet Ultra, combined with his natural romantic tendencies as the Victorian man of action, drew him inexorably down to the operational and even tactical levels of war as he sought to deal with what he came to believe were fundamental weaknesses in his Mideast commanders. The enemy's cards were, after all, in the hands of those commanders; and he could not grasp why they would not act with swift ruthlessness to close with and decisively destroy the enemy, as he would have done if he were at the center of battle. Moreover, the Chiefs were no more immune to Ultra than Churchill, and they too shared his picture of Rommel's desperate condition, persistently renewed by the intercepts of the German commander's frantic demands for more resources as well as his abuse of Italian incompetence. The constant stream of Enigma decrypts created images for them of a German army living on a shoestring and, based on their endorsements of the relief of both Wavell and Auchinleck, they apparently also believed that those generals could have dealt more conclusively with an enemy so evidently weak.[72]

What Churchill and the Chiefs of Staff did not always appreciate, however, was that Ultra was only as good as its interpreter, no matter what the level of war. The Prime Minister, himself, provided an example of this on 20 July 1944 while visiting Montgomery's headquarters on the Continent. During the visit he received his box of Enigma decrypts and proceeded to rummage enthusiastically through the contents which contained names and events that made it obvious to Montgomery's Chief Intelligence Officer that the plot against Hitler had failed. Equally obvious to him was the fact that the raw intelligence had no implications or meaning for Churchill.[73]

At the operational and tactical levels of war, Ultra could be almost as meaningless, if not misleading, without an understanding of the enemy's doctrine and tactics. There was Wavell's response, for instance, to Enigma decrypts concerning the arrival of Rommel and what constituted no more than a brigade group in North Africa in March 1941. Based on the size of the force and using staff estimates for the logistics efforts required by such a force for a successful approach march and attack, Wavell saw no possibility of German offensive actions in the near future. But he was ignoring the Blitzkrieg doctrinal evidence from Poland and Norway to France and the Balkans. That doctrine emphasized ruthless daring and opportunistic operations based on combined arms and the *Auftragstaktik*, both of which left the initiative in the hands of the commander and provided even a brigade group size unit a cohesion and offensive power much greater than its more loosely-knit British equivalent. "My ... great error," Wavell wrote in this regard after the war, "was that I made up my mind that the enemy could not put in any effective counter-stroke before May at the earliest."[74] By 30 March, forward German units had advanced well into Cyrenaica, and by early April, the British were in full retreat with the loss of the port of Benghazi and the abandonment of all Cyrenaica.

In a similar manner, there was no shortage of authoritative information regarding German intentions concerning Crete. By 14 May 1941, Enigma decrypts had furnished the British with the precise German order of battle for an attack on the island. "I should particularly welcome chance," Churchill telegraphed Wavell that same day, "for our high-class troops to come to close grips with those people under conditions where enemy has not got his usual mechanized advantages, and where we can surely re-inforce much easier than he can."[75] At one point, the Prime Minister considered, then rejected, sending the actual Enigma decrypts by air courier directly to General Freyberg, the Allied commander of the island, who was not even in the "Secret Circle." In the end, the Ultra information was passed in filtered form to Freyberg, who in short order was more fully aware of enemy plans than any previous Allied commander in the war. That the New Zealand general was well briefed on German intentions was attested to by a British intelligence officer who was sitting at breakfast with Freyberg "at the moment when we saw the gliders overhead and the parachutists dropping. He was very calm and simply remarked: 'They're dead on time.' "[76]

But Freyberg's calm was based on a misinterpretation of the copious information concerning the enemy. The Enigma decrypts warned in detail about both airborne and seaborne landings. The Allied general did not realize, however, how critical airfields were in both airborne and amphibious German doctrine for follow-on airlifts of troops and supplies. Without an airfield, there could be no quick reserves once the amphibious units as well as the limited force of 10,000 paratroopers were expended. Because that essential point was not understood, the Germans were able to seize Maleme airfield, which in turn inevitably meant the loss of Crete.[77]

Interpretation of Ultra information also played a key role in Churchill's dismissal of Wavell and Auchinleck because it intensified differences between both generals and the British leader. In Wavell's case, the affair began with what Ronald Lewin has called the "great black joke of the African campaign," the dispatch of General von Paulus, the future capitulator at Stalingrad, to Rommel's headquarters to advise on the siege of Tobruk. Paulus arrived on 27 April 1941 and after three days, personally called off Rommel's next attack, while dispatching a report to Berlin that confirmed the pessimistic outlook of the High Command, already immersed in Barbarossa. Caution and consolidation were the keys, Paulus wrote. The *Afrika Korps* was dangerously short of fuel, ammunition, food and equipment. The Italians would not run supply convoys across the Mediterranean to Benghazi. Until conditions improved, he concluded, no more German troops should be sent to Rommel's command.[78]

The Paulus message was deciphered at Bletchley and a summary passed to Wavell on 4 April. "Have you read my telegram of 4th inst.?" Churchill telegraphed to Wavell the next day. "Presume you realize the highly secret and authoritative character of this information? Actual text is more impressive, showing enemy thoroughly exhausted ... also definite forbidding of any advance ... except for reconnaissance without permission ...."[79] By 8 April, the entire Paulus telegram was in Wavell's hands. "At this time," Churchill wrote in his memoirs, concealing the Enigma source, "we had a spy in close touch with Rommel's headquarters, who gave us accurate information of the fearful difficulties of Rommel's assertive but precarious position."[80]

That "spy," of course, provided the catalyst for future disagreements. That same week in April, the "Tiger" convoy was moving through the Mediterranean with over 300 tanks for Wavell — a triumph for Churchill over the pessimistic advice of the Chiefs. The arrival of those "tiger cubs," as he called them, seemed to the Prime Minister, now more conscious of German than he was of British operational and logistical problems, the means for an early British offensive. Consequently, as has been demonstrated, Wavell's more cautious approach caused resentment in Churchill and intensified his doubts in Wavell's ability. These doubts, bred in earlier message exchanges and in the personality clashes revealed in their 1940 London meeting, were soon to increase in the campaigns in Greece, Crete, Iraq and Syria. Wavell, on the other hand, was well aware in the spring of 1941 that his army was much weaker than in the earlier campaigns against the Italians. The tanks from the Tiger convoy were in bad condition and would, in any case, have to be adjusted for desert warfare. There was also the matter of training crews not only to operate with armor in desert warfare, but to conduct the simple mechanical repairs necessary for extended operations.

Against that backdrop, there was no chance on either side of an objective, dispassionate examination of Rommel's predicament as revealed by the Enigma decrypts. The advantage provided by those decrypts was nullified by an increasingly impatient Prime Minister's desire to press Ultra's evidence beyond what was militarily possible in short order at the operational level and by Wavell's skeptical acquiescence to pressures from his political chief for what he knew was a premature campaign. The result was Operation Battleaxe, which began on 15 June 1941. "I think it right to inform you," Wavell reported to the CIGS prior to the operation in a message which further increased Churchill's ire, "that the measure of success which will attend this operation is in my opinion doubtful." [81] He, of course, was right. Battleaxe was a disaster, a classic example of how a multitude of other considerations could affect Ultra's impact on campaigns and major operations at the operational level.

In Auchinleck's case, the problems with Ultra interpretations began in December 1941 when Rommel initiated a series of counterattacks, the decisions for which he kept from Berlin and Rome and therefore from the British. By 29 January 1942, Benghazi had fallen again and by early February, the Eighth Army had been driven from the Cyrenaican bulge and had fallen back on the Gazala line just west of Tobruk. During that period, Churchill attempted to keep up with what he considered inexplicable reverses in terms of his Ultra information. "You have no doubt seen," he telegraphed Auchinleck on 28 January 1942, "most secret stuff about Rommel's presumed intentions .... This seems to reinforce importance of our holding on. I am most anxious to hear further from you about defeat of our armour by inferior enemy numbers. This cuts very deep." [82]

The pressure from Churchill steadily increased during the next months as Auchinleck repositioned his forces on the Gazala line. Much of that, of course, was fueled by the disastrous chain of events in the Far East culminating in the fall of Singapore. But the major source of the pressure at the operational level was the Prime Minister's selective use of Ultra intelligence. "In your appreciations," he signaled to Auchinleck in mid-March after examining Enigma decrypts, "you estimate possible by March 1 that enemy may have in Libya 475 medium tanks and by April 1, 630. We now know ... that ... Panzer Army Africa had in forward area... barely half the number you credited them with." [83] But those figures were misleading. To begin with, there was always the matter of tanks in various stages of echelon repair from the regimental workshop back to the rear depots located near the ports. More importantly, Churchill's numbers were based on situation reports to the OKW by a commander who never hesitated to concoct the most pessimistic picture of his strength in armor and fuel in order to support his constant and strident complaints to Germany. Thus, the Eighth Army's March assessment, based as it was on lower grade code intercepts, photo reconnaissance, prisoner interrogation and other methods, probably provided a clearer intelligence picture in terms of relative armor strength at the operational and tactical levels than did Ultra.

Churchill's pressure on Auchinleck reached a new intensity the following autumn as he repeatedly attempted to exhort the field commander to go on the offensive with Operation Crusader. But in addition to logistics problems, Auchinleck was also confronted with a major policy difference that once again highlighted the problems Ultra could raise between London and the major commands in the field. This time it involved not only interpretation of intelligence, but grand strategy as well, centering on Air Chief Marshal Tedder, Air Officer Commander-in-Chief Middle East. Like the other major commanders in that theater, Tedder received Ultra decrypts by that time directly from Bletchley Park. As a result, he knew the exact order of battle and positions of both the German and Italian Air Forces in the theater – the same information available from Ultra in London. But there the similarity ended. Tedder and his staff differed from Churchill and the Air Staff over the probable percentage of aircraft that were serviceable as well as the likelihood of Luftwaffe reinforcements from the Eastern Front. Based on his more pessimistic analysis in both those areas, Tedder concluded that Crusader, scheduled to begin on 1 November 1941, would not be possible that month.

On 16 October, Churchill dispatched a senior Air Chief Marshal to Cairo with a personal letter for Auchinleck disputing the field interpretation of intelligence and, more particularly, strategy. "The Air Staff here knows just as much and in some ways more than the Air Intelligence in Egypt," the Prime Minister wrote. "Their conviction is that you will have a substantial numerical superiority in the battle zone .... Moreover ... the Russian front ... will certainly not be stabilized for some weeks, if then, and thereafter several more weeks must elapse before any effective transference can be made of German Air Units already battered and worn."[84] Before the letter reached Cairo, Churchill was in receipt of a letter from Auchinleck requesting that Crusader be postponed to 18 November.

When Crusader began on 18 November, the initial advantage lay with Auchinleck who knew from Ultra that Rommel was in Athens. But that was as far as Enigma decrypts could help in a tactical situation – a fact not completely understood by Churchill who continued his pressure on his field commander throughout the battle based on, as he put it, "usual source." Most of the major events in the complicated six-day battle were the result of on the ground, immediate and improvised decisions in response to the rapidly changing tactical situation. The Ultra signals that Auchinleck received, on the other hand, reflected Rommel's problems with fuel and air cover – all confidence-building information that did not illuminate the tactical situation. That situation was better served by such conventional means as interception of German battlefield conversations, direction-finding and prisoner interrogation.[85]

DECEPTION

One can always do what one wants to if it takes people by surprise.

Churchill in Harriman and Abel, *Special Envoy to Churchill and Stalin, 1941–1946*, p. 202

Indeed, if Churchill had not been Prime Minister, he would have been a member of the LCS.

Cave Brown, *Bodyguard of Lies*, p. 274

Like Ultra, deception operations appealed to both facets of Churchill's Victorian heritage. On the one hand, making the enemy think you were going where you were not was in keeping with the idea that war could be a game, in which trickery and subterfuge would only add to the fun of the sport. Moreover, such operations were clearly part of the "Great Game," and Churchill's romantic impulses never failed to respond to the many intelligence and cloak and dagger aspects involved with deception. On the other hand, the British leader also realized early on that deception was a critical force multiplier in total war, whether on the defensive or offensive. Most importantly for him, in this regard, strategic deception was a critical element in the plans for the allied reentry of Europe. And operations in support of this type of deception, Churchill knew, would require a strong centralized hand to coordinate all the theaters of war. Finally, deception at any level involved surprise; and surprise, as the British leader never forgot, could not only save immediate casualties, but could prevent the type of extended, attritive conflict he had experienced first hand in the previous war. "There are manoeuvres in time, in diplomacy, in mechanics, in psychology," he wrote after that war; "all of which are removed from the battlefield; but react often decisively upon it, and the object of all is to find easier ways than sheer slaughter of achieving the main purpose."[86]

Given Britain's initial situation in the Second World War, it was only natural that Churchill would have been involved in passive defensive deception measures at the outset, whether at the Admiralty or Downing Street. Three days after the war began, for example, he pointed out to his First Sea Lord that air reconnaissance had become a major factor since the previous war. As a consequence, he directed that dummy ships be built in harbors throughout England in order to introduce an "element of mystery which if rightly used, might draw long exhausting and futile attacks upon worthless targets, while the real ships are doing their work elsewhere."[87] In a similar manner, Churchill was also involved in the use of phony targets during the Battle of Britain, which led the Germans to attack nonexistent airfields and factories. In another variant of this type of deception late in the war, the British used the German agents they controlled in Britain under the "double cross" system to deceive the Germans as to the location of the actual hits with the V-weapons. In this manner, they generally succeeded in moving the target areas for both the V-1 and V-2 away from London.[88]

Churchill's philosophy on defensive deception operations was summed up in his thoughts concerning their importance in maintaining the secrecy of allied convoys. Those operations, he minuted to the Ministers concerned in April 1941, were particularly necessary because "where so much is visible and must be known, the continued fabrication and dissemination of false information is a necessary part of security. All kinds of Münchhausen tales can be spread about to confuse and baffle the truth. Sun helmets or winter clothing should be hawked about and calculated leakages made of false and sometimes true intentions."[89]

Churchill's primary focus, however, was on strategic deception and its principal goal: diversion of the enemy. That goal meant for him that all civilian and military efforts should be concentrated in such operations on persuading the opponent that the actual major operations and campaigns would occur in entirely different locations – even in different countries and different theaters. That was to be accomplished by creating an imaginary threat either through suggestion or simulation which would cause the enemy to divert large forces from the area where the principal offensive was to occur. How important the concept of diversion was to the Prime Minister was demonstrated in his bitter reaction as he watched Allied forces land in southern France two months after Overlord as part of Operation Anvil. "If you reflect upon what I have said at different times on strategic operations," he wrote to his wife, "you will see that Eisenhower's operations [in Normandy] have been a diversion for this landing instead of the other way around as the American Chiefs of Staff imagined .... One of my reasons for making public my visit was to associate myself with this well-conducted but irrelevant operation."[90]

Strategic deception involves preparing and executing plans, making sure the enemy is aware of the implementing operations, and evaluating the enemy's reaction. At different times during the war on various operations, Churchill was involved to some degree in all those facets of deception. But it was in his enthusiastic and imaginative commitment to the central coordination of those elements that the British leader made his greatest contribution to strategic deception. Ironically, all that began with a memorandum by Wavell in 1940, recommending that the Chiefs of Staff coordinate all cover and deception plans of the theater commanders so that

they should not only have the maximum effect in their own theatre, but should fit in with the general plan of campaign of the other theatres. Every operation in every part of the world, however distant, and however disparate the conditions, would have its effect on every other operation. Therefore ... if it was possible to deceive the enemy in one theatre, that deception, especially on the strategic plane, could not be effective and might even be dangerous if its effect on operations in other theatres were not controlled.[91]

Wavell's memorandum, combined with the obvious success of the British general's deception operations against the Italians in late 1940 and early 1941, caused Churchill to establish the London Coordinating Section (LCS) in April 1941 as the agency to plan, coordinate and control deception operations. From that time on, all British war planning staffs throughout the world were required to have a deception section directly linked to the LCS.[92] Soon, a constant stream of message traffic containing new ideas for deception began to pour from the LCS to the various theaters of war. And although many talented people would become involved, there was no doubt as to the primary source of inspiration for the LCS. "It was Churchill who had all the ideas," the Deputy Director of the LCS recalled. "It was his drive, his brilliant imagination, and his technical knowledge that initiated all these ideas and plans ...."[93]

There were seven members of the LCS with a hierarchy that was strictly patrician. Colonel John Bevan, the director after June 1942, was a grandson of the founder of Barclay's Bank as well as a Military Cross winner from World War I. His personal assistant was Lady Jane Pleydell-Bouverie, and his deputy was Colonel Sir Ronald Evelyn Leslie Wingate, the nephew of Kitchener's intelligence officer, who the night before Omdurman had provided the young Churchill with a meal. Bevan was an extraordinarily able officer, "truly great and well-loved" in the words of one subordinate, who increased the stature of the LCS by 1943 to a point where it influenced many of the activities of other British secret organizations. Moreover, by that time, the Director of LCS was also able to exercise his authority not only through his bureaux around the globe, but through the American counterpart to the LCS, the Joint Security Control, a JCS organization established in May 1942.[94]

Ultimately, Bevan acquired his greatest power because Churchill had complete confidence in him and because both the Prime Minister and the President delighted in deception operations. "Bevan and Churchill," the Pentagon representative to the LCS recalled, "sparked each other off and pulled out what were all the old tricks of Eton and Harrow and polished them up for the task at hand."[95] On occasions, Bevan even had Churchill and Roosevelt make their personal movements and statements conform to deception parameters. In 1944, for instance, both leaders continued the dissimulations of Fortitude, the deception plan for Normandy, after the invasion occurred. "I have also to announce to the House," Churchill stated after informing Commons on 6 June of the 5 June liberation of Rome, "that during the night and early hours of this morning *the first of a series of landings* in force on the European continent has taken place .... *In this case*, the liberating assault fell on the coast of France." And that same day, Roosevelt concluded his address to the American people in a similar manner. "The Germans appear to expect landings elsewhere," he stated. "Let them speculate. We are content to wait on events."[96]

Much of Bevan's success in strategic deception was due to Ultra. The Enigma decrypts provided advance knowledge of where specific enemy units were stationed and allowed immediate monitoring of enemy reactions to deception attempts which might confirm the success of the operations. Nowhere was this better illustrated than in Operation Mincemeat. The basic intent of that deception plan was to make the Germans believe that following the conquest of Tunisia, allied forces would invade, not Sicily, but the Greek Peloponnesus, with the ultimate objective of advancing through the Balkans. The key to Mincemeat was a letter to Alexander informing him that Sicily would be used as a cover for the landings in Greece. That letter, along with one from Mountbatten making it clear that Sardinia was the target of the second amphibious operation, was placed in a briefcase attached to the corpse of an imaginary Major Martin and floated ashore on 30 April 1943 from a submarine off the coast of Spain. In his briefing to Churchill on Mincemeat, Bevan had stressed some of the problems associated with the deception, particularly the fact that the tide might be wrong, thus preventing the body from washing ashore. "[W]ell, in that case," Churchill replied, "you'll have to take him on another swim, won't you."[97]

Within two weeks of what Churchill called Major Martin's swim, Ultra confirmed that the deception concerning "the man who never was" had been accepted as genuine by Hitler. That same day, Churchill, who was in conference in Washington, received a confirming message: "Mincemeat swallowed rod, line and sinker by right people and from best information they look like acting on it."[98] How the enemy "was acting" on the deception was indicated by the information received between early May and 10 July, when the Allied invasion of Sicily was launched, that indicated a significant movement of German air and land forces into Greece. Equally important, Ultra revealed what the enemy had not done, and that was to reinforce Sicily.[99]

In addition to Ultra, Churchill was not averse to using existing plans to deceive the Germans. From 1941 to 1943, for instance, a series of deception threats were originated against Norway. In one instance, in an attempt to convince Auchinleck to begin the Crusader offensive earlier, Churchill described the use of a deception operation against Norway that would help the British commander exploit his success in North Africa. "Winter clothing is being issued to the troops assigned," he concluded on 16 October 1941. "This forms a real cover."[100] How effective such deceptions were is difficult to gauge. Certainly they were not hindered by Churchill's known enthusiasm for action in the north. Equally certain was the fact that the Prime Minister's obsession with the opportunities offered to an invader by Norway, was more than matched by that of Hitler, who squandered divisions in that country that could have been extremely effective in either Russia or France.[101]

In the case of Torch, the North African invasion, Churchill dusted off two aborted invasion plans for deception use: Jupiter for northern Norway and Sledgehammer for the 1942 cross-Channel invasion. "All depends upon secrecy and speed," he telegraphed Roosevelt .... "Secrecy can only be maintained by deception."[102] The use of Sledgehammer also illustrated how invaluable Churchill's direct involvement in strategic deception could be. For if the cross-Channel deception were to be effective, as he reminded Stalin in their August 1942 Moscow meeting, there must be no recriminations over the lack of a Second Front in 1942.

> It would be injurious to all common interests, especially Russian interests, if any public controversy arose in which it would be necessary for the British Government to unfold to the nation the crushing argument which they conceive themselves to possess against "Sledgehammer." Widespread discouragement would be caused to the Russian armies, who have been buoyed up on this subject, and the enemy would be free to withdraw further forces from the West. The wisest course is to use "Sledgehammer" as a blind for "Torch," and proclaim "Torch" when it begins as the second front. This is what we ourselves mean to do.[103]

Torch also demonstrated Churchill's concern for security in deception operations. When Colonel Bevan briefed the cover plan for the invasion, the Prime Minister termed the deception "well considered," but added his "great fear that with all the talk that is here and in the United States, the enemy will find out that we are going to North Africa." Because of those concerns, Churchill directed the LCS to transpose names from the actual area of invasion to the principal locale of the Sledgehammer deception plan. Casablanca was to be called Dunkirk, with Oran to be Calais and Algiers to be Boulogne. Moreover, a small map was to be produced of the African coast with the substituted French names. "Thereafter," he concluded, "no one should use the guilty names in conversation."[104]

That concern for deception security, as in other cases of intelligence security, was not always a primary factor with Churchill. At Eisenhower's insistence, for example, and only after overcoming the Prime Minister's reluctance, the War Cabinet ruled on 17 April 1944 that foreign diplomats would not be permitted to send or receive uncensored messages. All the representatives of the Allied governments in Britain protested at the restriction vigorously to the government. As a consequence, Churchill was further agitated when Eisenhower stated that he wanted to maintain the ban after D-Day. To the British leader's immediate objection, the American general pointed out that if the ban were lifted after D-Day, the Germans would realize that Overlord was the primary attack, thus compromising the deception of Fortitude. If normal diplomatic traffic recommenced, Eisenhower concluded, Hitler "would deduce the fact that from that moment he is safe in concentrating his forces to repel the assault we have made." Churchill responded that he could not agree to an indefinite diplomatic ban and proposed that it be continued until D-Day plus seven. Eisenhower resisted, and in the end the restriction continued until D + 13.[105]

Churchill's contretemps with Eisenhower illustrated how central deception had become to the invasion of Europe in 1944. In their joint message to Stalin at the end of the Casablanca Conference in January 1943, both Western leaders had explained that centrality as they built up their forces to re-enter the Continent. "These concentrations will certainly be known to our enemies," they emphasized, "but they will not know where or when, or on what scale, we propose striking. They will therefore be compelled to divert both land and air forces to the shores of France, the Low Countries, Corsica, Sardinia, Sicily, the heel of Italy, Yugoslavia, Greece, Crete and the Dodecanese."[106] Churchill's hand was in evidence throughout the message. Only diversion and surprise would bring off the largest amphibious operation in history by making the fog of war work for the allies. Only a gigantic, seamless deception net covering all theaters would prevent the accumulation of opposing forces locked in attritive combat.

The result was Plan Jael, a code name specifically selected by Churchill, for the Europe-wide deception plan. Jael was the woman in the Song of Deborah in the Old Testament who kills a Canaanite commander after welcoming him into her home by driving a tent peg through his temple, pinning him to the ground as he sleeps. On 30 November 1943, the last day of the Teheran Conference and Churchill's 69th birthday, the British leader proposed Jael for 1944, concluding that "truth is so precious that she should always be attended by a bodyguard of lies."[107] As a result, deception agreements were written into the conference's military conclusions which stipulated "that a cover plan to mystify and mislead the enemy ... should be concerted between the staffs concerned."[108]

The result of this top down political-military emphasis was a finely coordinated overarching deception plan, renamed "Bodyguard" in December 1943 by LCS to reflect Churchill's remark at Teheran. Only the well-oiled centralized deception machinery launched by Churchill with his establishment of the LCS could have produced and coordinated the 36 subordinate plans for Bodyguard as well as the myriad associated stratagems.

Basically, however, there were two principal parts to Bodyguard. Plan Zeppelin called for the sustained threat of two British phantom armies to pin down the large German forces in the Balkans. As a result, there were still some 24 enemy divisions throughout that area on D-Day.

Fortitude North called for containing German forces in Scandinavia by means of a phantom army ostentatiously assembled in Scotland and the threat of an Anglo-Russian invasion of northern Norway agreed during Bodyguard negotiations in Moscow by Bevan in February 1944. There was some German skepticism concerning the joint invasion, but not enough to affect Fortitude North; and it was not until 16 June that Hitler ordered two divisions from that area to France — and even then only to the Pas de Calais. That, of course, was a tribute to the success of the most important deception plan, Fortitude South, which kept the other half of Rommel's Army Group B, the 15th Army, away from Normandy, spread roughly between the Scheldt and the Seine with the principal concentration at the Pas de Calais. And although Hitler had a last minute intuitive feeling about Normandy, his commanders in the west, to include von Rundstedt and Rommel, remained convinced long after D-Day that the Pas de Calais was the key to Overlord.[109]

SCIENCE AND TECHNOLOGY

Lastly, let none be alarmed at the objection of the Arts and Sciences becoming depraved to malevolent or luxurious purpose and the like for the same can be said of enemy worldly Good.... Only let mankind regain their rights over nature assigned to them by the gift of God, and obtain that power whose exercise will be governed by right Reason and true Religion.

Francis Bacon, *Novum Organum*, 1620

The campaign of 1919 was never fought; but its ideas go marching along ... and should war come again to the world it is not with the weapons and agencies prepared for 1919 that it will be fought, but with developments and extensions of these which will be incomparably more formidable and fatal.

Thoughts and Adventures, pp. 186–187

Science and technology played a critical role in the British "Great Game" in the Second World War. Ultra, as has already been demonstrated, was a quintessential example of not only how critical that role could be, but how important the Prime Minister's support, organization and decision-making process was for that role despite a lack of scientific expertise. "I knew nothing about science," Churchill recalled in his memoirs, "but I knew something of scientists, and had much practice as a Minister of handling things I did not understand. I had, at any rate, an acute military perception of what would help and what would hurt, of what would cure and what would kill."[110] In fact, Churchill recognized more than any other political leader of the time the importance of technological surprise in total war which could only come from an overall political direction that brought scientists and technologists together with members of the armed services.

In the end, it was Churchill's curiosity, imagination and reasoning power coupled with his administrative ability that formed the basis for many of the inventions and countermeasures concerned with technological surprise in World War II. He did not, for instance, invent the artificial harbor known as "Mulberry," or the pipeline under the Channel, code named "Pluto," or H_2S, a blind bombing device. But he was able in such cases to appreciate the possibilities for technological surprise and provide the authority of his office to the scientists, often spurring them to achieve the "impossible." There were, of course, some problems when a scientific scheme had a fundamental defect. At such times, Churchill's Victorian and personal traits of doggedness, optimism and faith that technicians could do anything resulted in research and experiment being pushed beyond the point where it was clear that the scientific result would be barren. But on balance, as in the military field, there were enough constraints to keep such developments under control, while harnessing the vast stimulation of the Prime Minister's matchless imagination and energy to the efforts at creating and defending against technological surprise.

Victorian Tension

It is the duty of scientists, like all other people, to serve the state and not to rule it because they are scientists.
Churchill in Eade, *Churchill by his Contemporaries*, p. 387

On the night of 19 March 1941, while Churchill was giving a dinner at Downing Street for two American guests, a heavy air raid on London began. The Prime Minister immediately took his guests to the roof of the Air Ministry and as they watched the fires and explosions, quoted to them from Tennyson's description of aerial warfare in "Locksley Hall":

Heard the heavens fill with shouting,
and there rain'd a ghastly dew
From the nations' airy navies
grappling in the central blue.[111]

Churchill's reaction was indicative of the influence that his Victorian upbringing continued to have on his perception of science and technology. To begin with, there was his Positivist faith in science as a means of progress. Allied to this was his belief that if enough time and resources were devoted to a project, it would be successful. In October 1940, for instance, as pressures mounted during the Battle of Britain, Churchill focused on air defense, directing that the "very highest priority" must be focused on "the Radio sphere," using "Scientists, Wireless Experts, and many classes of highly-skilled labour and high-grade material .... Not only research and experiments, but production must be pushed hopefully forward from many directions, and after repeated disappointments we shall achieve success."[112]

That type of faith was illustrated by Churchill's total involvement throughout the war in the project to create artificial harbors. In 1917, he had proposed such a harbor in connection with a possible landing behind the German lines in Flanders. In the next war, the idea of Mulberry became the basic assumption for the 1944 cross-Channel invasion of Europe. But only because of the personal direction of Churchill, who kept a working model of the project next to the War Room in Whitehall. "Don't argue about it," he admonished the Combined Operations planners over a particularly difficult technical problem. "The difficulties will argue themselves."[113] In the end, that type of perseverance and faith produced a device that was decisive for the Allies. Strategically, Mulberry provided the planners with the freedom to select landing zones well away from the heavily fortified harbors on the Continent; psychologically, it gave the Allied leaders a degree of confidence, without which they might never have attempted what they perceived as an extremely hazardous cross-Channel operation. As it was, that "single brilliant technical device," as Albert Speer described it, allowed the Allies to bypass the Atlantic Wall, thus rendering the German defense system irrelevant.[114]

On a smaller scale of technological surprise, Churchill had also come away from the First World War with the firm conviction that science must serve the front-line combatant directly. That conviction, coupled with his fascination for gadgets and his very real short-term need for special weapons in the summer of 1940, resulted in the creation of an unorthodox section called MD 1, so named because it was the first department established directly under the Minister of Defence. The organizational linkage was no accident. Both Churchill and Lindemann were convinced from Watson-Watt's triumph with radar that one man or a small group of men cut off from the bureaucratic morass could achieve similar accomplishments. Hence, MD 1 and its Chief, Colonel Millis Jefferis, who was responsible through Lindemann directly to Churchill as Minister of Defence. This special connection to the Prime Minister ensured almost unlimited support for Jefferis and his organization at Whitchurch, where he created a self-contained experimental station and proving ground complete with fully equipped workshops, factories, and firing ranges. From the Whitchurch station came such invaluable inventions as the Limpet magnetic mine and its smaller version, the Clam, the "L" delay-action fuse, and the Jefferis Shoulder Gun which as the PIAT (Projector Infantry Anti-Tank) became standard equipment.[115]

Churchill's personal connection to MD 1 was indispensable throughout the war. As an organization outside the civil and military bureaucracy, it not surprisingly occasioned a great deal of resistance. When that occurred, the Prime Minister would not interfere until, as in the case of MD 1's anti-tank device, known as the Sticky Bomb, the impasse could not be resolved. At that point, he would bring his supportive powers to bear as he did very succinctly in a memorandum concerning that device. "Sticky Bomb. Make one million. WSC."[116] At other times, his support could be even more immediate. "As Prime Minister," he told the MD 1 personnel, after a successful firing demonstration of a weapon at Chequers in 1940, "I instruct you to proceed with all speed with the development of this excellent weapon. As First Lord of the Treasury, I authorise expenditure of £5,000 on this work to tide you over until proper financial arrangements are made."[117]

The guiding hand behind such demonstrations was Lindemann, whose love of gadgetry and surprise at least equalled the Prime Minister's. Their common delight in such matters, not to mention one aspect of the decision-making process, was illustrated at a dinner at Chequers one night in July 1940. After listening to reports from the military guests which displeased him, Churchill turned to Lindemann and demanded: "Prof! What have *you* got to tell me today?" An uneasy look spread along the faces of the other dinner guests as Lindemann slowly and with great pride produced a Mills hand grenade from his pocket. "This, Prime Minister, is the inefficient Mills bomb," he replied, "issued to the British infantry .... Now *I* have designed an improved grenade, which has fewer machined parts and contains a fifty percent greater bursting charge." Churchill was ecstatic. "Splendid, Prof, splendid!" he shouted. "That's what I like to hear." And turning to General Dill: "C.I.G.S.! Have the Mills bomb scrapped at once and the Lindemann grenade introduced." Dill attempted to explain that contracts for millions of the Mills grenades had been signed in both the United States and England and that it would be impractical to alter the design. But the Prime Minister brushed the arguments aside.[118]

At the strategic level, this impulsiveness could have adverse results, particularly when combined with Churchill's deep-seated perception of science and technology as a panacea for deterring and surprising the enemy. In some cases, the Prime Minister's impulses were checked early on in the project. In July 1943, for example, Churchill asked the Chiefs to examine, under the code name Habbakuk, the possibility of turning icebergs into floating air bases that would be virtually unsinkable because of their massive size. The Habbakuk iceberg bases would include installations built from frozen wood pulp and could be used not only against Norway, but eventually Japan as well. In the end, the project never went beyond the memorandum stage because of a general skepticism, the nature of which could be gauged by one scientist's proposal to use the term " 'mili-habbakuk' as a new unit for measuring impracticability."[119]

In other cases, such as the dispatch of the *Repulse* and the *Prince of Wales* to "exert a paralysing effect upon Japanese naval action," Churchill's romantic view of the power of technology overrode the advice of his advisers.[120] In a similar manner, the Tiger tanks were valuable and timely reinforcements in the Middle East. But to Churchill with his overactive imagination, those reinforcements seemed to be the answer to all of Wavell's problems. Moreover, with new developments in armor, the idea of a modern-day Cambrai was never far from the British leader's thoughts. In June 1940, he initiated a crash project to create a new type of tank with 500 to 600 models due by March 1941 over and above the current armor programs. The result was the A22 model, the "Churchill" tank, literally ordered off the drawing board and, as a consequence, requiring major reworking as the first models began to emerge from the production line. As late as November 1941, the War Office reported that without at least 16 modifications, those products of Churchill's impetuous and impulsive directive would be useless not only for the Middle East, but for sustained operations in Britain as well.[121]

There was also a ruthless, pragmatic side to Churchill's approach to technological surprise, placed in even sharper relief by his disillusioned realization after the first total war that "Science herself may destroy all that makes human life majestic and tolerable."[122] That disillusionment continued to contribute to his ambivalent feelings on the matter throughout the war. "There is no doubt," he wrote Eden after learning for the first time the full extent of the mass extermination of the Jews, "that this is probably the greatest and most horrible crime ever committed in the whole history of the world, and it has been done by scientific machinery ...."[123] Nevertheless, that type of misuse of science only emphasized how high the stakes had become in total war. For example, there was always the possibility, however unfounded, that the Germans might win the race to build an atomic bomb. In June 1943, just as evidence was mounting concerning the German rocket threat, Churchill received a report from an agent in Switzerland intimating that the Germans were planning a devastating air attack on Britain for August, using "bombs of terrific destructive power" and "other undefined methods hitherto unexpected..." The peace of mind of the Prime Minister, whose own imagination could soar concerning new technology and weapons, was not helped by the normally imperturbable Lindemann's opinion that the "undefined methods" might include atomic bombs.[124]

Churchill, of course, viewed the threat as one to national survival from the beginning of the war and would often vent his combative indignation against those who would not take full advantage of technological surprise. As First Lord in December 1939, for instance, he was angered to read a note prepared by the Air Staff that opposed, for legal reasons, his scheme for mining the Rhine River. In place of the note's formal title, Churchill wrote: "Some funkstick in the Air Ministry running for shelter ...." And where the Air Staff had pointed out that the operation was "unprofitable," he scrawled, "Don't irritate them dear!"[125] Other attempts were also ruthlessly pursued. At the end of June 1940 as the invasion seemed imminent, Churchill approved a scheme to send fire ships into German-held French ports to "scatter burning all over the harbour, possibly with most pleasing results."[126] This was followed in August by Operation Razzle, the dropping of incendiary pellets into German forests.[127] Neither operation was successful; but both demonstrated the willingness of the British leader to use any means in total war to effect some form of technological surprise that would aid national survival.

Nowhere was this better illustrated than in Churchill's consideration of the use of bacteriological and chemical weapons. In February 1944, the Prof. recommended that Britain should stockpile N-Bombs, a weapon containing "N" spores to which there was "no known cure and no effective prophylax." Churchill agreed, believing that if the Germans possessed that type of weapon, "the only deterrent would be our power to retaliate." At the same time, Churchill reaffirmed his belief that the Germans would not use poison gas during the impending Normandy invasion, although "the temptation to use it on the beaches might conceivably be strong enough to override prudence." Once again, deterrence was the key, with any use of enemy gas to be followed by the immediate "full delivery power of our Strategic Air Forces to drench the German cities and towns where the war industry exists."[128]

In terms of poison gas, Churchill's considerations went beyond just deterrence. On 30 June 1940 as invasion seemed near, Churchill asked Ismay to investigate the use of mustard gas "or other variants" on the beaches against German forces. And in a discussion concerning the matter with a visitor to Chequers the next day, Churchill summed up his rationale which personified the amalgam of his romantic-realistic tendencies. "I have no scruples," he remarked, "except not to do anything dishonourable."[129] Even this rationalization disappeared in July 1944 during the height of the V-1 assault, when the stability of the Home Front was decisively threatened. Not only were the suspense and strain from the V-1 more prolonged than the Blitz, but as Churchill noted, "the blind, impersonal nature of the missile made the individual on the ground feel hopeless."[130] Added to this was increasing information on the production of V-2 rockets. For Churchill, as he told his Chiefs, the use of poison gas could not be discounted against the unknown rocket threat that he knew was developing at the mouth of the Peene River in Mecklenburg and that could be a matter of "life or death to us ...."

It is absurd to consider morality on this topic when everybody used it in the last war without a word of complaint from the moralists or the Church. On the other hand, in the last war the bombing of open cities was regarded as forbidden. Now everybody does it as a matter of course. It is simply a question of fashion changing as she does between long and short skirts for women ....

If the bombardment of London really becomes a serious nuisance and great rockets with far-reaching and devastating effect fell on many centres of Government and labour, I should be prepared to do anything that would hit the enemy in a murderous place. I may certainly have to ask you to support me in using poison gas. We could drench the cities of the Ruhr and many other cities in Germany in such a way that most of the population would be requiring constant medical attention .... I do not see why we should always have all the disadvantages of being the gentlemen while they have all the advantages of being the cad. There are times when this may be so but not now.

I quite agree that it may be several weeks or even months before I shall ask you to drench Germany with poison gas, and if we do it, let us do it 100 percent. In the meanwhile, I want the matter studied in cold blood by sensible people and not by that particular set of psalm-singing uniformed defeatists which one runs across now here now there.[131]

The Joint Planning Staff provided a comprehensive critique on 26 July that argued against the use of poison gas and noted the improbability of Germany's initiating biological warfare. "I am not at all convinced by this negative report," Churchill responded in a memorandum on 29 July. "But clearly I cannot make head against the parsons and the warriors at the same time. The matter should be kept under review and brought up again when things get worse."[132] Nevertheless, the Joint Planning Staff's critique was effective, and the subject of using poison gas either for technological surprise or as a deterrent was not raised again, even when the V-2 attacks began.

Surprise and Countermeasures

> The fox knows many things, but the hedgehog knows one big thing.
>
> Archilochus

> This was a secret war, whose battles were lost or won unknown to the public, and only with difficulty comprehended, even now, to those outside the small high scientific circles concerned.
>
> Churchill, *The Second World War*, Vol. II, p. 381

Churchill depended heavily on the Prof in his dealings with the scientific and technological aspects of intelligence and surprise − a natural result of Lindemann's status for over 20 years as Churchill's trusted friend and confidant. Moreover, as has been demonstrated, there was the Prof's ability to simplify and synthesize. "Lindemann could decipher the signals from the experts on the far horizons," Churchill wrote, "and explain to me in lucid homely terms what the issues were .... Anyone in my position would have been ruined if he had attempted to dive into the depths which not even a lifetime of study could plumb. What I had to grasp were the practical results, and ... so I made sure ... that some at least of these terrible and incomprehensible truths emerged in executive decisions."[133] That this type of facility in communication was as critical as in the dealings of the military hierarchy with the Prime Minister, was demonstrated in the visit of Niels Bohr, the great Danish physicist. Bohr had urged the meeting on Churchill in order to explain the dangers of the atomic bomb once it was produced. The problem, however, was that the physicist tried to be precise with Churchill, and as a consequence his clarity suffered. The result was that the Prime Minister believed Bohr to be a muddled thinker, primarily concerned about loss of atomic secrets to the Russians.[134]

The essence of the Churchill–Lindemann duo was a focus on the problem at hand. "Assemble your ideas and facts," Churchill directed the scientist in his efforts to develop a proximity fuse, "so that I may give extreme priority and impulse to this business."[135] During the Battle of Britain, Churchill used this focus to impel innovations to help air defense, such as experimental searchlight control radar. "Some must be in action during the next moon phase," he minuted Ismay in September 1940. "Report to me how this will be achieved. Use all necessary authority."[136] That same month, as he surveyed the myriad war-related projects underway, he reemphasized the importance of the scientific community in waging total war. "The multiplication of the high-class scientific personnel," he wrote, "as well as the training of those who will handle the new weapons and research work connected with them, should be the very spear-point of our thought and effort."[137]

The primary vehicle for that scientific focus, as it was for other war efforts, was the committee. In the autumn of 1940, for instance, Churchill formed the Night Air Defence Committee with himself in the chair in his capacity as Minister of Defence. In another example, in order to combat the rising shipping losses, he formed the Cabinet Anti-U-boat Warfare Committee, which again included himself in the chair and again, in addition to Service Chiefs and Ministers, also included a high level group of scientists. The purpose of the committee, as Churchill fashioned it, was threefold: to bring under the committee's purview every aspect of the U-boat battle, no matter how trivial; to provide a forum for settling inter-Service differences; and, most importantly, to assess and implement the results of an intense scientific investigation concerning the Battle of the Atlantic. The result of such dynamism and organization, as one member of the committee's scientific group later recalled, was an "anti-submarine campaign ... waged under closer scientific control than any other campaign in the history of the British Armed Forces ...."[138]

To all this were added the problems, so familiar to Churchill from the previous war, of when and where to introduce instruments for technological surprise in order to achieve maximum effect. The introduction of the navigational radar instrument known as H_2S into Bomber Command's aircraft was a case in point. At Lindemann's insistence, the device was used against cities as well as U-boats, the latter by 1943 undoubtedly the greatest threat to Britain. The result was the German discovery of the secret from the first downed British aircraft, and it was left up to Dr. R.V. Jones, then Deputy Director of Intelligence at the Air Ministry, to convince the Germans that this was not the same device used so successfully at sea by Coastal Command. "Only a great deal of luck in the way of almost incredible slowness on the part of the Germans," Jones wrote, "together with some skilful deception, thereafter enabled us to use it successfully against the U-boats."[139]

Deception could, of course, also be used to disguise the effectiveness of British countermeasures to German technical surprises. There were, for example, the elaborate efforts Churchill directed as First Lord to convince the Germans that their magnetic mine, which had been initially so effective against British shipping, was still a powerful weapon even though in fact effective countermeasures had been devised. By 24 December 1939, de-magnetization experiments had proved successful enough to prompt a triumphant telegram from Churchill to Roosevelt. That same day, he minuted the Admiralty that "wherever ships are lost by mines in future it will be well to state that they are sunk by magnetic mines whenever this possibility exists."[140] Unfortunately, in that particular case, the process of demagnetisation of ships became known because of the publicity given the subject when the *Queen Elizabeth* arrived at New York.[141]

The use of the means of friendly technological surprise by the enemy had been one of Churchill's key considerations in his call for the decisive introduction of the tank in the First World War. That concern was compounded by the advances of modern technology in the next war, which further complicated his decision process. There was, for example, the classic case of "Window," the tin foil strips which could be dropped to simulate a bombing raid on the German radar screen. That scheme had been raised by Lindemann in 1937 and proposed by Churchill at that time to the government's Air Defence Research Committee. In 1942, the Prime Minister supported experiments under the Prof's direction which clearly indicated that Window was not only effective, but as Air Chief Marshal Portal indicated in a staff conference on 23 June 1943, would save one-third of the British bomber casualties. Portal was supported by R.V. Jones and opposed by Watson-Watt, the inventor of radar, who had apparently developed, in Jones' description, "a bridge on the River Kwai attitude toward radar, and it hurt him to think of radar being neutralized, even German radar."[142]

Churchill's major concern, however, was whether the Germans might not use Window in conjunction with a renewal of heavy bomber raids on Britain. Despite reassurances by Portal, the British leader was still unwilling to commit himself to Window as late as 2 July. "This is one of those cases," he wrote Portal on 2 July, "which ought to be proved three-ply before the plunge is taken. You must excuse my being cautious, but I feel it my duty to be completely convinced."[143] The conviction came at an acrimonious staff meeting on 17 July when Churchill turned to the head of Fighter Command and asked him for his advice since he would have to "carry the can" if Britain's defenses failed. That commander did not discount the fact that his defenses might be neutralized, but acknowledged that he would take responsibility since the focus must now be on reducing losses in Bomber Command. "Very well," Churchill concluded the meeting, "let us open the Window."[144]

The Window decision was instructive for a number of reasons. For one thing, it showed a Prime Minister actively engaged with his scientific and military advisers, rationally and cautiously considering all aspects of a complicated issue concerning scientific intelligence and technological surprise. For another, it demonstrated the openness of the entire decision-making process by the participation of Dr. Jones. Jones was a backbencher at the 23 June meeting when he was spotted by Churchill. "Mr. Jones," the Prime Minister called out, "very glad to see you here."[145]

That effusive greeting had its inception on 23 May 1940, the day that Jones informed Lindemann of the possibility that the Germans had developed a system of intersecting radio beams for the purpose of guiding bombers accurately to their targets. The information on that possibility began to accumulate rapidly thereafter. An Ultra intercept of 5 June, when decyphered four days later, pinpointed an area named Retford under the code name of "Knickebein," literally translated as crooked legs. The analysts examining the Enigma decrypt on 9 June realized that two airfields had been bombed near Retford on the evening subsequent to the dispatch of the coded message. On 11 June, there was further confirmation from a captured German flier who revealed under interrogation that Knickebein was a device for dropping bombs automatically when an airplane reached the point where two radio beams intersected. Jones continued to investigate other leads, becoming increasingly convinced that Knickebein was a device using radio beams to direct German bombers upon precise targets in Britain.[146]

On 21 June 1940, Jones was abruptly summoned to 10 Downing Street where he was ushered into the Cabinet Room before an assembly that included not only the Prime Minister and the Prof, but an imposing array of military and scientific leaders that included Professor Tizzard and Robert Watson-Watt. Nevertheless, the young scientist was not overwhelmed. "Although I was only 28," he recalled later, "and everyone else round the table much my senior in every conventional way, the threat of the beams was too serious for our response to be spoilt by any nervousness on my part."[147] Moreover, as he listened to comments around the table, it became apparent to Jones that there was little comprehension of the situation. Consequently, when Churchill addressed a question on some detail to him, Jones ignored it and asked if it would help if he told the entire story from the start. "Churchill seemed somewhat taken aback," he recalled, "but after a moment's hesitation said, 'Well, yes it would!' And so I told him the story."[148]

Churchill was enthralled with Jones' tale. "For twenty minutes or more he spoke in quiet tones," the Prime Minister later recounted, "unrolling his chain of circumstantial evidence the like of which for its convincing fascination was never surpassed by tales of Sherlock Holmes or Monsieur Lecoq."[149] As he listened, lines from the *Ingoldsby Legends*, first published in 1840 but still popular towards the end of the Victorian era, "jingled" in his mind:

> But now one Mr. Jones
> Comes forth and depones
> That, fifteen years since, he had heard certain groans
>
> On his way to Stone Henge (to examine the stones
> Described in a work of the late Sir John Soame's)
>
> That he'd followed the moans,
> And, led by their tones,
> Found a raven a-picking a Drummer-boy's bones![150]

Jones was, of course, unaware of the Ingoldsby Legend playing through the mind of the British leader. But he was aware of the impression he was making on Churchill, particularly in the discussions of possible countermeasures. "Here was strength, resolution, humour, readiness to listen, to ask the searching question and, when convinced, to act," he wrote. "He was rarely complimentary at the time .... In 1940 it was compliment enough to be called in by him at the crisis; but to stand up to his questioning attack and then to convince him was the greatest exhilaration of all."[151] The advantages of that type of immediate accessibility to a leader of Churchill's imagination, power and intense interest in the possibilities offered by science were described by the British leader in his memoirs.

> Being master, and not having to argue too much, once I was convinced about the principles of this queer and deadly game, I gave all the necessary orders that very day in June for the existence of the beam to be assumed, and for all countermeasures to receive

absolute priority. The slightest reluctance or deviation in carrying out this policy was to be reported to me. With so much going on I did not trouble the Cabinet, or even the Chiefs of Staff. If I had encountered any serious obstruction, I should of course have appealed and told a long story to those friendly tribunals. This, however, was not necessary, as in this limited and at that time almost occult circle obedience was forth-coming with alacrity, and on the fringes all obstructions could be swept away.[152]

The obstructions were indeed swept away. As a result of the 21 June meeting, Jones was directed to continue his research. "If our good fortune holds," he wrote a week after the meeting, "we may yet pull the Crooked Leg."[153] That was accomplished before the end of the summer. Not only was the beam located, but shortly after it became operational, it was successfully "bent." For the two critical months of September and October 1940, as Churchill noted, "the German bombers wandered around England bombing by guesswork, or else being actually led astray."[154]

The bending of the beam, Martin Gilbert has noted, "was a triumph for the persistence of R.V. Jones, and for Churchill's own willingness to believe in the beam, and to give authority to those who insisted it could be countered."[155] It was also a triumph for the cross-currents set in motion for the Prime Minister so many years before in the Victorian era. There was the romantic belief in science and technology as progressive entities that made the British leader alive to their possibilities. "Alone among politicians," Jones pointed out in this regard, "he valued science and technology as something approaching their true worth ...."[156] That appreciation governed Churchill's essentially nineteenth-century generalist approach to the scientific specialists of the twentieth century and was one of the reasons that Jones, with his "extraordinary intuition, based on encyclopaedic knowledge," appealed to the British leader.[157]

At the same time, there was Churchill's realistic appreciation of how the civil-military powers that he possessed as a twentieth-century total warlord could aid scientific intelligence and countermeasures. "It makes me very proud of our country," the British leader wrote to Jones in this regard after the war, "that there were minds like yours playing so keenly around the unknowable, and I am also glad that ... I was able to bring these deadly beams into relation with the power of the British State."[158] For Jones, as he continued his scientific exploration during the war, there was never any doubt concerning the vivid reality of that power in support of his endeavors. After his initial and successful meeting with Churchill, the young scientist felt that there was an intense appreciation of scientific intelligence at the very top − so strong, that he could have appealed to the Prime Minister on any issue with confidence. And he was right. "Your name," Churchill informed him, "will open all doors."[159]

6

CONCLUSION

I found, in brief, that all great nations learned their truth of word, and strength of thought in war; that they were nourished in war, and wasted by peace; taught by war, and deceived by peace; trained by war, and betrayed by peace: – in a word, that they were born in war, and expired in peace.

Ruskin, "Crown of Wild Olive"

One man, still carrying with him the British Island in its most remarkable efflorescence of genius and energy, stood against this kind of accommodation. Marlborough, harassed and hampered upon every side, remained unexhausted and all-compelling.

Marlborough, Vol. V, p. 242

Total war is a phenomenon of the twentieth century, requiring an all-encompassing coordination of the government, the military and the people – the elements of Clausewitz' "remarkable trinity." The quintessential example of such a conflict is the Second World War, and the quintessential example of a leader in total war is Winston Churchill. For six years, he led Great Britain through that cataclysm, the most ferocious conflict in the history of man. In the end, he and his nation emerged triumphant. There were many strange and wonderful factors in that final victory, not the least of which was the paradoxical fact that Britain was led in that greatest of twentieth-century wars by a man of the nineteenth century. And in fact, in the final paradox, it was because Churchill had spent his formative years in the Victorian era that he was so well prepared to lead his nation in total war.

As a product of the last 25 years of the Victorian period, Churchill inherited the basic tension of that era between emotional, often irrational, romanticism and earnest, rational pragmatism. To this were added general Victorian beliefs in such shibboleths as the British Empire and the Whig version of British history, the latter with its inexorable movement of Britain through successive stages of progress, most clearly demonstrated in Churchill's youth by the almost daily discoveries in science and technology. Compounding all that were the personality traits formed by a boy raised in patrician elegance, but cruelly neglected by his parents. From that early adversity emerged an egocentric, ambitious, self-absorbed young man, who before the turn of the century had acquired the power of total concentration on any project and a lifelong determination to overcome his physical and psychological weaknesses.

That determination fueled a fundamental, obstinate combativeness in Churchill's nature, which, in turn, was encouraged by the era in which he grew up. Late Victorians venerated the heroic, combative "men of action" who maintained the far-flung Empire in the many battles and campaigns that occurred in every year of Churchill's youth. War was a sporting game, an extension of the manly ethos of the public schools, accepted by the majority of the young patricians who officered the British Army. To that sporting game was added the "Great Game," the early burgeoning efforts at intelligence operations by the British Army, which were noted and appreciated by the young Churchill because of his combat experiences in Cuba as well as in three Victorian wars, and because of his instinctive, romantic attraction to secret cloak and dagger operations.

Despite his experiences in the Boer War, the totality of World War I was as much a shock for Churchill as it was for the average British citizen. To begin with, there was the mass attritive warfare on the Western Front, which he experienced first hand during his Antwerp and Ostend expeditions, his tenure as a battalion commander, and his many visits to the front as Munitions Minister. Because of those experiences, Churchill became determined during World War I to return decisiveness to the battlefield as it had been in the Victorian era. That determination, in turn, led to a refocus on the "Great Game" and the potential for changes in that game because of developments in science and technology. In that regard, with his overactive and romantic imagination, Churchill was quick to appreciate the potential of signal intelligence. At the same time, he was rationally and pragmatically ready to translate his vision into the organizational efforts that resulted in the evolution of Room 40. In a similar manner, he was alive to the possibilities for a return to maneuver warfare offered by surprise, whether by deception, diversion or the introduction of new technology.

World War I also demonstrated to Churchill the growing importance of the people in total war. As a member of Asquith's War Cabinet, he was aware of the problems associated with mass conscription. Equally important, particularly later as Minister of Munitions, he was conscious of the many issues associated with the Home Front, where every aspect of the normal citizen's life was controlled by the government and affected by the war. It was a new and singular element which he realized, after speaking to striking munitions workers, could be marshalled to great effect to serve the total objectives of modern war.

At the same time, the Great War also served notice that organization for total war would require absolute authority at the top if all the civil-military sinews of modern conflict were to be brought together in a focused, rational effort. In particular, Churchill was struck by the need for policy to dominate strategy. The converse situation in Germany during the Ludendorff–Hindenburg dictatorship and its disastrous results had a profound effect on him. A variant of that situation concerned the problems that British policy-makers had with their field commanders. For Churchill, the "frock–brass hat" disputes, with the military often recruiting public support for its position, was an uneven linkage of the elements of the Clausewitzian trinity that almost led to the bankruptcy of national strategy. Only full political-military authority could dictate the proper relationship of the elements of the "remarkable trinity" in total war.

Throughout the interwar years, Churchill contemplated the lessons from his first encounter with total war. Some would never be fully absorbed. He would always be ambivalent about science and technology. Despite the horrors in those fields unleashed by total war, there was always that deep undercurrent of Victorian faith in science as a means of progress. And war could never completely become the "cruel game" for Churchill. There would always be the vivid memories of the limited Victorian wars coupled with his small boy's enthusiasm for what he called "the bangs."[1] But the major lessons endured. There was a renewed appreciation of the "Great Game" as a means of avoiding attritive bloodbaths. And there was an abiding belief in the need to control and mesh the elements of the Clausewitzian trinity, if there were to be victory in total war.

When war came and Churchill took the reins of his nation's leadership, he applied those lessons to the "remarkable trinity." That the application worked, however, was due to the fundamental Victorian tension that still formed the basis of his character. In his approach to government, there was a rational system of organization that soon provided him with more power over civil and military authorities than any Prime Minister in British history had ever possessed. And yet his romantic reverence for such institutions as Parliament and the Monarchy would never have allowed him to subvert that power. Those institutions were part of that broad Whig mosaic that allowed Churchill to see himself in, and thus draw sustenance from, a long historical picture of Britain's struggles against external despots. Finally, in terms of government, the advantages of the dialectic between the elements of the Victorian tension in Churchill were never better displayed than in his formation of the Grand Alliance and the relationships he established with such disparate leaders as Roosevelt and Stalin.

That Victorian dialectic was also beneficial as Churchill exerted his firm control of policy over strategy throughout the war. The romantic, impulsive, heroic man of action in him often led to interference at the operational and tactical levels of war and proposals for untenable offensive schemes that were only defeated by supreme efforts on the part of his Chiefs of Staff. At the same time, Churchill's bold and adventurous spirit, combined with his vivid imagination and a willingness to take calculated risks, far outstripped the more limited strategic outlook of many of his military subordinates and inspired them to greater offensive efforts. In a similar manner, his ultimate deference to his Chiefs of Staff on most contentious military issues demonstrated the rational, pragmatic side of the Prime Minister who, while maintaining the superiority of policy, realized that strategy must ultimately be coordinated and implemented by military officials who believe in it if it is to be successful.

Churchill's power base was evident throughout the war in the aid and direction he provided in adjusting the "Great Game" to modern total conflict. On the one hand, his romantic nature responded to all cloak and dagger operations, whether it was exotic espionage excursions by SOE in foreign countries or the domestic turn around of foreign agents in the Double Cross system. Added to that was the small boy's perpetual delight in tricking and diverting the enemy – all of which he could indulge with his personal involvement in deception plans. Finally, there was his deep-seated Victorian appreciation of science coupled with his World War I experiences that demonstrated what scientific breakthroughs could mean, particularly in the areas of signal intelligence and other aspects of technological surprise. The result was informed involvement from the very top throughout the war in esoteric projects ranging from Ultra and Mulberry to Knickebein and Window.

On the other hand, Churchill approached the "Great Game" with a rational appreciation of the need to support all aspects of intelligence in total war. "No British statesman in modern times," Christopher Andrew has pointed out in this regard, "has more passionately believed in the value of secret intelligence. None has been more determined to put it to good use."[2] It was that appreciation, for instance, that led Churchill to institutionalize the central coordination of strategic deception plans from all theaters of war. And it was that appreciation that caused him to provide the full power of his office to support instantly and unstintingly, throughout the war, the many scientific and technological projects associated with intelligence and surprise. Only in such a milieu could a young scientist like R.V. Jones have made such an immediate contribution to scientific intelligence. Only in such a milieu could the full brunt of the power of a modern nation state have been brought to bear by a leader who could recite a Victorian nonsense verse in his head, while being briefed on the latest enemy intelligence.

Ultimately, however, it was the relatively new emergence and expanded role of the people in the "remarkable trinity" that provided the key to Churchill's most important contribution to total war. For it was primarily because of the British national will that Britain survived in World War II. And that national will owed its existence to a nineteenth-century man in his seventh decade, who in his dealings with the British people closed off the rational pragmatic side of his Victorian inheritance and allowed his emotional, romantic picture of his country and its citizens full rein.

It was a picture that did not reflect the contemporary world of 1940. Instead, Churchill created an imaginary world steeped in Victorian visions with such power and coherence and imposed it on the external world with such irresistible force that for a short time it became reality. Imagination can be a revolutionary force that destroys and alters concepts. But as Churchill demonstrated, imagination can also fuse previously isolated beliefs, insights and mental habits from an earlier time into strongly unified systems. In those systems he created romantic ideal models in which by dint of his energy, force of will and fantasy, facts were so ordered in the collective mind as to transform the outlook of the entire British population.

It was a picture that ignored the changes in Britain since the "palmy days" of his youth despite the warnings, as Kipling noted in *Puck of Pook's Hill*, that "Cities and Thrones and Powers" scarcely endured "in Time's eye." But it was that very assumption of Victorian perpetuity, much like that of the flower in the same Kipling poem, that brought Churchill to his fullest glory.

> This season's Daffodil
> She never hears
> What change, what chance, what chill,
> Cut down last year's;
> But with bold countenance,
> And knowledge small,
> Esteems her seven days' continuance
> To be perpetual.

In the end, it is the heroic, romantic side of Churchill's Victorian inheritance that is the essence of his famous public image, which in turn is no longer distinguishable from his inner essence. He remains, in short, a Victorian man, larger than life, as Isaiah Berlin has pointed out,

> of bigger and simpler elements than ordinary men, a gigantic historical figure during his own lifetime, superhumanly bold, strong and imaginative, one of the two greatest men of action his nation has produced, an orator of prodigious powers, the saviour of his country, a mythical hero who belongs to legend as much as to reality, the largest human being of our time.[3]

189

NOTES

CHAPTER 1

1. Winston B. Churchill. *A Roving Commission* (New York: Charles Scribner's Sons, 1951), p. 6. See also Herbert Tingsten, *Victoria and the Victorians*, trans. David Grey and Eva Leckstoern Grey (London: George Allen & Unwin, Ltd., 1972), pp. 450, 454–455 and William Manchester, *The Last Lion: Winston Spencer Churchill; Visions of Glory: 1874–1932* (Boston: Little, Brown & Company, 1983), p. 43.
2. Tingsten, p. 449.
3. Ibid., p. 455. See also Manchester, pp. 44 and 69 and Charles Eade (ed.), *Churchill by his Contemporaries* (New York: Simon & Schuster, 1954), pp. 221–222.
4. Churchill's emphasis. The different spellings of Sir George's name are also apparently Churchill's doing. 12 January 1887 letter. Randolph S. Churchill, *Winston S. Churchill. Vol. I. Youth. 1874–1900* (Boston: Houghton Mifflin Company, 1966), p. 98.
5. Ibid., pp. 171, 256, 176 and 523. See also Randolph Churchill, *Companion Volume.* Volume I. Part II, 1896–1900 (Boston: Houghton Mifflin Company, 1967), pp. 1209 and 329. Hereafter known as C.V. I, II.
6. These words hung on a wall plaque in the London Coordinating Section (LCS), the principal deception authority in Churchill's organization during World War II. Anthony Cave Brown, *Bodyguard of Lies* (New York: Harper & Row, Publishers, 1975), p. 9. See also Gerald Morgan, "Myth and Reality in the Great Game," *Asian Affairs. Journal of the Royal Central Asian Society*, Vol. 60 (New Series Vol. IV), Part 1 (February 1973), p. 55.
7. Rudyard Kipling, *Kim* (New York: Doubleday & Company, 1901), p. 299, Morgan, p. 55 and Christopher Andrew, *Her Majesty's Secret Service* (New York: Viking, 1986), p. 35.
8. "So the great game goes on," Churchill said in a speech on 31 October 1898, "and gentlemen it is for you to say that it shall go on – that it shall not be interrupted until we are come through all the peril and trial ...." R. Churchill, Vol. I, p. 408. See also Andrew, p. 448.
9. Jerome H. Buckley, "Symbols of Eternity: The Victorian Escape from Time," *Victorian Essays*, eds. Warren D. Anderson and Thomas D. Clareson (Oberlin, Ohio: Kent State University Press, 1967), p. 1.
10. John Colville, *The Churchillians* (London: Weidenfeld & Nicolson, 1981), p. 64.
11. Winston S. Churchill, *Savrola. A Tale of the Revolution in Laurania* (New York: Random House, 1956), p. 34. See also Buckley, p. 1.
12. Winston S. Churchill, *The World Crisis. 1911–1914* (New York: Charles Scribner's Sons, 1928), p. 1 and Manchester, p. 11. "Renown awaits the Commander who first in this war restores artillery to its prime importance upon the battlefield, from which it has been ousted by heavily armoured tanks." Winston S. Churchill, *The Second World War. Vol. III. The Grand Alliance* (Boston: Houghton Mifflin Company, 1950), p. 498. After initial citation of each volume, entire series hereafter referred to as *World War II* with appropriate volume number.
13. Manchester, p. 12.
14. 23 February 1945. Churchill was in a somber mood listening to "The Mikado" after returning from the Yalta Conference. John Wheeler-Bennett (ed.), *Action This Day. Working with Churchill* (New York: St. Martin's Press, 1969), p. 93.
15. Lord Moran, *Churchill. Taken from the Diaries of Lord Moran: The Struggle for Survival, 1940–1965* (Boston: Houghton Mifflin Company, 1966), p. 717.
16. The visitor was Anthony Montague Browne. Ibid., p. 722.

NOTES

CHAPTER 2

1. Walter Houghton, for instance, addresses the age in *The Victorian Frame of Mind 1830–1870* (New Haven: Yale University Press, 1957) as that encompassed by his title. See also Tingsten, p. 17. "There is no such thing as a Victorian society or a Victorian culture." Eugene C. Black, *Victorian Culture and Society* (London and Basingstoke: The Macmillan Press Ltd., 1973), p. ix.
2. Black, p. 279.
3. Gertrude Himmelfarb, *Victorian Minds* (New York: Alfred A. Knopf, 1968), p. 219.
4. Tingsten, p. 22.
5. Ibid., pp. 22–24 and 209–210.
6. Winston S. Churchill, *Thoughts and Adventures* (London: Odhams Press Ltd., 1949), p. 39.
7. Winston S. Churchill, *Great Contemporaries* (London: Thornton Butterworth Ltd., 1937), p. 242.
8. Ibid., p. 141.
9. *Roving Commission*, p. 252. At the time of his capture, Churchill had soft-nose Mauser bullets in his pocket. To his Boer captors, he pretended that he had just found them. Ibid., p. 253. See also Tingsten, p. 346.
10. Winston L. Spencer Churchill, *The Story of the Malakand Field Force. An Episode of Frontier War* (New York and Bombay: Longmans, Green & Co., 1901), p. 230.
11. Asa Briggs, *Victorian People*, revised edition (Chicago: The University of Chicago Press, 1979), p. 123 and Houghton, p. 221.
12. Winston Spencer Churchill, *London to Ladysmith via Pretoria* (London and Bombay: Longmans, Green & Co., 1900), p. 173.
13. Randolph S. Churchill, *Winston S. Churchill, Vol. II. 1901–1914. Young Statesman* (Boston: Houghton Mifflin Company, 1967), p. 16.
14. Briggs, p. 143.
15. Houghton, p. 254.
16. "When I was young," Churchill told Lord Moran in August 1944, "for two or three years the light faded out of the picture. I did my work. I sat in the House of Commons, but black depression settled on me." Moran, p. 179. See also Anthony Storr, "The Man," *Churchill Revised. A Critical Assessment* (New York: The Dial Press, Inc., 1969), p. 230.
17. Winston S. Churchill, *Marlborough. His Life and Times. Vol. II. 1702–1706* (New York: Charles Scribner's Sons, 1933), p. 245 and *Marlborough. Vol. IV. 1704–1705* (New York: Charles Scribner's Sons, 1935), p. 144.
18. Storr, p. 232 and Manchester, p. 24.
19. Winston S. Churchill, *The World Crisis 1915* (New York: Charles Scribner's Sons, 1929), p. 234. Churchill, of course, remained an incredibly hard worker all his life, regardless of depression. See, for example, Maurice Ashley, *Churchill as Historian* (New York: Charles Scribner's Sons, 1968), p. 7, who worked as a researcher for Churchill in the late 1930s: "He expected me to work hard but not a quarter as hard as he worked himself."
20. Himmelfarb, p. 291.
21. Emphasis added. R. Churchill, Vol. II, p. 685. See also Manchester, p. 70.
22. Houghton, p. 265.
23. *Thoughts and Adventures*, p. 235. Years before he began painting, Churchill apparently recognized the painting metaphor for romantic action and impulsiveness. Admiral Fisher recalled of Churchill prior to World War I that "it was rather sweet: he said his penchant for me was that I painted with a big brush!" A.L. Rowse, *The Later Churchills* (London: Macmillan & Co., Ltd., 1958), p. 393.
24. *Thoughts and Adventures*, p. 235; Eade, p. 256.
25. Manchester, p. 36. "Churchill was a romantic," his son noted. "Tears easily came to his eyes when he talked of the long story of Britain's achievement in the world and the many deeds of heroism which had adorned it." R. Churchill, Vol. II, p. 706. Churchill could also put tears to his own use. "One night," Eisenhower recounted long after the Second World War, "there was something that he wanted to do in Italy; and I was

telling him the impossibility. And he painted a terrible picture if we didn't do it. I'll never forget the terms he used. He said, 'If that should happen I should have to go to His Majesty and lay down the mantle of my high office.' And there were tears streaming down. But within ten seconds he was telling a joke." James Nelson (ed.), *General Eisenhower on the Military Churchill* (New York: W.W. Norton & Co., Inc., 1970), p. 18.

26. Houghton, pp. 291–292.
27. *Great Contemporaries*, p. 239.
28. Houghton, p. 294. H.G. Wells once likened Churchill to Gabriele D'Annunzio, the soldier, novelist, poet, historian and, above all, the romantic champion of lost causes. R.W. Thompson, *The Yankee Marlborough* (London: George Allen & Unwin, Ltd., 1978), p. 37.
29. Edgar Johnson, "Dickens and the Spirit of the Age," *Victorian Essays*, p. 29.
30. Janet and Peter Phillips, *Victorians at Home and Away* (London: Croom Helm Ltd., 1978), pp. 47–49.
31. R. Churchill, Vol. I, pp. 107–108. See also *Roving Commission*, p. 18.
32. The film was "Lady Hamilton." Martin Gilbert, *Winston Churchill, Vol. VI. Finest Hour. 1939–1941* (Boston: Houghton Mifflin, 1983), p. 1156. Churchill also found "vastly entertaining" a fictional story about another man of action, C.S. Forester's Captain Hornblower. Ibid.
33. *Roving Commission*, pp. 13 and 77. Churchill read Stevenson's *Kidnapped* five years later while concealed in a South African mine at Witbank, during his escape from the Boers. Rowse, p. 347.
34. *Roving Commission*, p. 180.
35. J.H. Plumb, "The Historian," *Churchill Revised*, p. 133. See also H. Butterfield, *The Whig Interpretation of History* (New York: Charles Scribner's Sons, 1951).
36. Winston S. Churchill, *History of the English Speaking Peoples. Vol. I. The Birth of Britain* (New York: Dodd, Mead & Co., 1966), p. 137.
37. Plumb, pp. 134–135. Regicide notwithstanding, all of English history to include the Civil War was part of a great design. In October 1912, Churchill as First Lord of the Admiralty, submitted Oliver Cromwell as a name for one of the four capital ships of 1912–13. George V turned the proposal down; and after a series of letter exchanges on the subject, Churchill wrote the King's Private Secretary on 1 November 1912: "His Majesty is the heir of all the glories of the nation, & there is no chapter of English history from which he should feel himself divided." R. Churchill, Vol. II, p. 629.
38. Plumb, p. 135.
39. Herman Ausubel, *The Late Victorians* (New York: D. Van Nostrand Co., Inc.), p. 135.
40. Houghton, p. 305.
41. R. Churchill, Vol. I, p. 61.
42. Phillips, p. 166.
43. Manchester, p. 128. Two of Churchill's other favorites from Haggard were *She* and *Jess*, which he apparently read as early as 1887 as a 13-year-old and was still reading ten years later as a subaltern in India. See C.V. I, II, pp. 136–137, 144 and 721.
44. Houghton, pp. 210–211.
45. Phillips, p. 166.
46. Tingsten, p. 144; Black, pp. xv and xxi.
47. Tingsten, p. 458. Churchill portrayed Gordon as a hero in his *The River War* of 1899. See also the *Daily Mail* review concerning the section on Gordon at Khartoum: "Nothing could exceed Mr. Churchill's admiration of the hero, nor his anger at the hero's desertion." R. Churchill, Vol. I, p. 443. This does not mean, however, that Churchill was ignorant about Gordon's faults. See, for example, his 30 March 1899 letter after talking to Lord Cromer as research for *The River War*. Ibid., p. 426.
48. C.V. I, I, p. 135. In a 31 May letter in which he asked his mother to intercede with his school to allow him to attend the festival. Churchill ended: "P.S. Remember the 'Jubilee.'" R. Churchill, Vol. I, p. 85.
49. C.V. I, I, p. 135; Manchester, p. 129; Phillips, p. 168 and R.C.K. Ensor, *England 1870–1914* (London: Oxford University Press, 1960), p. 177.

50. *Malakand Field Force*, p. 220.
51. C.V. I, II, p. 784.
52. *Malakand Field Force*, p. 139; Phillips, pp. 163–164.
53. C.V. I, II, p. 839.
54. Gilbert, VI, p. 836.
55. F.W. Deakin, "Churchill the Historian." Third Winston Churchill Memorial Lecture. University of Basel, 10 January 1969, p. 1.
56. Ibid., p. 14. For the cakes episode, see *History of the English Speaking Peoples*, Vol. I, p. 114.
57. Lionel Hastings Ismay, *The Memoirs of General Lord Ismay* (New York: the Viking Press, 1960), p. 142.
58. S.W. Roskill, *Churchill and the Admirals* (New York: William Morrow & Co., Inc., 1978), p. 224.
59. Ashley, pp. 216–217.
60. Robert E. Sherwood, *Roosevelt and Hopkins. An Intimate History* (New York: Harper & Brothers, 1950), p. 241.
61. From A.G. Gardiner's *Pillars of Society*. "He will write his name big on our future," Gardiner wrote, "let us take care he does not write it in blood." Martin Gilbert, *Winston Churchill. Vol. III. The Challenge of War 1914–1916* (Boston: Houghton Mifflin, 1971), p. 132.
62. *Roving Commission*, p. 113.
63. Carter, p. 178.
64. Isaiah Berlin, *Mr. Churchill in 1940* (Boston: Houghton Mifflin Co., 1949), p. 15. Winston S. Churchill, *The Second World War. Vol. II. Their Finest Hour* (Boston: Houghton Mifflin Co., 1949), p. 155. In describing Savrola, Churchill often described himself: "To live in a dreary quiet and philosophic calm in some beautiful garden far from the noise of man and with every diversion that art and intellect could suggest, was, he felt, a more agreeable picture. And yet he knew that he could not endure it." *Savrola*, p. 28. Compton Mackenzie later commented that *Savrola* "is the day dream of a man of action, and if some accident or illness had deprived the author of the opportunity to remain a man of action, that author might have written many more romances and left an eminent name as a romancer." Eade, p. 60.
65. Storr, p. 238.
66. Manchester, p. 119 and Arthur Bryant, *The Turn of the Tide* (New York: Doubleday & Co., 1957), pp. 12–13.
67. *Thoughts and Adventures*, p. 256; *Pascal's Pensées*. Trans. W.F. Trotter. Introduction by T.S. Eliot (New York: E.P. Dutton, 1958), p. 2.
68. R. Churchill, Vol. II, p. 329.
69. Moran, p. 57.
70. Eade, p. 147. See also Arthur M. Schlesinger, *The Age of Roosevelt: The Coming of the New Deal* (Boston: Houghton Mifflin, 1959), p. 52, who states that FDR "worked by apprehending through intuition a vast constellation of political forces .... Situations had to be permitted to develop, to crystallize, to clarify .... Only then at the long frazzled end, would the President's intuitions consolidate and precipitate a result."
71. C.P. Snow, *Variety of Men* (New York: Charles Scribner's Sons, 1967), p. 167 and Taylor, pp. 17, 21–22 and 26–27.
72. *World Crisis 1915*, p. 324.
73. John Kennedy, *The Business of War*, ed. Bernard Fergusson (London: Hutchinson & Co., 1957), p. 236.
74. Robert Rhodes James, "The Politician," *Churchill Revised*, p. 95.
75. *Savrola*, p. 157.
76. The two weekly magazines that Dickens successfully published at the time were also full of enthusiastic articles concerned with scientific progress, current inventions, and advances in industrial processes. Johnson, p. 30.
77. Winston S. Churchill, *World Crisis 1911–1914*, p. 4.
78. Houghton, pp. 35–37.

79. Eade, p. 379. In a letter signed "Truth" to the Editors of the *Harrovian*, Churchill made a plea for electric lights at his school a few years later. "Gas has two duties to perform – to light and to warm," he wrote. "Harrow gas does neither – it only smells." 17 November 1888 letter. C.V. I, I, p. 314.

80. R. Churchill, Vol. I, p. 60.

81. *Roving Commission*, p. 25.

82. To Hore-Belisha, Eade, p. 339. See also Ibid., pp. 379–390. In August 1944, Churchill's physician rebuked the Prime Minister for running risks. "I cannot understand what is afoot," was the reply, "unless I see for myself." Moran, p. 184.

83. C.V. I, II, p. 725.

84. The novel was *Helbeck of Bannisdale*. 5 August 1898 letter. Ibid., p. 958.

85. 16 September 1898 letter to Ian Hamilton, Ibid., p. 977 and *London to Ladysmith*, p. 196.

86. First published February 1900. *Savrola*, p. 64.

87. Manchester, p. 74.

88. Frederick Woods, *Young Winston's Wars. The Original Dispatches of Winston S. Churchill War Correspondent 1897–1900* (New York: Viking Press, 1972), pp. xxv and 128.

89. Violet Bonham Carter, *Winston Churchill. An Intimate Portrait* (New York: Harcourt, Brace & World, Inc., 1965), p. 210.

90. Eade, p. 378.

91. Barbara Tuchman, *The Proud Tower*. 3rd Printing (New York: The Macmillan Co., 1966), p. 59. In reaction to a situation in Latin America at one time, Queen Victoria was said to have ordered the British fleet to bombard La Paz, a city 200 miles from the sea and 12,000 feet above sea level. Kennedy, p. xi.

92. Tuchman, p. 29 and *Roving Commission*, p. 68. Brabazon was a die-hard Tory whose three fundamental tenets were Protection, Conscription, and the revival of the Contagious Diseases Acts – all of which formed his basis for judging governments and politicians. Brabazon was a well known eccentric in the army, often insolent to senior officers. "And what chemist do you get this champagne fwom?" he demanded one evening of a Mess President. In his farewell speech to his regiment, he referred to India as "that famous appendage of the Bwitish Cwown." *Roving Commission*, pp. 71, 69 and 102.

93. Manchester, p. 80.

94. Moran, p. 265.

95. Carter, p. 107. "Winston is a pasha," his wife once stated. Moran, p. 460. On Churchill's dexterity with bath faucets, see Martin Gilbert, *Winston S. Churchill, Vol. VII, Road to Victory 1941–1945* (Boston: Houghton Mifflin Co., 1986), p. 354. Churchill was often summoned from baths during emergencies such as the 1911 Sidney Street Siege and the Dogger Bank episode in 1914. Eade, p. 75. On 11 November 1944 Churchill and Eden were de Gaulle's guests at the Quai d'Orsay. Churchill was given a room with a gold bath, originally intended for Goering. Eden recalled later going into Churchill's suite and hearing the Prime Minister's voice coming through the open bathroom door: "Come in, come in, that is if you can bear to see me in a gold bath when you only have a silver one." Gilbert, VII, p. 1057.

96. Jack was wounded in the relief of Ladysmith and actually treated on the ship. *London to Ladysmith*, p. 320. See, as an example, Churchill's 9 August 1899 letter to Lord Salisbury asking Salisbury's permission for Churchill to dedicate *The River War* to him because of the Prime Minister's help in arranging his assignment to Kitchener's command. C.V. I, II, p. 1040. Equally revealing was Salisbury's reply of 13 August, which indicated that he did not need to see the proofs of the book unless Churchill criticized people of high position. Ibid. Lady Jeune also used her friendship with Sir Evelyn Wood to help Churchill obtain a posting to Egypt. As Lady St. Helier she was the future Clementine Churchill's great aunt. R. Churchill, Vol. II, p. 241. Even Churchill, in looking back on this era in later years, was astounded by some of the eccentricities of the age. In discussing Lord Curzon, a quintessential Victorian, Churchill recounted how Lady Curzon showed him a letter from her husband in India. The letter was a hundred pages long, all written, Churchill noted with incredulity, "in his graceful legible flowing hand. But a hundred pages!" *Great Contemporaries*, p. 281.

97. Winston S. Churchill, *Ian Hamilton's March* (London: Longmans, Green and Co., 1900), p. 31. How enduring those combinations could be was demonstrated in 18 November 1941 when Churchill welcomed General Alanbrooke as the new CIGS, referring in his letter to his "old friendship for Ronnie and Victor, the companions of gay subaltern days and early wars." Both men were brothers of Alanbrooke. Churchill had met Victor in the 4th Hussars in 1895–96; and he and Ronnie Brooke had gone through combat together in the Boer War, fighting at Spion Kop, Vaal Krantz and the Tugela, and galloping into Ladysmith together on the night of that town's liberation. Gilbert, VI, p. 1235 and *World War II*, II, p. 265.

98. *Roving Commission*, p. 19.

99. Manchester, p. 188. The closest Lord Randolph ever came to complimenting his son publicly was when he introduced him to Bram Stoker, a ministerial secretary and the future author of *Dracula*. "He's not much yet," he told Stoker, "but he's a good 'un'." Ibid., p. 187.

100. *Roving Commission*, p. 73.

101. *Savrola*, p. 32.

102. G.W. Steevens' admiring article, "The Youngest Man in Europe" in the *Daily Mail*. Eade, p. 46.

103. Manchester, p. 25.

104. Berlin, p. 17. "No other man who made so great a mark upon his times," one contemporary commented, "passed from first to second childhood without maturity intervening." Thompson, p. 29.

105. Manchester, pp. 13–14.

106. Winston S. Churchill, *The River War. An Historical Account of the Reconquest of the Soudan* (London: Longmans, Green and Co., 1902), p. 21. See also R. Churchill, Vol. I, p. 232.

107. Winston B. Churchill, *Marlborough, His Life and Times. Vol. I. 1650-1688* (New York: Charles Scribner's Sons, 1933), p. 29.

108. Gilbert, VII, p. 28.

109. 11 January 1899 letter. R. Churchill, Vol. I, p. 427; Storr, p. 250.

110. James, p. 64.

111. Eade, p. 46.

112. R. Churchill, Vol. II, p. 1; Storr, p. 251.

113. 5 September 1897 letter. C.V. I, II, p. 784.

114. The first time occurred in India to another officer, the second time to the son of a station-master in South Africa, and the last time to the American novelist, Winston Churchill, whom he met in Boston in 1900. In the latter case, the two Churchills had lunch, then walked to a bridge over the Charles River, and paused to talk. The English Churchill said to his American namesake, who was three years older: "Why don't you go into politics? I mean to be Prime Minister of England: it would be a great lark if you were President of the United States at the same time." R. Churchill, Vol. I, pp. 339–341.

115. 28 July 1914 letter. R. Churchill, Vol. II, p. 694.

116. Winston S. Churchill, *The Second World War. Vol. I. The Gathering Storm* (Boston: Houghton Mifflin Co., 1948), p. 667. "This cannot be by accident," he told his physician in World War II, "it must be design. I was kept for this job." Moran, p. 827.

117. 19 January 1898 letter. C.V. I, II, p. 862. See also his 26 January 1898 letter to his mother. "I hope the book will please you. After all it is your applause that I covet more than any other." Ibid., p. 864. And his 27 January 1898 letter to his brother Jack: "Write and tell me all you think about the book. Say nice things." Ibid., p. 866. See also Manchester, p. 24.

118. *World Crisis 1911–1914*, p. 78.

119. Ibid., pp. 85–86. Churchill also referred to the incident as "a memory which is very precious to me." Ibid., p. 86. All the more so because Churchill had relieved Wilson as First Sea Lord when Churchill had assumed office as First Lord of the Admiralty in 1911. Wilson worked in the Admiralty in an unofficial capacity during World

War I until Churchill's dismissal. Wilson had won a VC at Tarnai in the Sudan where, after exhausting the ammunition for his Gatling gun, he used the broken hilt of his sword to knock the Dervish spearmen down. Ibid., p. 80.

120. Original emphasis. Carter, pp. 104 and 116. A lifelong trait. In 1958, Brendan Bracken commented that Churchill "would go to the stake for a friend." Moran, p. 796.

121. Churchill's 22 April 1894 letter of explanation to his typically outraged father. C.V. I, I, p. 470. Confirmed by Captain Armstrong's 17 August 1908 letter. Ibid, p. 471.

122. 22 December 1897 letter. C.V. I, II, p. 839. Churchill admired this trait all his life. "He had a singular power of concentration," he wrote approvingly of Birkenhead in the 1930s, "and five or six hours sustained thought upon a particular matter was always within his compass." Great Contemporaries, p. 179.

123. Moran, p. 265.

124. Liddell Hart, p. 221.

125. Carter, p. 115.

126. Bernard Darwin, The English Public School (London: Longmans, Green and Co., 1929), p. 26.

127. Houghton, p. 203; Tingsten, p. 51.

128. Tingsten, p. 51.

129. Paul Fussell, The Great War and Modern Memory (New York: Oxford University Press, 1975), pp. 25–26.

130. Roving Commission, p. 39. Anthony Trollope reacted to his years at Harrow in a similar manner. "The indignities I endured are not to be described ... Nor did I learn anything – for I was taught nothing." T.W. Bamford, Rise of the Public School (London: Thomas Nelson and Sons, Ltd., 1967), p. 225. See also Rupert Wilkinson, The Prefects (London: Oxford University Press, 1964), p. 5. Churchill did not like General Montgomery's practice of making his men in World War II conduct a pre-breakfast three-mile run every morning, since he considered this reminiscent of Victorian public school fetishes. Colville, p. 154.

131. R. Churchill, Vol. I, p. 203.

132. R. Churchill, Vol. II, p. 28. See also R. Churchill, Vol. I, p. 282.

133. Churchill's phrase in his 6 March 1915 letter to Sir Edward Grey. World Crisis 1915, p. 205; Storr, pp. 235–236.

134. Letter to Lord William Beresford (Uncle Bill), 2 October 1897. C.V. I, II, p. 798. Churchill had attempted to reach a young fir tree in his leap from the bridge at Bournemouth. "The argument was correct," he wrote later, "the data were absolutely wrong." As a result, he was unconscious for three days and spent three months in bed. Roving Commission, pp. 29–30. On the shoulder dislocation, see Ibid., p. 101.

135. Moran, p. 184. Churchill was well aware of the dangers in the Johannesburg episode. "According to all the laws of war my situation, if arrested, would have been disagreeable .... No courtmartial that ever sat in Europe would have had much difficulty in disposing of such a case." Roving Commission, p. 347. Either Churchill or Lord Moran later confused the town in the incident with Ladysmith. Moran, p. 203. See also Ian Hamilton March, pp. 269–274.

136. 18 December 1940. Gilbert, VI, p. 949.

137. Manchester, pp. 55, 54 and 222.

138. 5 September 1897 letter. R. Churchill, Vol. I, p. 339 and C.V. I, II, p. 785. For the 27 August 1897 letter, see C.V. I, II, p. 781. Churchill used sporting metaphors in a larger context as well. Upon the death of Queen Victoria, he wrote to his mother from Canada referring to Edward VII's ascension to the throne: "I am glad he got his innings at last, and am most interested to watch how he plays it." 22 January 1901 letter. C.V. I, II, p. 1231. On the good fight, when Lucile asks Savrola how he knows he will triumph, he replies: "Because we have got might on our side, as well as moral ascendancy." Savrola, p. 82.

139. 4 December 1897 letter. C.V. I, II, pp. 833–834.

140. Malakand Field Force, p. 90.

141. 2 November and 22 December 1897 letters. C.V. I, II, pp. 815 and 839.

NOTES

142. 19 September 1897 letter in pencil to his mother. R. Churchill, Vol. I, p. 346.
143. 11 August 1898 letter to Captain Haldane. C.V. I, II, p. 964. Churchill was never shy about his desire for decorations. In his midlife memoirs, he wrote: "In the closing decade of the Victorian era the Empire had enjoyed so long a spell of almost unbroken peace that medals ... were becoming extremely scarce in the British Army .... How we longed to have a similar store of memories to unpack and display ... to a sympathetic audience." *Roving Commission*, p. 74. For other examples concerning ribbons and medals, see 27 September 1897 and 19 September 1897 letters. C.V. I, II, pp. 794 and 792.
144. 19 September 1897 letter. R. Churchill, Vol. I, p. 346 and C.V. I, II, p. 793. "The general who avoids all 'dash,' who never starts in the morning looking for a fight and without any definite intention, who does not attempt heroic achievements, and who keeps his eyes on his watch, will have few casualties and little glory." *Malakand Field Force*, p. 294.
145. Wood, pp. xxv-xxvi. It was, however, all relative. "Babies deaths are the least sad of all partings .... A strong man full of hope and enthusiasm seems to me a greater cause for sorrow when he is stricken down." 21 February 1900 letter to his quasi-fiancée, Pamela Plowden, from Colenso. C.V. I, II, p. 1151.
146. 8 September 1898 letter. C.V. I, II, p. 976.
147. *Malakand Field Force*, p. 208.
148. Wood, p. 138.
149. 4 September 1898 letter. R. Churchill, Vol. I, p. 404. See also his 29 December 1898 letter to his mother on Kitchener. "A vulgar common man – without much of the non-brutal elements in his composition." Ibid., p. 425.
150. *London to Ladysmith*, p. 98.
151. Wheeler-Bennett, p. 106. See, however, Snow, p. 165, who points out that Churchill's magnanimity was based on an aristocratic indifference that negated the fundamental ingredient of generosity. In World War I, there was one exception to Churchill's philosophy: General Monro, a Westerner whose supreme conception, in Churchill's words, was "killing Germans." At Gallipoli, he was "an officer of swift decision. He came, he saw, he capitulated." *World Crisis 1915*, pp. 515–516. Churchill later spoke of General Monro to Violet Asquith. "I should like him to starve," he told her, "to starve without a pension in a suburban hovel facing a red-brick wall." Carter, p. 348.
152. 2 October 1897 letter, C.V. I, II, p. 797.
153. *Malakand Field Force*, p. 88. See also Churchill's popular account in his novel *Savrola* when a subaltern in the Lauranian army recalls a campaign in Africa: "It was damned good fun .... My squadron had a five-mile pursuit. The lance is a beautiful weapon." *Savrola*, p. 73.
154. *Malakand Field Force*, p. 241.
155. Ibid., p. 288. In *Savrola*, when told that it will be necessary for government troops to fire on a crowd in order to create a diversion, the Major in charge replies: "Excellent, it will enable us to conclude those experiments in penetration, which we have been trying with the soft nosed bullet." *Savrola*, p. 11.
156. "Whether I hit him or not, I cannot tell. At any rate he ran back two or three yards and plumped down behind a rock." *Roving Commission*, p. 142.
157. All quotes from Churchill's 4 September 1898 letter to his mother. R. Churchill, Vol. I, pp. 400-404. But see also his letter to Ian Hamilton two weeks later. "The dismounted fire was more practical," Churchill again acknowledged. "But British cavalry so seldom get a chance that they must aim at the magnificent rather than the practical – and another fifty or sixty casualties would have made the performance historic – and have made us all proud of our race & blood." C.V. I, II, p. 981. The combination of romanticism and practicality was still evident in Churchill's account over three decades later, in which he noted proudly that "the British too fought with sword and lance as in the days of old," while also describing how he reloaded the clip of his Mauser after piercing the Dervish line. *Roving Commission*, pp. 193–194.
158. Wood, p. xxiv.

159. Churchill concluded "that such slaughter is inseparable from war, and that if the war be justified, the loss of life cannot be accused." *River War*, p. 360. Such emotion, of course, was easy to sustain when natives comprised the majority of casualties. See, for instance, Churchill's letter to his mother on 4 September 1898: "I am just off with Lord Tullibardine to ride over the field. It will smell I expect as there are 7,000 bodies lying there. I hope to get some spears etc." C.V. I, II, p. 974.
160. Woods, p. 122.
161. Manchester, p. 317.
162. *London to Ladysmith*, pp. 309 and 429. C.V. I, II, p. 1147. Once, after observing the effect of one Boer artillery piece, Churchill conjectured on the effect of an entire Boer battery, and concluded presciently: "Yet in a European war there would have been not one, but three or four batteries. I do not see how troops can be handled in masses under such conditions, even when in support and on reverse slopes." Ibid, p. 420.
163. *Ian Hamilton's March*, p. 10.
164. Ibid., p. 294.
165. Ibid., p. 386.
166. Ibid., p. 244. The Boer War remained a Victorian conflict for Churchill. On 20 September 1940, after a particularly grueling day that included a visit to one of the worst bombed areas of London, Churchill sat up late at night, reminiscing about the Boer conflict, "the last enjoyable war." Gilbert, VI, p. 800.
167. Andrew, pp. 21 and 24–25. While serving as a cavalry officer in India in 1884, Baden-Powell wrote *Reconnaissance and Scouting*, a handbook on obtaining vital military information by infiltrating enemy territory. Cecil D. Eby, *The Road to Armageddon. The Martial Spirit in English Popular Literature, 1870–1914* (Durham and London: Duke University Press, 1987), p. 63.
168. Andrew, p. 26. War, of course, was also subsumed in the public-school spirit for Baden-Powell whose young boys in organizations ranging from boys' clubs and boys' brigade, to the Boy Scouts were ready to be unleashed by 1914 to give, as he summed it up, "the big bully a knock-out blow, so that other nations can live afterwards in peace and freedom." Mark Girouard, "When Chivalry Died," *The New Republic*, Vol. 185, No. 13 (30 September 1981), p. 28.
169. Himmelfarb, p. 250.
170. C.V. I, I, p. 608.
171. *River War*, p. 186. Andrew, p. 21. The Director of Intelligence at Omdurman was Colonel Wingate. R. Churchill, Vol. I, p. 395. Wingate was the uncle of the Deputy Director of the London Coordinating Section in World War II.
172. 16 September 1898 letter to Ian Hamilton. C.V. I, II, p. 977.
173. Manchester, p. 275. For Churchill's report to Kitchener, see R. Churchill, Vol. I, p. 399.
174. Ausubel, pp. 38 and 84.
175. Briggs, p. 296.
176. Phillips, p. 180. W.E. Henley's popular "Invictis," of course, with its "I am the master of my fate, I am the captain of my soul," was the counterpoint to Hardy. A favorite poem of Franklin Roosevelt.
177. Tingsten, p. 24.
178. C.V. I, II, p. 774.
179. Girouard, pp. 25–26.
180. Ibid., p. 26. Note the similarity in sentiment to that expressed at the end of *Peter Pan* when Captain Hook offers the captive children freedom if they will enlist in his crew and proclaim "Down with King Edward!" as an oath of allegiance. At that point, Wendy rallies the boys. "I have a message to you from your real mothers," she cries out, "and it is this, 'We hope that our sons will die like English gentlemen.' " Eby, p. 135.
181. Eyewitness accounts of the *Titanic* were exaggerated. There was an almost unanimous tendency of Anglo-Saxon witnesses to assume that anyone who acted badly during the disaster was an Italian or another type of foreigner. Girouard, p. 27.
182. Ibid.

NOTES

CHAPTER 3

1. Girouard, pp. 25–26.
2. Nivill's unit was the 8th East Surreys. The connection between Nivill's feat and Newbolt's poem, "Vitai Lampada" was illustrated by a poem written about the event which concluded: "The fear of death before them/Is but an empty name/True to the land that bore them/The SURREY's play the game." Fussell, p. 28.
3. Girouard, p. 28.
4. Ibid., p. 29; Phillips, p. 189.
5. Girouard, p. 29.
6. Ibid., p. 30.
7. *Great Contemporaries*, p. 139.
8. Carter, p. 188.
9. Ibid., p. 190.
10. *Thoughts and Adventures*, p. 51. Nevertheless, upon returning to England after the 1906 maneuvers, he wrote his Aunt Leonie: "I am very thankful there is a sea between that army and England." R. Churchill, Vol. II, p. 191. At the conclusion of the 1909 maneuvers, Churchill paid his respects to Wilhelm II. "This ... was the last occasion on which I ever spoke to the Emperor, though it was not to be my last contact with the German Army." *Thoughts and Adventures*, pp. 54–55.
11. R. Churchill, Vol. II, pp. 558 and 561–562.
12. The comment was by Lieutenant RN Richard Davies, later Admiral, VC. R. Churchill, Vol. II, p. 683. See also Ibid., pp. 597 and 592–593. *World Crisis 1911–1914*, p. 139.
13. A paragraph later in the same letter detailing war preparations, Churchill wrote: "The two black swans on St. James's Park lake have a darling cygnet–grey, fluffy, precious & unique." R. Churchill, Vol. II, p. 694.
14. Gilbert, III, p. 31.
15. *World Crisis, 1911–1914*, p. 225.
16. Churchill's emphasis. Ibid., p. 211. "I feared to bring this matter before the Cabinet, lest it should mistakenly be considered a provocative action likely to damage the chances of peace .... I only therefore informed the Prime Minster, who at once gave his approval." Ibid., p. 225.
17. Basil Liddell Hart, "The Military Strategist," *Churchill Revised*, p. 185.
18. Ibid., p. 187.
19. *World Crisis 1911–1914*, pp. 394–395.
20. Ronald Lewin, *Churchill as Warlord* (New York: Stein & Day, 1973), p. 12.
21. Carter, p. 275.
22. Ibid., p. 274. Nevertheless, Kitchener was determined that Antwerp should resist as long as possible and wrote that he was prepared to commission Churchill as a Lieutenant General, the rank necessary to supervise the military operation which involved at least two Major-Generals. Gilbert, III, pp. 113–144. "Of course without consulting anybody," Asquith, who understood his impulsive subordinate, later wrote, "I at once telegraphed to him warm appreciation of his mission and his offer, with a most decided negative saying we could not spare him at the Admiralty." Carter, p. 274.
23. Ibid.
24. Ibid., p. 295.
25. R. Churchill, Vol. II, p. 19. Carl von Clausewitz, *On War*, edited and translated by Michael Howard and Peter Paret (Princeton: Princeton University Press, 1976), p. 89.
26. Winston S. Churchill, *The World Crisis 1916–1918*, Part I (London: Thornton Butterworth Ltd., 1927), pp. 237 and 240.
27. Martin Gilbert, *Winston Churchill. Vol. IV. The Stricken World 1916–1922* (Boston: Houghton Mifflin Co., 1975), p. 50.
28. R. Churchill, Vol. II, pp. 26–27.
29. *Thoughts and Adventures*, p. 100.
30. Ibid., p. 92.

31. *World Crisis 1916–1918*, Pt. 2, pp. 364–365. The convoy issue had two sequels that for Churchill confirmed his view of the military's resistance to innovation and technological change. In return for acquiescing to the convoy system, the First Sea Lord demanded in return that the overall naval task should be reduced by the abandonment of the Salonica operation and the withdrawal of the Allied armies from the Balkan theater. This would save, he maintained, some 400,000 tons of shipping. Lloyd George was on the point of agreement when a civil official in the Foreign Trade Department produced a paper demonstrating that this tonnage could be saved by bringing all Allied supplies from the United States instead of all over the world. The scheme was adopted and as Churchill pointed out, it was the Salonican forces that produced the surrender of Bulgaria in October 1918 which in turn produced the final collapse of Germany. But for this, Churchill concluded, the German armies would have retreated to the Meuse or the Rhine and the war would have dragged on another year. *Thoughts and Adventures*, pp. 99–100.

32. *World Crisis 1915*, p. 6. Churchill never deviated from this view. After his second encounter with total war, he wrote: "It is not possible in a major war to divide military from political affairs. At the summit they are one." *World War II*, III, p. 28.

33. Ibid., p. 526.

34. Gilbert, III, p. 543.

35. Ibid., IV, p. 111.

36. *World Crisis 1916–1918*, Pt. 1, p. 244.

37. Ibid., p. 243.

38. Both quotes, *World Crisis 1915*, pp. 404–405.

39. Ibid., pp. 526–527.

40. Gilbert, III, p. 643.

41. Ibid., VI, p. 521.

42. Ibid., III, p. 755.

43. Ibid., p. 254.

44. Ibid., p. 777.

45. Ibid., VI, p. 521.

46. *World Crisis 1916–1918*, Pt. 2, p. 563. For the 1 August 1916 memorandum on casualties, see Ibid., Pt. 1, pp. 187–192.

47. Ibid., Pt. 2, p. 570.

48. *World Crisis 1915*, p. 5.

49. *Thoughts and Adventures*, pp. 58–59.

50. All quotes from Christopher Andrew, *Her Majesty's Secret Service* (New York: Viking, 1986), p. 150.

51. Ibid., pp. 35 and 60–61. In October 1914, Churchill as First Lord was convinced of German invasion preparations and sought means "to get early intelligence for the sailing of the expedition." Ibid., p. 77. Between 1871 and 1914, there were over sixty popular narratives published dealing with the invasion or attempted invasion of England. In those accounts, Germany was normally the invader (forty-one times), followed by France with eighteen and Russia with eight. Eby, p. 11. See also Chapter 2, "Paper Invasions," Ibid., pp. 10–37.

52. R. Churchill, Vol. II, p. 594.

53. For Churchill's scenario, see his 16 April 1913 memorandum entitled "The Time Table of a Nightmare." Ibid., pp. 595–607. Churchill did not see much potential fighting capability in the British civil population. Ibid., p. 609.

54. *World Crisis 1911–1914*, p. 503. Christopher Andrew points out that when the SKM was declassified in 1980, it showed no signs of sea-stains, thus indicating that it was "probably recovered from the *Magdeburg* more prosaically than Churchill was led to believe" and that Churchill's account was "probably romanticised." Andrew, p. 89. In *World Crisis 1911–1914*, p. 504, Churchill quoted from the German official history to demonstrate that the enemy was apparently well informed on the subject: "Even if doubt were to exist that the British Admiralty were in possession of the whole secret ciphering system of the German Fleet, it has been cleared away by the reliable news from Petrograd, that after the stranding of the *Magdeburg* off Odensholm the secret

papers of that ship, which had been thrown overboard, were picked up by the Russians and communicated to their Allies."
55. *World Crisis 1916–1918*, Pt. 1, pp. 118–119.
56. Patrick Beesly, *Room 40* (London: Hamish Hamilton, 1982), p. 16. Beesly points out that "Excessively Secret" would have been a more accurate description. Ibid. Andrew, p. 90.
57. Beesly, p. 40.
58. Andrew, p. 91. See also Beesly, p. 36, who thought Hall "looked rather like a peregrine falcon ...."
59. Ibid., p. 135.
60. *World Crisis 1911–1914*, pp. 505–506. "This decision ... was," Churchill pointed out, "in the light of subsequent events, much to be regretted, but it must be remembered that the information on which the Admiralty was acting, had never yet been tested ...." Ibid.
61. Ibid., p. 508.
62. Andrew, p. 98. For Churchill's description of the fiasco, see *World Crisis 1911–1914*, pp. 508–519. "Thus ended," Churchill wrote of the raider's escape in the fog, "this heart shaking game of Blind Man's Buff." Ibid., p. 519.
63. Ibid., p. 520.
64. Ibid., pp. 520–521.
65. *World Crisis 1916–1918*, Pt. 1, p. 118. But see Beesly, p. 69, who also points out: "The problem for the British was that Room 40's information was now so good, that signs of any German movement could be detected in advance and could not be ignored if the Grand Fleet was to be sailed in time to intercept any offensive operation. That the movements, throughout 1915, always turned out in the end to be purely local ones, to cover minesweeping in the Helgoland Bight, or to guard against possible British attacks, could rarely be ascertained until the *Hochseeflotte* was already on its way back to port. It was all most frustrating both for those who credited the Germans with more aggressive intentions than they in fact possessed, and equally for those longing to bring on the great naval battle which would ensure Britannia's supremacy once and for all."
66. *World Crisis 1915*, p. 125.
67. Ibid., p. 127.
68. Ibid., p. 128.
69. Ibid., p. 137. For a description of the battle, see Ibid., pp. 130–137.
70. Gilbert, IV, p. 8 and Ashley, p. 101.
71. Gilbert, IV, p. 62.
72. Manchester, p. 11.
73. Gilbert, IV, p. 62.
74. Ibid., pp. 105 and 23.
75. *World Crisis 1915*, p. 64. Liddell Hart has pointed out that "without Churchill's impulsion, and the naval experiments he initiated, however misguided, the new idea might never have survived the chill of that first winter in official Army quarters." Liddell Hart, p. 196. On Churchill's role in creating a Naval Air Service, see H. St. George Saunders, *Per Ardua: The Rise of British Air Power 1911–1939* (London: Oxford University Press, 1944), Chapters 1–4.
76. *World Crisis 1915*, pp. 69–70.
77. 18 June memorandum. Ibid., p. 425.
78. Ibid., p. 71.
79. 9 November 1916 memorandum. *World Crisis 1916–1918*, Pt. 2, p. 564.
80. 24 September 1915 memorandum. *World Crisis 1915*, p. 496. See also Churchill's 1917 memorandum on trench mortars in *World Crisis 1916–1918*, Pt. 2, p. 555.
81. *World Crisis 1915*, p. 80.
82. *World Crisis 1916–1918*, Pt. 1, p. 185.
83. *World Crisis 1915*, p. 82.
84. *World Crisis 1916–1918*, Pt. 2, p. 567.
85. Winston S. Churchill, *The Unknown War* (New York: Charles Scribner's Sons, 1931), p. 311.

86. *World Crisis 1916–1918*, Pt. 1, p. 254.
87. *World Crisis 1915*, p. 300.
88. Ibid, p. 65.
89. *World Crisis 1916–1918*, Pt. 2, p. 561.
90. Ibid., p. 564.
91. Ibid., p. 345. Churchill later commented: "Accusing as I do without exception all the great ally offensives of 1915, 1916, and 1917, as needless and wrongly conceived operations of infinite cost, I am bound in reply to the question, What else could be done? And I answer it, pointing to the Battle of Cambrai, 'This could have been done.' This in many variants, this in larger and better forms ought to have been done, and would have been done if only the Generals had not been content to fight machine-gun bullets with the breasts of gallant men, and think that that was waging war." Ibid., p. 348.
92. Ibid., p. 504.
93. Original emphasis. Ibid., pp. 505 and 507. Churchill knew Sir Henry Rawlinson from Omdurman where the future general had been on Kitchener's staff. In World War I, they had watched together the battle around Soissons in September 1914 from a haystack. Later, Rawlinson had arrived at Antwerp to take over command from Churchill before the evacuation of that city.
94. Ibid., pp. 517–518.
95. *Great Contemporaries*, p. 326.
96. *Thoughts and Adventures*, p. 113.
97. Gilbert, IV, p. 915.
98. Ibid., p. 914.
99. *Thoughts and Adventures*, p. 197.
100. *Great Contemporaries*, p. 23.
101. Ibid., p. 103.
102. *Marlborough*, III, p. 98.
103. Winston S. Churchill, *The Aftermath* (New York: Charles Scribner's Sons, 1929), pp. 480–481.
104. *Thoughts and Adventures*, pp. 198–199.
105. Ibid., p. 198; *Aftermath*, p. 479.
106. *Thoughts and Adventures*, p. 200.
107. Ibid.
108. Ibid., p. 201 and *Aftermath*, p. 479.
109. *Roving Commission*, p. 180.
110. Eade, p. 302. See also Fussell, p. 21.
111. Gilbert, IV, p. 911.
112. In Sassoon's book, *Siegfried's Journey*, Ibid., p. 151. In August 1918, while in France, Churchill recited some of Sassoon's anti-war poetry to his brother Jack, who warned him that Sassoon might write a poem about him. "I am not a bit afraid of Seigried [sic] Sassoon," Churchill replied. "That man can think. I am afraid only of people who cannot think." Ibid., p. 140.
113. All quotes in the paragraph from *World Crisis 1916–1918*, Pt. 2, pp. 496, 501 and 426.
114. Ibid., pp. 410, 412 and 435. Freyberg, who won the VC and the DSO with two bars in World War I, remained a hero to Churchill, who was to place him in command of Crete in the next war. One day in the interwar years while visiting with Freyberg, Churchill asked the New Zealander to show him his wounds. "He stripped himself," Churchill recounted, "and I counted twenty-seven separate scars and gashes." *World War II*, III, p. 273.
115. *Great Contemporaries*, p. 190.
116. Ibid., pp. 310, 302 and 312. At one point in his room at the French Ministry of War, Clemenceau tried out a speech on Churchill that he was later to give in the tribune. The speech included the phrases that Churchill was later to transform with such good results in 1940: "I will fight in front of Paris; I will fight in Paris; I will fight behind Paris." Ibid., p. 312.
117. *Marlborough*, III, p. 116.

118. Ibid., IV, p. 215. Duke John wrote to Sarah on 20 July: *"The kindness of the troops to me has transported me ...."* Marlborough's emphasis. Ibid., p. 220.
119. Ashley, p. 152. Churchill's romantic, combative vision was sometimes even too large for the earlier men of action. In writing on the Duke of Monmouth whose rebellion was crushed at Sedgemoor on 5 July 1685 and who was later beheaded, Churchill noted: "It is amazing he did not resolve to die on the field with all these earnest simples he [had] drawn to their fate." *Marlborough*, I, p. 221.
120. *World War II*, II, p. 678. Hobart was brought back to active duty and commanded an armored division, in which capacity, as Churchill pointed out, he "rendered distinguished service to the very end of the war." He was knighted in 1943. Gilbert, VI, p. 863.
121. Martin Gilbert, *Winston Churchill, Vol. V, the Prophet of Truth, 1922–1939* (Boston: Houghton Mifflin Co., 1977), p. 319. In the summer of 1939, Churchill was working on his *History of the English Speaking Peoples*. "It has been a comfort in this anxious year," he wrote on 9 July, "to retire into past centuries." Ibid., p. 1086.
122. *Marlborough*, IV, p. 129.
123. Ibid., III, p. 112.
124. *Aftermath*, p. 1.
125. Ibid., p. 479.
126. *Great Contemporaries*, p. 323.
127. *Thoughts and Adventures*, pp. 201 and 196.
128. Ibid., p. 202.
129. Both quotes, Ibid., p. 483.
130. *Great Contemporaries*, p. 57.
131. *World Crisis 1916–1918*, Pt. 1, p. 57.
132. *Aftermath*, p. 483.
133. *World War II*, I, p. 4. On 26 April 1945, Churchill read a telegram from the British Ambassador to Brussels in which were described the current efforts to capture or at least detain the Hapsburg heir, Archduke Otto. Churchill immediately wired that it was no part of British policy to "hunt down" the Archduke or any other royalty. "I am of the opinion," he concluded, "that if the Allies at the peace table at Versailles had not imagined that the sweeping away of long-established dynasties was a form of progress, and if they had allowed a Hohenzollern, a Wittelsbach, and a Hapsburg to return to their thrones, there would have been no Hitler." Gilbert, VII, p. 1314.
134. *Great Contemporaries*, p. 320.
135. *Aftermath*, p. 2.
136. *World Crisis 1916–1918*, Pt. 1, p. 243.
137. Winston S. Churchill, *Marlborough. His Life and Times, VI. 1708–1722* (Charles Scribner's Sons, 1938), p. 90.
138. Ibid., p. 124.
139. *World Crisis 1915*, p. 6.
140. *World Crisis 1916–1918*, Pt. 2, p. 454.
141. *Aftermath*, p. 2.
142. *World Crisis 1915*, p. 425.
143. *World Crisis 1916–1918*, Pt. 1, pp. 238–239.
144. *Great Contemporaries*, p. 254.
145. *World Crisis 1916–1918*, Pt. 1, p. 239.
146. Ashley, p. 104; *World Crisis 1916–1918*, Pt. 1, p. 214.
147. *Great Contemporaries*, p. 118.
148. *Marlborough*, III, p. 113.
149. *Thoughts and Adventures*, p. 108.
150. *World Crisis 1916–1918*, Pt. 2, p. 378.
151. "I never thought you would allow it," he wrote to Lloyd George. Andrew, p. 287. Other quotes in paragraph, Ibid., pp. 286–287.
152. Ibid., p. 258.
153. Ibid., pp. 268–269.

154. Ibid., pp. 315–316. Churchill was unsuccessful. In the future, only the Foreign Office received complete sets of intercepts.
155. Ibid., p. 355 and Gilbert, V, p. 298. Morton was shot through the heart at the Battle of Arras in April 1917. Ibid., VI, p. 298. Gilbert also lists 1929 *vice* Andrew's 1931, as the year Morton began at the IIC. The relationship between the two men was furthered by Morton's proximity at Edenbridge to Churchill at Chartwell.
156. Andrew, p. 355.
157. Ibid. See also Gilbert, V, p. 662, who concluded that the advantage provided by Morton's intelligence, "combined with the information on British policy which he received both officially and secretly from the Ministers themselves ... gave Churchill a unique position in British public life for some one without Cabinet office."
158. *Marlborough*, III, p. 338. See also Ibid., p. 337, Ibid., II, p. 183 and Ibid., IV, p. 128.
159. Ibid., III, p. 61.
160. *Thoughts and Adventures*, p. 190.
161. Gilbert, V, p. 438.
162. *Marlborough*, IV, p. 65.
163. Ibid.
164. Ibid., p. 67.
165. Ibid., p. 87. See also Ibid., p. 83. For an even more complex but equally successful deception plan by Marlborough, see Churchill's description of the preparations for the battle of Elixem in the summer of 1705. The deception plan was also designed to fool his own allies, the Government and States-General of the Dutch Republic, which did not want the coalition commander to take chances with his allied forces. Ibid., pp. 205 and 109.
166. *Thoughts and Adventures*, pp. 188–190.
167. Ibid., pp. 206–207. The only note of pessimism concerned what he called robotization, a condition in which man surrenders his freedom and ordering of life to a government of scientists and impersonal planners. He was influenced by Karel Čapek's play, *Rossum's Universal Robots* (RUR), which he had seen a few years earlier. His views, of course, anticipated those in Huxley's *Ape and Essence* and Orwell's *1984*. As for the creations in RUR, Churchill concluded that "Robots could be made to fit the grisly theories of Communism." Ibid., p. 211.
168. Gilbert, V, p. 443. See also Colville, p. 31 and R.V. Jones, *Most Secret War* (London: Hamish Hamilton, 1978), p. 14.
169. Gilbert, V, p. 421.
170. Ibid., p. 653.
171. Ibid., p. 743.
172. *Marlborough*, III, pp. 107–108.
173. Eade, p. 384.
174. Gilbert, V, p. 751 and VI, p. 845. Radar was the US term for Radio Direction and Ranging adopted in 1943. The existence of radar was not publicly acknowledged until 1941 when it was referred to as Radiolocation. Its original name was RDF – Radio Direction Finding. Gilbert, VI, p. 659.
175. Ibid., p. 773.
176. All quotes in paragraph from Ibid., pp. 1051, 950 and 946.

CHAPTER 4

1. Wheeler-Bennett, p. 15. In his 1861 essay on "The American Constitution at the Present Crisis," Bagehot referred to Lincoln in this regard as "an unknown and probably an inferior man ...." Norman St. John-Stevas (ed.), *Bagehot's Historical Essays* (Garden City, N.Y.: Anchor Books/Doubleday & Company, Inc., 1965), p. 378. "If the wit of man had been set to devise a system specially calculated to bring to the head of affairs an incompetent man at a pressing crisis," Bagehot wrote of the U.S. Constitution, "it could not have devised one more fit; probably it would not have devised one as

NOTES

fit." Ibid., p. 474. After Lincoln's assassination, Bagehot revised his estimate. "It is not merely that a great man has passed away, but he has disappeared at the very time when his special greatness seemed almost essential to the world ...." Ibid., p. xxxvi.

2. Lewin, pp. 10–11 and 23 and Snow, p. 153.
3. Plumb, pp. 164–165. "Churchill was infused with the sense of history. He felt that he represented not only the living electorate but also the mighty hosts of the dead, who had made the immense and majestic national heritage which he must tend and improve and hand on to the generations yet to come. He stood between the past and the future and felt that he must not fail either." Lord Beaverbrook, "Lloyd George and Churchill," *History Today*, August 1973, p. 553.
4. *Marlborough*, I, p. 82.
5. *World War II*, II, p. 262. Berlin, p. 13.
6. *Marlborough*, I, p. 85.
7. Stalin listened to Churchill discourse on his ancestor and then with what the note taker referred to as a "sly mischievous look," replied, "I think England had a greater general in Wellington, who defeated Napoleon, the greatest menace of all time." Gilbert, VII, p. 203.
8. Winston S. Churchill, *The Second World War. Vol. V. Closing the Ring* (Boston: Houghton Mifflin Co., 1951), p. 106.
9. Moran, p. 202.
10. Gilbert, VI, p. 37.
11. Ibid., p. 664.
12. Ibid., p. 1273.
13. Liddell Hart, p. 206; Lewin, p. 18.
14. Wheeler-Bennett, p. 203. In discussing the fall of Singapore in his memoirs, Churchill admitted that "it had never entered into my head that no circle of detached forts of a permanent character protected the rear of the famous fortress. I cannot understand how it was I did not know this." Winston S. Churchill, *The Second World War. Vol. IV. The Hinge of Fate* (Boston: Houghton Mifflin Co., 1950), p. 49.
15. Ismay, p. 158; Berlin, pp. 17–18. As an example, see Churchill's wartime praise for Rommel as "a great general" and his description of the negative reaction in some quarters to that praise. "This childishness is a well-known streak in human nature," he concluded, "but contrary to the spirit in which a war is won or a lasting peace established." *World War II*, IV, p. 67.
16. Moran, p. 107.
17. *World War II*, V, p. 85.
18. Arthur Bryant, *The Turn of the Tide* (New York: Doubleday & Co., Inc., 1957), p. 579.
19. L.F. Ellis, *The War in France and Flanders, 1939–1940* (London: HMSO, 1953), p. 167.
20. *World War II*, II, p. 230.
21. Ismay, p. 131.
22. Lewin, p. 50.
23. Moran, p. 35.
24. Gilbert, VI, p. 1112.
25. Ibid., pp. 588–589.
26. Ibid., VII, p. 158.
27. Moran, pp. 85–86.
28. Gilbert, VII, p. 1227 and Moran, p. 282.
29. Moran's response was hardly reassuring: "Heaven is as near by sea as by land." Moran, p. 15. See also Ibid., p. 40: "The P.M. is always a little apprehensive in the air ...." "I must confess," Churchill wrote, "that I felt rather frightened." *World War II*, III, p. 708.
30. Gilbert, VII, p. 1017.
31. Reported by the senior British intelligence officer at MacArthur's headquarters in the Far East to Menzies (C). Ibid., p. 217.
32. Hans J. Morgenthau, "Henry Kissinger, Secretary of State," *Encounter*, November 1974, p. 61.

33. Jones, p. 107.
34. Gilbert, VI, p. 697.
35. Storr, p. 258.
36. Kennedy, *The Business of War*, p. 316.
37. Gilbert, VI, pp. 694–695.
38. *Savrola*, p. 53.
39. Ismay, pp. 128–129. According to Ismay, Gamelin winced when Churchill slapped him on the shoulder. Ibid., p. 128.
40. Ibid., p. 141.
41. Gilbert, VI, p. 507.
42. W. Averell Harriman and Elie Abel, *Special Envoy to Churchill and Stalin, 1941–1946* (New York: Random House, 1975), p. 205. Harriman expressed his disquietude at Churchill's remarks – to which the Prime Minister replied: "You must come with me in the boat and see the fun." Ibid.
43. Nelson, p. 17.
44. Ibid., p. 18; James, p. 125.
45. Kennedy, p. 275.
46. Storr, p. 259.
47. Gilbert, VI, p. 659.
48. Cunningham was rebuked, but remained unrepentant, reasserting that "on this occasion the Italian destroyers *had* fought well." Roskill, p. 169.
49. *Great Contemporaries*, p. 265. Churchill had had enough of dictators by the time the war ended. When he returned to his *History of the English Speaking Peoples* after the war, he changed Cromwell into a villain despite the fact that the Lord Protector had been a patriot. For Churchill, after five years of war, the fact remained that Cromwell was as much a dictator as Hitler. Ashley, p. 33.
50. *Marlborough*, I, p. 258; Gilbert, VI, p. 81.
51. Snow, p. 125.
52. Gilbert, VI, p. 844.
53. Ibid., p. 672.
54. Eade, pp. 338 and 353.
55. Colville, p. 143.
56. Brendan Bracken, July 1958. Moran, p. 796. "Provided a man was brave and patriotic and had a sense of duty, his other defects were easily overlooked." Colville, p. 11.
57. Roskill, p. 83.
58. Ibid., p. 177.
59. Ashley, p. 230.
60. Gilbert, VI, p. 62.
61. Nelson, p. 19. See also Eade, p. 163.
62. Lewin, p. 41; Ismay, p. 189.
63. Gilbert, VII, p. 466. The Inter-Services Security Board working under the direction of the JIC issued and coordinated code names. These names were kept on a central index by the board and allotted in blocks to different Government Departments. Both used and projected code names were kept on a separate index card system and never typed out as a complete list. Churchill was allotted 32 code names on 22 Jan. 41. Ibid., VI, p. 966.
64. Manchester, p. 10.
65. Gilbert, VII, p. 354; Manchester, p. 10.
66. Excised section of Fuller's manuscript provided by Professor Jay Luvaas, U.S. Army War College.
67. Gilbert, VI, p. 828. See also Liddell Hart, p. 175. Lord Moran described Churchill's August 1944 visit to General Alexander's command in Italy: "Yesterday Alex whisked him off to an American battery with a new nine-inch gun, where he was invited to fire the first shot – a very noisy performance which, however, gave him great satisfaction." Moran, p. 184.

NOTES

68. Lewin, p. 247. When Churchill asked Eisenhower if he could go in with the initial wave at Normandy, Eisenhower turned him down, adding: "And I think it's rather unfair to give me another burden on a day like this." Nelson, p. 38.
69. Winston S. Churchill, *The Second World War. Vol. VI. Triumph and Tragedy* (Boston: Houghton Mifflin, 1953), p. 15. Note the similarity with Churchill's 1916 letter to his wife after visiting his battalion front.
70. Arthur Bryant, *Triumph in the West* (Westport, Conn.: Greenwood Press, 1959), p. 334; *World War II*, VI, pp. 416–417.
71. Gilbert, VII, p. 806.
72. Manchester, p. 10; Eade, p. 91.
73. Lewin, pp. 21–22. Still, Churchill left the impression that he would have preferred a field command and like his 1914 offer to give up his position as First Lord, would have laid down the reins of his office for such a command. On 25 May 1941, with problems in Crete mounting and the *Bismarck* not yet caught, a frustrated Churchill stated that if he could be "put in command" in Wavell's place, he would gladly lay down the Premiership, "yes, and even renounce cigars and alcohol." Gilbert, VI, p. 1095. "I envy you," he said to Alexander on 20 August 1944, "the command of armies in the field. That is what I should have liked." Moran, p. 184.
74. Gilbert, VII, p. 167. For the description of his welcome on Tripoli, see Ibid., p. 330.
75. Kennedy, p. 294; Lewin, p. 249.
76. Kennedy, p. 169.
77. *Marlborough*, III, p. 101.
78. Gilbert, VII, p. 75.
79. Kennedy, pp. 79–80.
80. Colville, p. 125.
81. Bryant, *Turn*, p. 415; Rowse, p. 493. "Speaking as one amateur to another," Churchill began a telegram to FDR on 1 April 1942, Gilbert, VII, p. 82.
82. *Marlborough*, IV, p. 214.
83. Kennedy, p. 146.
84. C.P. Snow, *Science and Government* (Cambridge, Mass.: Harvard University Press, 1961), p. 4.
85. Gilbert, VI, p. 829.
86. Ibid., p. 594; A.J.P. Taylor, "The Statesman," *Churchill Revised*, pp. 41–42; Lewin, p. 32; Wheeler-Bennett, p. 235.
87. Ismay, p. 160. "I clearly remember," Ismay wrote Churchill after the war, "that one of the first things that you said to me after you had assumed the office of Minister of Defence was 'we must be very careful not to define our powers too precisely'. In point of fact, they were, as you know, never defined, but the system worked admirably." Gilbert, VI, p. 322. "In calling myself, with the King's approval, Minister of Defence," Churchill wrote, "I had made no legal or constitutional change. I had been careful not to define my rights and duties." *World War II*, II, p. 16.
88. Lewin, p. 34.
89. "I became accountable," Churchill wrote of the Dardanelles, "for an operation the vital control of which had passed to other hands." *Thoughts and Adventures*, p. 7. Later, he wrote that at the Dardanelles "a supreme enterprise was cast away, through my trying to carry out a major and cardinal operation of war from a subordinate position." *World War II*, II, p. 15.
90. In his memoirs, Ismay demonstrated how the 1940 organization would have prevented the Dardanelles campaign from occurring as it did. Ismay, p. 165. Lewin, p. 32.
91. Ismay, p. 166; Gilbert, VI, p. 326; Lewin, p. 32.
92. Colville, p. 124. Lord Moran termed Ismay "a perfect oil-can." Moran, p. 121.
93. Gilbert, VI, p. 323; Ismay, pp. 160–165.
94. John Martin's term in Wheeler-Bennett, p. 163; Lewin, pp. 33–34.
95. Herbert Goldhammer, *The Adviser* (New York: Elsevier, 1978), p. 89.
96. Ibid., p. 91; Gilbert, VI, p. 659.
97. Gilbert, VI, p. 324; Wheeler-Bennett, p. 234.

98. *World War II*, III, p. 122.
99. Ismay, p. 162; Lewin, pp. 60–62. For another example, the Pacific War Council, see Gilbert, VII, p. 54. See also Ibid., p. 697 for Churchill's 31 March 1944 founding of the Overlord Preparation Committee.
100. Gilbert, VI, p. 1125; Ismay, pp. 193–194. See also John Connell, *Wavell. Scholar and Soldier* (New York: Harcourt, Brace & World, Inc., 1964), p. 506 for Wavell's reaction to this help for work, which along with his military duties, he had "tackled single-handedly for two years."
101. Gilbert, VI, p. 1195. Eight days later, samples of the Cuban cigars were actually sent out to be tested for poison. "Lord Cherwell [Lindemann] hopes that you will not smoke any of the cigars until the result of the analysis is known," Colville minuted Churchill on 23 September 1941. "He points out that ... a surprisingly large number of Nazi agents and sympathizers exist in that country." Ibid.
102. Ibid., p. 659.
103. Wheeler-Bennett, p. 235.
104. Originally written for his 10 May 1942 broadcast to the nation, then deleted. Gilbert, VII, 107.
105. *Marlborough*, III, pp. 314–315.
106. Gilbert, VII, p. 251. In May 1943, Moran commented: "King and country, in that order, that's about all the religion Winston has. But it means a lot to him." Moran, p. 207.
107. Gilbert, VI, pp. 703–705. Churchill did not relinquish the pressure on the Duke, refusing to allow him to visit the United States until after that country's entry into the war. After an interview with an American magazine that was defeatist and pro-Nazi in tone, Churchill referred indirectly to the abdication crisis in his censuring letter of 17 March 1941: "I could wish, indeed, that your Royal Highness would seek advice before making public statements of this kind." The message ended: "I should always be ready to help as I used to in the past." Ibid, p. 709. In May 1943, while visiting in Washington, Moran noted of Churchill that "when they tell him that the Duke has asked for an appointment, the P.M. sighs and arranges the day and hour." Moran, p. 103.
108. Gilbert, VI, p. 696.
109. Ibid, p. 792; Eade, p. 67.
110. Eade, pp. 79–80. Churchill used his wartime authority to make sure that the Chamber was rebuilt almost exactly as it had been before. R. Churchill, II, p. 4. Churchill, of course, had spent almost his entire adult life in the Commons, and had long since polished his oratorical skills in that House. Nevertheless, he practiced each speech as if it were his first. One day while Churchill was soaking in the bath, his valet responded to what he thought was his master's call. "I wasn't talking to you, Norman," Churchill told him. "I was addressing the House of Commons." Thompson, p. 247.
111. Gilbert, VI, p. 1083.
112. Ibid., VII, p. 133. See also Ibid., pp. 51–52 and John Connell, *Auchinleck* (London: Cassell & Co., Ltd., 1959), p. 448.
113. Gilbert, VII, p. 139.
114. Ibid., p. 140; Rowse, p. 490. "Nearly all of them," Ismay wrote in his memoirs, of the MPs in the Commons during the debate, "appeared to have elementary ideas about the conduct of total war." Ismay, p. 257.
115. Gilbert, VII, p. 722.
116. Ibid.
117. Ibid., p. 1346.
118. Fraser Harbutt, *The Iron Curtain. Churchill, America and the Origins of the Cold War* (New York: Oxford University Press, 1986), p. 35.
119. Gilbert, VI, p. 358. See Churchill's description of his reaction to Pearl Harbor: "I knew the United States was in the war, up to the neck and in to the death. So we had won after all!" *World War II*, III, p. 606.
120. Lewin, p. 35.
121. Churchill and FDR had been introduced at a Gray's Inn dinner when Roosevelt visited

London in 1918. In September 1939, FDR began a correspondence with Churchill who was then First Lord. Colville, p. 88; Lewin, p. 36.

122. Winston S. Churchill, *Marlborough. His Life and Times. Vol. V. 1705–1707* (New York: Charles Scribner's Sons, 1937), p. 129.

123. Ibid., III, p. 352. "No one can comprehend the battle of Blenheim unless he realizes that Eugene and Marlborough were working like two lobes of the same brain." Ibid., VI, p. 62.

124. *World War II*, III, p. 663. "Both of them had the spirit of eternal youth." Ismay, p. 256.

125. Berlin, pp. 31–32, 36–38.

126. Gilbert, VI, p. 1159. *World War II*, III, p. 432.

127. One of his Private Secretaries noted that after the speech on the trip back by car to Downing Street, Churchill sang "Ole Man River." Gilbert, VI, p. 743. Stephen Roskill has pointed out that Churchill's vision of an eternal union of the English speaking peoples was "as much a chimera as Hitler's 'Thousand Year Reich'." Roskill, p. 277.

128. Gilbert, VII, p. 493.

129. Moran, p. 16.

130. Gilbert, VII, pp. 274–275.

131. Ibid., p. 790.

132. Ibid., VII, p. 1301.

133. Original emphasis. Ibid., VI, p. 689.

134. Harbutt, pp. 21–22.

135. Ismay, p. 217. "He seemed so ill and frail," Ismay wrote of Hopkins, "that a puff of wind would blow him away." Ibid., p. 214; Lewin, p. 63; Sherwood, p. 247.

136. Original emphasis. Sherwood, p. 243.

137. Moran, p. 6.

138. Lewin, pp. 63–64.

139. Ibid., pp. 37–38. Churchill was very much aware of this commercial aspect. During his May 1943 visit to Washington, Halifax suggested that the subject of Britain's Lend Lease debt might arise. "Oh, I shall like that one," he replied. "I shall say, yes by all means let us have an account if we can get it reasonably accurate, but I shall have my account to put in too, and my account is for holding the baby alone for eighteen months, and it was a very rough brutal baby I had to hold." Gilbert, VII, p. 410.

140. Harbutt, p. 40.

141. Ibid., p. 33; Taylor, p. 39.

142. *World War II*, III, pp. 371–373; Rowse, p. 483.

143. Ismay, p. 134.

144. Lewin, p. 80.

145. Gilbert, VII, p. 98. PQ13 had left Iceland for Russia on 1 April. Five out of 17 ships were sunk and a principal escort vessel, a cruiser, badly damaged. Ibid., 87.

146. Lewin, p. 142.

147. Gilbert, VII, p. 109.

148. Ibid., p. 151.

149. *World War II*, IV, p. 475.

150. Gilbert, VII, p. 186.

151. Beaverbrook, p. 549.

152. Eade, p. 285.

153. Gilbert, VI, p. 665.

154. Ibid., p. 840.

155. Ibid., VII, p. 810.

156. Ibid., p. 835.

157. Ibid., VII, p. 409. On 27 March 1944, Harold Nicolson noted in his diary: "The fact is that the country is terribly war-weary, and the ill success of Anzio and Cassino is for them a sad augury of what will happen when the Second Front begins." Ibid., p. 721.

158. Ibid., p. 780. At another point, Churchill read in the *Yorkshire Post* that a home-owner had been fined for borrowing coal from a neighbor. He immediately directed the Minister of Fuel and Power to "put a stop to nonsense like this," adding that such

actions of "bureaucratic folly" were "only typical of a vast amount of silly wrong-doing by small officials or committees." Ibid.
159. Ibid., VI, p. 853. Churchill's scheme for compensating bombed-out home-owners was approved by the War Cabinet on 3 September 1940. Ibid., p. 769. See also Ibid., pp. 760–761.
160. Ibid., p. 663.
161. Churchill's radio broadcast had an astonishingly wide audience. One night in Hamburg, William Joyce, the turncoat "Lord Haw Haw," returned to his broadcasting office and found work at a standstill. When he asked what was happening, he was told to be quiet – "Churchill's broadcasting." Eade, p. 350.
162. Ibid., p. 353.
163. Gilbert, VI, pp. 602–603.
164. Sherwood, p. 239.
165. Lewin, p. 163. But see Alanbrooke's 4 November 1942 diary entry. "P.M. delighted. At 3.30 p.m. he sent for me again to discuss the project of ringing church bells. I implored him to wait a little longer till we were quite certain we should have no cause for repenting ringing them." Bryant, *Turn*, p. 421.
166. *Marlborough*, III, p. 16.
167. *World War II*, II, p. 194. Churchill forgot to lift the ban until the end of July 1940. The announcement was made after *The Times* on 25 July had quoted a US newspaper report describing the sinking. Gilbert, VI, p. 685. See also Ibid., pp. 564–565.
168. Gilbert, VII, p. 117.
169. Ibid., VI, pp. 1217 and 1219.
170. Ibid., p. 830. See also Ibid., p. 673.
171. Plumb, p. 167.
172. Ibid., p. 137.
173. *World War II*, II, p. 330.
174. Ashley, p. 49.
175. Ismay, p. 156. See also Churchill's 10 May 1942 speech. Gilbert, VII, p. 81. Churchill never deviated from this view. At the end of November 1954, his 80th birthday celebration culminated in a unique ceremony in Westminster Hall where both Houses of Parliament assembled to honor him. To this honor, Churchill replied: "I have never accepted what many people have kindly said, namely, that I inspired the nation. Their will was resolute and remorseless, and, as it proved, unconquerable. It fell to me to express it, and if I found the right words, you must remember that I have always earned my living by my pen and by my tongue. It was the nation and the race dwelling all round the globe that had the lion's heart. I had the luck to be called on to give ... the roar." Rowse, pp. 515–516. See also *Savrola*, p. 36, in which Savrola asks, "Do you think I am what I am, because I have changed all those minds, or because I best express their views? Am I their master or their slave?"
176. Berlin, pp. 26–27; Thompson, p. 26.
177. *World War II*, II, p. 279.
178. Snow, *Variety*, p. 150. See also Berlin, pp. 28–29.
179. Gilbert, VII, pp. 1347–1348.
180. Liddell Hart, p. 220.
181. Lewin, pp. 27–28; Connell, *Auchinleck*, pp. 268–269 and 305.
182. Alex Danchev, " 'Dilly-Dally,' or Having the Last Word: Field Marshal Sir John Dill and Prime Minister Winston Churchill," *Journal of Contemporary History*, Vol. 22, No. 1 (January 1987), p. 22.
183. Ismay, p. 270; Colville, p. 136.
184. Gilbert, VI, p. 1071.
185. Bryant, *Turn*, p. 136.
186. Kennedy, pp. 60–61. One morning at 2 a.m., Churchill offered Dudley Pound a whiskey and soda. "I never drink spirits in the morning," the First Sea Lord replied. "I'll have a glass of port." Ibid., p. 229.
187. Lewin, p. 13. Attlee believed that it was because of "Winston's knowledge of military

NOTES

men, his own military experience and flair, his personal dynamism and the sweeping
powers that any Prime Minister in wartime can have if he chooses to use them," that
"the deadly problem of civilians-versus-generals in wartime was solved." Andrew, p. 485.
188. Connell, *Wavell*, p. 256.
189. *World War II*, II, p. 43.
190. Ismay, p. 270.
191. Connell, *Wavell*, p. 501. Such problems were not confined to Wavell. On 18 October
1941 as he prepared for the 17−23 November 1941 Crusader offensive, Auchinleck
wrote Churchill that "the cruiser tanks of the 22nd Armoured Brigade arrived here
without having been modified for the desert ...." And the next day, the general further
informed the Prime Minister that "all the tanks on arrival had to be modified here
to fit them for desert. This process entails stripping each tank and the whole will occupy
three weeks." Ibid., p. 319; Lewin, pp. 13−14; Kennedy, p. 241.
192. Ismay, p. 16.
193. Gilbert, VII, p. 772.
194. Kennedy, p. 115. "The Army is like a peacock − nearly all tail," Churchill commented
at one meeting, to which Brooke replied: "The peacock would be a very badly balanced
bird without its tail." Ibid., p. 274.
195. Gilbert, III, p. 771.
196. Connell, *Wavell*, p. 306. In his reply, Wavell provided assurances that he would comply with Churchill's advice. "But the more I see of war," the CINC added, "the more
I am impressed by part that administration plays." Ibid.
197. Lewin, p. 133.
198. Gilbert, VII, p. 775.
199. *World War II*, IV, p. 383. Wheeler-Bennett, p. 200.
200. Moran, p. 41.
201. *London to Ladysmith*, p. 158.
202. Lewin, pp. 134−135. Gilbert, VII, pp. 47−48.
203. Moran, p. 29.
204. Gilbert, VII, p. 55. "One evening, months later, when he was sitting in his bathroom
enveloped in a towel, he stopped drying himself and gloomily surveyed the floor: 'I
cannot get over Singapore,' he said sadly." Moran, p. 29.
205. Roskill, p. 200. Churchill was also influenced in his ideas of deterrence by the effect
that the presence of the great German battleship *Tirpitz* in Norwegian waters had on
the dispositions of Britain's Home Fleet. Ibid., p. 196. Wheeler-Bennett, p. 202.
206. *World War II*, III, p. 547; Lewin, *War Lord*, p. 124; Roskill, p. 200.
207. Arthur Marder argued that Pound "feared neither God, man nor Winston Churchill."
Stephen Roskill, on the other hand, believed that Marder exaggerated. Roskill points
out that the relationship was often strained between the two men. "At times you could
kiss his [Churchill's] feet − at others you could kill him," Pound remarked on 9 June
1942 to A.V. Alexander, the First Lord. Roskill, p. 125. Marder describes how Pound
was a master at weaning or diverting Churchill from some of his more impracticable
projects. Arthur Marder, *Winston is Back: Churchill at the Admiralty* (London:
Longman, 1972), p. 5.
208. Danchev, p. 22.
209. *World War II*, V, p. 164.
210. Colville, p. 141. Cunningham had also been CINC Mediterranean and thus the reci-
pient of what he considered interference by Churchill at the operational level.
211. Danchev, p. 24. He replaced Sir Edmund Ironside, who had commanded the anti-Soviet
Archangel expedition in 1919 and had been the model for Richard Hannay in John
Buchan's *The Thirty-Nine Steps*. Colville, p. 141.
212. Danchev, p. 27 and Connell, *Wavell*, p. 256.
213. Dill and Churchill quotes from *World War II*, III, p. 422.
214. Kennedy, p. 60. On another occasion, as he watched the Chiefs file from his room
after a late night session, Churchill remarked to a member of his entourage: "I have
to wage modern war with ancient weapons." Ibid.

215. Kennedy, p. 116.
216. Kennedy, p. xv. See also Colville, pp. 124–128 and Wheeler-Bennett, pp. 162–165, 194–197.
217. "I wonder where we should be now," Dill commented later to Alanbrooke, "if Winston had his untrammelled way ...." Danchev, p. 29.
218. Danchev, pp. 33 and 35.
219. Thompson, p. 341.
220. Bryant, Turn, p. 213; Colville, p. 142; Kennedy, p. 203; Lewin, p. 126.
221. Moran, p. 304.
222. Lewin, p. 44.
223. Ibid., p. 79.
224. Ibid., p. 60.
225. Gilbert, VI, p. 1001. See Ibid., pp. 935 and 987. See also Kennedy, p. 63 and Roskill, p. 172.
226. Bryant, Turn, p. 209.
227. Ibid., p. 274.
228. Lewin, p. 84.
229. See Gilbert, VI, pp. 1012–1014, 1024 and 1028; Kennedy, p. 87; Ronald Lewin, The Chief (New York: Farrar, Straus, Giroux, 1980), pp. 80 and 103–104. See, in particular, Churchill's 20 February 1941 message to Eden in Athens: "Do not consider yourself obligated to a Greek enterprise if in your hearts you feel it will only be another Norwegian fiasco. If no good plans can be made please say so." Gilbert, VI, p. 1013. And Eden's 6 March 1941 message to Churchill from Athens: "Chief of Imperial General Staff and I, in consultation with the three Commanders-in-Chief ... are unanimously agreed that ... the right decision was taken in Athens." Lewin, Chief, p. 104.
230. Roskill, p. 197.
231. On the bad choice of Admiral Phillips, a non-believer in air power at sea, as the commander of the Eastern Fleet, see Roskill, p. 199. Churchill was aware of the problems air power could cause the navy, if for no other reason than the April 1940 experience in Norway. "It is absolutely necessary to have a comparatively small number of really fast fighter aircraft on our carriers," he wrote in November 1940. "Without these the entire movement of our ships is hampered." Geoffrey Till, Air Power and the Royal Navy 1914–1915 (London: Jane's Publishing Company, 1979), p. 106.
232. World War II, II, p. 440.
233. Lewin, War Lord, p. 55.
234. Roskill, p. 178.
235. Gilbert, VI, p. 1066.
236. Ibid., p. 1067. Lewin, Chief, p. 142. World War II, III, p. 248.
237. Gilbert, VI, p. 1085. "The Queen thanks Mr. Churchill most gratefully," Queen Elizabeth wrote from Windsor on 12 May, "for his kindness in sending news of the progress and safe arrival of Tiger. Even though he lacks a claw or two, it is to be hoped that he will still be able to chew up a few enemies." The Queen added: "Any risk was well worth taking." Original emphasis. Ibid., p. 1086.
238. Michael Howard, Grand Strategy, Vol. IV (London: HMSO, 1972), p. 208.
239. Lewin, p. 171.
240. Howard, p. 216.
241. Michael Howard, The Mediterranean Strategy in the Second World War (New York: Frederick A. Praeger, 1968), p. 69. "In after months," Eisenhower said many years later in reference to Torch, "I became absolutely certain that Mr. Churchill had been right in his argument for that particular operation; and so did General Marshall." Nelson, p. 33.
242. Lewin, p. 139.
243. World War II, V, p. 38.
244. Howard, Mediterranean, pp. 70–71.
245. Gilbert, VI, p. 477.
246. World War II, II, p. 428.

247. Connell, *Wavell*, p. 530.
248. Gilbert, VI, pp. 731–732. Connell, *Wavell*, p. 254.
249. Lewin, *Chief*, p. 25.
250. Gilbert, VI, p. 935. Connell, *Wavell*, p. 288. At the same time, Churchill was incensed by Wavell's opposition to "Workshop," the operation against the island of Pantellaria, to the extent that he apparently and incredibly made a suggestion to Eden, which the Foreign Minister recorded in his diary for 5 December 1940. "Winston unhappy at (Pantellaria) plan being turned down ... and proposed that I should go out to command in Middle East." Lewin, *War Lord*, p. 56.
251. *World War II*, II, p. 615. Connell, *Wavell*, p. 299; Gilbert, VI, p. 944.
252. Ian Stewart, *The Struggle for Crete 20 May – 1 June 1941. A Story of Lost Opportunity* (London: Oxford University Press, 1966), p. 478. See also Lewin, *The Chief*, p. 131, who also concludes that "in those last six months there was so much that could have been done."
253. Colville, p. 152.
254. Moran, p. 184.
255. Ibid., p. 186.
256. Ismay, p. 210.
257. Gilbert, VII, p. 122.
258. Description to Smuts. Ibid., VII, p. 667. On 24 February 1944, allied troops were still trapped on their bridgehead at Anzio. "My confidence in Alexander is undiminished," Churchill wrote, "though if I had been ... at his side ... at the critical moment I believe I could have given the necessary stimulus." Ibid., p. 695.
259. *World War II*, III, p. 574.
260. Gilbert, VII, p. 503.
261. Taylor, p. 43.
262. Kennedy, p. 275.
263. Gilbert, VI, p. 683.
264. Kennedy, p. 180.
265. Gilbert, VII, p. 463.
266. Kennedy, p. 268. In order to follow the defense of Tobruk, Churchill asked Ismay in April 1941 to secure the best air and ground photos of the area and to prepare a large-scale plan and a model of the city. Gilbert, VI, p. 1055.
267. In fact, Part III of the Directive was entitled "Tactical employment of the above force:" *World War II*, II, p. 430.
268. Connell, *Auchinleck*, p. 309.
269. Nelson, p. 17. Eisenhower noted in his memoir of the war that "Churchill always participated with the British Chiefs in the formulation and dispatch of instructions, even those that were strictly military, sometimes only tactical in character," Eade, p. 163.
270. *Marlborough*, III, p. 138.
271. Ibid., V, pp. 116 and 124.
272. Connell, *Auchinleck*, p. 250.
273. Ibid., p. 305. "He supplies drive and initiative," Colville noted of Churchill on 19 June 1941, "but he often meddles where he would better leave things alone and the operational side of the war might profit if he gave it a respite ...." And a week later, Eden commented on Churchill's "devastating effect on planning." Gilbert, VI, p. 1112.
274. Connell, *Auchinleck*, p. 473.
275. Kennedy, p. 61.
276. Bryant, *Turning*, p. 412. To other pressure from Churchill at this time, Montgomery told Alexander that he guaranteed complete success in October, but that "if a September attack was ordered by Whitehall, they would have to get someone else to do it. My stick was rather high after Alam Halfa! We heard no more about a September attack." Lewin, *War Lord*, p. 163. See, for instance, the earlier effect Churchill's tactical level 16 August 1940 General Directive had on Wavell. "It showed clearly," the general wrote, "that Winston did not trust me to run my own show ...." Connell, *Wavell*, p. 266.

277. The answer from the American general was that he did, but that his questions ought to show respect for Alexander's ability. In the end, Churchill agreed. Nelson, p. 27.
278. J.R.M. Butler, *Grand Strategy*, Vol. III, Part II (London: HMSO, 1964), p. 460; Kennedy, p. 135.
279. Lewin, *War Lord*, pp. 117–118 and 144.

CHAPTER 5

1. Eade, p. 91.
2. Gilbert, VI, p. 861; Danchev, p. 37.
3. Michael Handel (ed.), *Strategic and Operational Deception in the Second World War* (London: Frank Cass, 1987), pp. 32 and 35.
4. Andrew, pp. 484–485; F.H. Hinsley et al, *British Intelligence in the Second World War*, I (London: HMSO, 1979), p. 160.
5. Ibid.; Donald McLachlan, *Room 39. Naval Intelligence in Action 1939–45* (London: Weidenfeld and Nicolson, 1968), p. 247.
6. Ibid., pp. 262–263.
7. Andrew, p. 476; Gilbert, VI, p. 667. Churchill's romanticised concept of that type of warfare was illustrated by his reaction to the French resistance leader, Emmanuel d'Astier. "This is a remarkable man of the Scarlet Pimpernel type," he wrote to Roosevelt in 1944. Arthur L. Funk, "Churchill, Eisenhower, and the French Resistance," *Military Affairs*, Vol. XLV, No. 1 (Feb. 1981), p. 30.
8. Andrew, p. 477.
9. John W. Gordon, *The Other Desert War. British Special Forces in North Africa, 1940–1943* (New York: Greenwood Press, 1987), p. 117.
10. Andrew, p. 478; R.A. Haldane, *The Hidden War* (New York: St. Martin's Press, 1978), p. 149. After the Scapa Flow incident, Churchill was reluctant to even let British ships into the Clyde River. On 28 October 1939, he told Pound: "There are plenty of Irish traitors in the Glasgow area; telephone communication with Ireland is, I believe, unrestricted; there is a German ambassador in Dublin. I should expect that within a few hours of the arrival of these ships it would be known in Berlin that the British heavy ships were definitely out of the North Sea and could not return for more than sixty hours." Gilbert, VI, p. 71.
11. Andrew, p. 482.
12. McLachlan, p. 345.
13. Ronald Lewin, *Ultra Goes to War* (New York: McGraw-Hill, 1978), pp. 11 and 56–57.
14. Andrew, p. 465.
15. R. Churchill, Vol. II, p. 260. "Churchill was incapable of concealment," Beaverbrook wrote. "So much so that it was not possible to give him early notice of secret information." Beaverbrook, p. 548. In this regard, Violet Asquith apparently learned from some source during World War I of the Magdeburg German naval code decrypt episode. Carter, p. 284.
16. Lewin, *War Lord*, p. 176.
17. Wheeler-Bennett, p. 143 and Gilbert, VII, p. 38.
18. Dudley Clarke, *Seven Assignments* (London: Jonathan Cape, 1948), p. 197. When the connection with Gort was reestablished, Churchill continued the conversation more discreetly after prefacing his remarks: "There's somebody here who tells me I mustn't say what I was going to say." Ibid.
19. From those conversations, for instance, the Germans were aware of Allied expectations of an Italian armistice proposal. Alan Turing, the eccentric but brilliant decrypter from BP, devised a new scrambler that baffled the Germans. David Kahn, *Kahn On Codes* (New York: Macmillan Publishing Co., 1983), p. 37; Jack Haswell, *The Intelligence and Deception of the D-Day Landings* (London: BT Batsford Ltd., 1979), p. 158.
20. Gilbert, VI, p. 965. See also Ibid., 963–964.

21. Ibid., p. 896.
22. Ibid., pp. 750 and 823.
23. *World War II*, II, p. 654.
24. Hinsley, I, p. 295.
25. *World War II*, III, p. 356.
26. Lewin, *Ultra*, pp. 183–184.
27. Ibid., pp. 190–191.
28. McLachlan, p. 125.
29. Ibid., p. 129. "When estimating our existing tonnage," Harold Nicolson noted of Churchill in his diary in 1939, "he adds on the ships operating on the Canadian lakes." Gilbert, VI, p. 90.
30. Arthur J. Marder, *From the Dardanelles to Oran* (London: Oxford University Press, 1974), pp. 122–124. Pond apparently did not defend his subordinate, but did ensure that Talbot obtained command of the aircraft carrier *Furious*. Roskill, p. 95. See also McLachan, pp. 127–129; Patrick Beesly, *Very Special Intelligence* (London: Hamish Hamilton, 1977), pp. 37–38.
31. Gilbert, VI, p. 740.
32. McLachan, p. 134; Beesly, *Very Special Intelligence*, p. 36.
33. *World War II*, II, p. 498.
34. Sherwood, p. 257. See also Michael Handel, "The Politics of Intelligence," *Intelligence and National Security*, Vol. 2, No. 4 (October 1987), pp. 8–9.
35. Ibid., pp. 11–13.
36. Lewin, *Ultra*, p. 183.
37. Ibid.
38. Gilbert, VI, pp. 610–612; Andrew, p. 449.
39. Andrew, p. 454; Cave Brown, p. 19.
40. *Kahn*, p. 91. To the question why, if Ultra was so important, it didn't end the war earlier, Deutsch replied, "It did end sooner."
41. Lewin, *Ultra*, pp. 126–127.
42. Ibid., p. 127.
43. P.S. Milner-Barry, " 'Action This Day': The Letter from Bletchley Park Cryptoanalysts to the Prime Minister, 21 October 1941," *Intelligence and National Security*, Vol. 1, No. 2 (May 1986), pp. 272–273. See also Appendix 8, Hinsley, II, pp. 655–657; Andrew Hodges, *Alan Turing: The Enigma* (New York: Simon and Schuster, 1983), pp. 219–221, and Gilbert, VI, p. 1185.
44. In addition, Menzies also displayed his political astuteness in his dealings with the military and Foreign Office intelligence organizations by inviting the DNI, DMI and DAI to recommend candidates to fill three coordination positions in SIS. Nigel West, *MI5. British Secret Intelligence Service Operations 1909–1945* (London: Weidenfeld and Nicolson, 1983), pp. 137–139; Cave Brown, p. 815.
45. Hinsley, I, p. 295.
46. Gilbert, VI, p. 611 and Lewin, *Ultra*, pp. 185–186.
47. All described by Sir Arthur Benson, Morton's assistant at the time, to Ronald Lewin. Lewin, *Ultra*, p. 186. Morton's role declined after the winter of 1942–43. By that time, Ultra could work its way through the many arteries of what had evolved as a highly efficient political-military system of war administration. Moreover, the volume of intercepts by then was immense; and Churchill, as well, was increasingly a junior partner in the Grand Alliance. Ibid., p. 189. On the Secret Circle, see Gilbert, VI, p. 613.
48. Ibid., p. 1154.
49. Ibid., VII, p. 295.
50. Ibid., p. 459. At the conclusion of the August 1943 Quebec Conference, Churchill took a fishing holiday with his wife and one of his daughters in Canada. This posed immense problems for his Private Office in London. "Please telegraph urgently details and times of future movements," the 30 August message from the Private Office read, "in order transmission of news may be arranged, particularly information from 'C.' " Ibid., p. 485. For Churchill's fatherly affection for the members of the SLU who accompanied him throughout the remainder of the war, see Lewin, *Ultra*, p. 149.

51. Hinsley, II, p. 163. The boarding of U-110 remained a secret until 1959; and the capture of the Enigma machine was not known to the public until the 1970s. Ibid., I, pp. 336–339 and 565–569. See also S.W. Roskill's *The Secret Capture*, which was written to counter the claim that the U-505 captured by US forces in 1944 was the first boarding of a U-boat during the war. David Syrett, "The Secret War and the Historians," *Armed Forces and Society*, Vol. 9, No. 2 (Winter 1983), pp. 304–305.
52. Hinsley, II, pp. 228–233, 549–556, 566–567 and 747–752; Gilbert, VII, p. 438.
53. Ibid., VI, p. 849.
54. Churchill added that the reports to the attaché, M.G. Lee, "should not be broken off suddenly but should become less informative and padding used to maintain bulk." Ibid., p. 896. During this period, Churchill also added A.V. Alexander, the First Lord of the Admiralty and Anthony Eden to the list as well as the CINCs of Fighter Command and Bomber Commands. Ibid., p. 849.
55. Jones, p. 125.
56. Gilbert, VI, p. 1242; Hinsley, II, pp. 644–645. According to a former Bletchley Park worker in conversation with Martin Gilbert, the messages "were very pallid paraphrases reduced to officialese." Gilbert, VII, p. 238.
57. Hinsley, II, pp. 645–646.
58. Gilbert, VII, p. 360. See also Hinsley, II, p. 73, for slightly different wording. On 9 March 1943, after using Ultra to spring a successful trap on a German counterattack force at Medenine, Ultra began to reveal that the Germans were suspicious of British Intelligence's impressive achievements, although not, as it turned out, in terms of Enigma machine vulnerability. Ibid., pp. 593–596.
59. Kahn, p. 96. On the morning of 14 November 1940, the Air Staff sent a memorandum alerting Churchill to the upcoming raid which concluded: "We believe that the target areas will be ... probably in the vicinity of London, but if further information indicates Coventry, Birmingham or elsewhere, we hope to get instructions out on time." Hinsley, I, p. 317. Sir David Hunt and Sir John Martin have pointed out that Churchill abandoned a visit to Ditchley Park on the afternoon of 14 November and returned to Downing Street under the impression that the raid was to be directed against London. Ibid., p. 536. See also Appendix 9, Ibid., pp. 528–538 and Gilbert, VI, pp. 913–914.
60. Gilbert, VII, p. 779.
61. Ibid., pp. 779–780 and p. 11 and Hinsley, III, Part 1, pp. 165–166.
62. Hinsley, II, pp. 328–329; Gilbert, VII, pp. 55–56.
63. Gilbert, VI, p. 1234. See also Ibid., pp. 1239 and 1242–1244.
64. Hinsley, II, pp. 647 and 414. Gilbert, VII, p. 366.
65. Cave Brown, pp. 128–129.
66. Hinsley, II, pp. 75 and 55.
67. Sir Stafford Cripps was the Ambassador. He refused at first to deliver the message and then finally on 19 April handed it to the Soviet Foreign Minister, an action which Churchill realized diminished the immediacy of the message. Gilbert, VI, pp. 1050–1051. On 25 February 1942, Churchill informed Roosevelt that prior to Pearl Harbor, British Intelligence had been able to read some of the US diplomatic messages and to warn the President that "our enemies" might be able to do the same. "From the moment we became allies," Churchill added, "I gave instructions that this work should cease." Ibid., VII, p. 53.
68. Hinsley, II, p. 59.
69. Ibid., p. 73.
70. Gilbert, VII, p. 235.
71. Hinsley, II, p. 59.
72. Lewin, *Ultra*, pp. 190–191; Lewin, *War Lord*, p. 75.
73. Richard Lamb, *Montgomery in Europe 1943–1945. Success or Failure* (New York: Franklin Watts, 1984), p. 144.
74. Lewin, *Ultra*, p. 160.
75. Gilbert, VI, p. 1088. The previous month, Wavell evidently believed that the British Ultra cover was blown, since he suspected that Enigma references to Crete might be

part of a German deception plan to conceal a move toward Cyprus and Syria. Hinsley, I, p. 417.

76. Lewin, *Ultra*, p. 157; Gilbert, VI, p. 1085. Freyberg was only made commander of the allied troops in Crete on 5 May. Ibid., p. 1082.

77. Ibid., VI, p. 1088; Lewin, *Ultra*, p. 158.

78. Ibid., p. 162.

79. Gilbert, VI, p. 1080. Beginning the previous March, Wavell had begun to receive Enigma decrypts directly from Bletchley Park. Ibid., p. 1081; Lewin, *Ultra*, pp. 162–163; Hinsley, I, p. 395.

80. *World War II*, III, p. 334.

81. Ibid., p. 339. See also Lewin, *Ultra*, p. 163.

82. Ibid., p. 171.

83. Ibid., p. 174.

84. Gilbert, VI, p. 1217. As it turned out, it was not until 5 December that Hitler ordered an Air Corps transferred from Russia to the Sicily–Tripolitania area, and then only in response to Torch. Ibid., p. 1252.

85. Ibid., pp. 1245, 1239 and 1242; Lewin, *Ultra*, p. 169.

86. *World Crisis 1911–14*, p. 498.

87. Gilbert, VI, p. 10. Churchill later suggested that there might be a possibility of using the dummy ships to benefit the sailors by fitting recreation rooms or movie theaters in the false hulls. "I like to think," he added, "that in the long dark winter at Scapa they might add to the amenities as well as the protection of the Fleet." Ibid., p. 13.

88. J.C. Masterman, *The Double Cross System* (New Haven: Yale University Press, 1972), pp. 179–181.

89. Gilbert, VI, p. 967.

90. Ibid., VII, p. 899.

91. Ronald Wingate, *Not in the Limelight* (London: Hutchinson, 1959), pp. 188–189. Dudley Clarke was Wavell's representative to the March 1941 Chiefs of Staff meeting, out of which the LCS emerged. David Mure, *Master of Deception* (London: William Kimber, 1980), p. 83.

92. Cave Brown, pp. 2 and 50.

93. Wingate, p. 185. In referring to Churchill, Wingate also commented on "the power of his personality and the minute and detailed attention which he devoted to every aspect of operational planning," and which made every member of the staff feel "that he was at their elbow most of the time." Ibid.

94. Dennis Wheatley, "Deception in World War II," *RUSI*, Vol. 121, No. 3 (September 1976), p. 87. Wingate was also a cousin of Orde Wingate and T.E. Lawrence. Cave Brown, p. 8. See also Ibid., p. 270. Mure, pp. 131 and 196.

95. Cave Brown, p. 270.

96. Emphasis added. Ibid., p. 675. A similar speech was prepared for de Gaulle, since the LCS was well aware that the Germans would closely monitor the French leader's broadcast for signs of Allied strategy. But de Gaulle rejected the script and in his own speech not only insulted the Grand Alliance, but declared that the Normandy landings constituted *the* invasion. "The *supreme battle* has begun," he broadcast. "After so much struggle, fury, suffering, this is the *decisive* blow, the blow we have so much hoped for." Emphasis added. Ibid. In terms of Bevan's power, one subordinate commented "that in the last years of the war he could have asked the Chiefs of Staff for a battleship with an escort of destroyers to be sent anywhere and they would have let him have it." Wheatley, p. 87.

97. Gilbert, VII, p. 405; Lewin, *Ultra*, pp. 279–280.

98. Ibid., p. 405.

99. Lewin, *Ultra*, pp. 279–280.

100. Gilbert, VI, p. 1218.

101. Lewin, *War Lord*, p. 85. In July 1943 Churchill contemplated a right and left hand strategy calling for advances up the Italian boot and a northern Norway invasion – all of which would not leave enough troops for Overlord. In that case, he proposed, Overlord should become the deception plan for Jupiter. Gilbert, VII, p. 445.

102. Ibid., p. 155.
103. Ibid., p. 190.
104. Ibid., p. 228.
105. Imposing the ban, however, evidently provided a clue to Hitler in terms of the Overlord timing. When he learned of the ban in late April, he remarked that "the English have taken measures that they can sustain for only six to eight weeks." Stephen E. Ambrose, *Ike's Spies. Eisenhower and the Espionage Establishment* (New York: Doubleday & Company, Inc., 1981), p. 91.
106. Gilbert, VII, p. 312.
107. *World War II*, V, p. 338. Cave Brown, pp. 9 and 388–389. Churchill later explained that Stalin had originated the saying, terming it "a Russian proverb." Churchill's use of the phrase was apparently meant to please Stalin by using the Russian leader's own quote. Sir David Hunt to Martin Gilbert. Gilbert, VII, p. 586.
108. Cave Brown, p. 389.
109. Gilbert, VII, pp. 700, 812, 833 and 837. For "Plan 'Bodyguard,' Overall Deception Plan for the War against Germany," COS Paper # 779 (Operations) (Final), 23 January 1944, see Ibid., p. 701. Lewin, *Ultra*, p. 314. Cave Brown, p. 434.
110. *World War II*, II, pp. 337–338.
111. Gilbert, VI, p. 1038.
112. Ibid., p. 845.
113. Alfred Stanford, *Force Mulberry* (New York: William Morrow & Co., 1951), p. 39, and Guy Hartcup, *Code Name Mulberry* (New York: Hippocrene Books, Inc., 1977), p. 28.
114. Hartcup, p. 141.
115. Frederick Winston Smith, *The Professor and the Prime Minister* (Boston: Houghton Mifflin, 1962), pp. 234–235; R. Stuart Macrae, *Winston Churchill's Toyshop* (New York: Walker and Co., 1971), p. 96, and Lewin, *War Lord*, p. 52.
116. Macrae, pp. 125 and 169.
117. Macrae, p. 86. At weapons demonstrations, Churchill's bodyguard always carried a stengun for the Prime Minister's use on the nearest target whenever there were lulls in the proceedings. Ibid., p. 167.
118. Gilbert, VI, p. 684.
119. Churchill chose the code name from the biblical text: "Behold ye among the heathen, and regard, and wonder marvellously: for I will work a work in your days which ye will not believe, though it be told you." Ibid., VII, p. 446.
120. Ibid., VI, p. 1296. "They had been sent to these waters," Churchill wrote of the two ships, "to exercise that kind of vague menace which capital ships of the highest quality whose whereabouts is unknown can impose upon all hostile naval calculations." *World War II*, III, pp. 615–616.
121. Lewin, *War Lord*, p. 51.
122. Eade, p. 387.
123. Gilbert, VII, p. 847.
124. Lewin, *War Lord*, p. 206.
125. Gilbert, VI, pp. 90–91.
126. Ibid., p. 815.
127. Ibid., p. 711.
128. All quotes in paragraph, Ibid., VII, p. 776. See also Julian Lewis, "Churchill and the 'Anthrax Bomb,'" *Encounter*, Feb. 1982, 18–28.
129. Gilbert, VI, p. 618.
130. *World War II*, VI, p. 35.
131. Gilbert, VII, pp. 840–841.
132. Ibid., VII, p. 865. At the end of May 1942, Churchill had issued a declaration that if the Germans used gas on the Russian front, Britain would also use it. He had not consulted the Chiefs, and their study produced as a result of that declaration showed that the British Isles were more vulnerable to gas attack than Germany. Moreover, in overseas theaters such as Egypt, Britain was relatively unprepared for defense against gas and even more so for offensive operations.

133. *World War II*, II, pp. 337–338.
134. Bohr told R.V. Jones: "It was terrible! He scolded us like two schoolboys." Jones, p. 477; Snow, *Variety*, pp. 156–157.
135. Gilbert, VI, p. 615.
136. Ibid., p. 768.
137. Ibid., p. 770.
138. P.M.S. Blackett, *Studies of War* (London: Owen and Boyd, 1962), p. 238.
139. Jones, p. 249.
140. Gilbert, VI, p. 97. The countermeasures were due to the recovery of unexploded mines. On one was painted: "Geb ich ein gut Geleite, Churchill hat dann grosse Pleite." ("Guide me on my way aright. Then Churchill will be in sad plight.") Ibid., p. 98.
141. *World War II*, I, p. 711.
142. Jones, p. 290; Gilbert, VII, p. 434.
143. Ibid., pp. 434–435.
144. Jones, p. 297. Window was first used on the 24 July 1943 night attack on Hamburg to great effect. It was unanticipated by the Germans and for some time reduced bomber losses by half. "On the whole," Churchill concluded, "it may be claimed that we released it about the right time." *World War II*, IV, p. 289.
145. Jones, p. 297.
146. Churchill used "curtsey" as a translation of Knickebein. *World War II*, II, p. 384; Gilbert, VI, pp. 102 and 283; Jones, pp. 92–95.
147. Jones, p. 101.
148. Ibid.
149. *World War II*, II, pp. 384–385.
150. Ibid., p. 385.
151. Jones, p. 107. Churchill telephoned Jones in 1946 and while discussing other matters, asked: "Do you know that there is a poem about you in the *Ingoldsby Legends*?" and then proceeded to recite the verses that eventually appeared in his memoirs. Ibid., p. 521.
152. *World War II*, II, pp. 386–387.
153. Gilbert, VI, p. 583.
154. *World War II*, II, p. 387. One officer in Churchill's Defence Office sent his family to the country during this period to escape the London raids. They were astonished to see on one occasion more than 100 bombs fall in fields over 10 miles from the nearest town. The officer, unaware of Knickebein, recounted this to his colleagues, some of whom were in the small inner circle privy to the sensitive "beam" information. "The very few who knew," Churchill summed up the episode, "exchanged celestial grins." Ibid. See also Gilbert, VI, p. 1082, for the very successful beam bend on 8 May 1941 in which German bombers dropped 235 bombs on empty fields many miles distant from their actual target at the Rolls-Royce works in Derby.
155. Ibid., p. 757.
156. Jones, p. 107.
157. Ibid., p. xiii.
158. Written on the flyleaf of *Their Finest Hour*, presented by Churchill to Jones. Ibid., p. 81.
159. Ibid., p. 531. Churchill continued to look after Jones in later years. The Prime Minister, for instance, insisted after the war while visiting the University of Aberdeen that the officials give the Chair of Natural Philosophy to Jones, the man, he told the University Lord Provost, who "Broke the Bloody Beam." Ibid., p. 516.

CHAPTER 6

1. Liddell Hart, p. 175.
2. Andrew, p. 48.
3. Berlin, p. 39.

BIBLIOGRAPHY

Ambrose, Stephen E. *Ike's Spies. Eisenhower and the Espionage Establishment.* New York: Doubleday & Company, Inc., 1981.

Andrew, Christopher. *Her Majesty's Secret Service.* New York: Viking, 1986.

Ashley, Maurice. *Churchill as Historian.* New York: Charles Scribner's Sons, 1968.

Ausubel, Herman. *The Late Victorians.* New York: D. Van Nostrand Company, Inc., 1955.

Bagehot, Walter. *Bagehot's Historical Essays,* ed. Norman St. John-Stevas. Garden City, N.Y.: Anchor Books, Doubleday & Company, Inc., 1965.

Bamford, T. W. *Rise of the Public School.* London: Thomas Nelson & Sons Ltd., 1967.

Beaverbrook, Lord. "Lloyd George and Churchill," *History Today.* August 1973.

Beesly, Patrick. *Room 40.* London: Hamish Hamilton, 1982.

— *Very Special Intelligence.* London: Hamish Hamilton, 1977.

Berlin, Isaiah. *Mr. Churchill in 1940.* Boston: Houghton Mifflin Company, 1948.

Black, Eugene C. *Victorian Culture and Society.* London and Basingstoke: The Macmillan Press Ltd., 1973.

Blackett, P. M. S. *Studies of War: Nuclear and Conventional.* New York: Hill and Wang, 1962.

Briggs, Asa. *Victorian People,* revised edition. Chicago: The University of Chicago Press, 1979.

Bryant, Arthur. *The Turn of the Tide.* New York: Doubleday & Co., Inc., 1957.

— *Triumph in the West.* Westport, Conn.: Greenwood Press, 1959.

Buckley, Jerome H. "Symbols of Eternity: The Victorian Escape from Time," *Victorian Essays,* eds. Warren D. Anderson and Thomas D. Clareson. Oberlin, Ohio: Kent State University Press, 1967.

Butler, J. R. M. *Grand Strategy.* Vol. III, Part II. London: H.M.S.O., 1964.

Butterfield, H. *The Whig Interpretation of History.* New York: Charles Scribner's Sons, 1951.

Carter, Violet Bonham. *Winston Churchill. An Intimate Portrait.* New York: Harcourt, Brace & World, Inc., 1965.

Cave Brown, Anthony. *Bodyguard of Lies.* New York: Harper & Row, Publishers, 1975.

Churchill, Randolph S. *Winston S. Churchill. Volume I. Youth. 1874–1900.* Boston: Houghton Mifflin Company, 1966.

— *Winston S. Churchill. Companion Volume I. Part I. 1874–1896.* Boston: Houghton Mifflin Company, 1967.

— *Winston S. Churchill. Companion Volume I. Part II. 1896–1900.* Boston: Houghton Mifflin Company, 1967.

— *Winston S. Churchill. Volume II. 1901–1914. Young Statesman.* Boston: Houghton Mifflin Company, 1967.

Churchill, Winston S. *The Aftermath.* New York: Charles Scribner's Sons, 1929.

— *Great Contemporaries.* London: Thornton Butterworth Ltd., 1937.

— *History of the English Speaking Peoples. Volume I. The Birth of Britain.* New York: Dodd, Mead & Co., 1966.

— *Ian Hamilton's March.* London: Longmans, Green & Co., 1900.

BIBLIOGRAPHY

— *London to Ladysmith via Pretoria.* London and Bombay: Longmans, Green & Co., 1900.

— *Marlborough. His Life and Times. Volume I. 1650–1688.* New York: Charles Scribner's Sons, 1933.

— *Marlborough. His Life and Times. Volume II. 1688–1702.* New York: Charles Scribner's Sons, 1933.

— *Marlborough. His Life and Times. Volume III. 1702–1704.* New York: Charles Scribner's Sons, 1935.

— *Marlborough. His Life and Times. Volume IV. 1704–1705.* New York: Charles Scribner's Sons, 1935.

— *Marlborough. His Life and Times. Volume V. 1705–1708.* New York: Charles Scribner's Sons, 1937.

— *Marlborough. His Life and Times. Volume VI. 1708–1722.* New York: Charles Scribner's Sons, 1938.

— *The River War. An Historical Account of the Reconquest of the Soudan.* London: Longmans, Green, & Co., 1902.

— *A Roving Commission.* New York: Charles Scribner's Sons, 1951.

— *Savrola. A Tale of the Revolution in Laurania.* New York: Random House, 1956.

— *The Second World War. Volume I. The Gathering Storm.* Boston: Houghton Mifflin Company, 1948.

— *The Second World War. Volume II. Their Finest Hour.* Boston: Houghton Mifflin Company, 1949.

— *The Second World War. Volume III. The Grand Alliance.* Boston: Houghton Mifflin Company, 1950.

— *The Second World War. Volume IV. The Hinge of Fate.* Boston: Houghton Mifflin Company, 1950.

— *The Second World War. Volume V. Closing the Ring.* Boston: Houghton Mifflin Company, 1951.

— *The Second World War. Volume VI. Triumph and Tragedy.* Boston: Houghton Mifflin Company, 1953.

— *The Story of the Malakand Field Force. An Episode of Frontier War.* New York and Bombay: Longmans, Green, & Co., 1901.

— *Thoughts and Adventures.* London: Odhams Press Limited, 1949.

— *The Unknown War.* New York: Charles Scribner's Sons, 1931.

— *The World Crisis. 1911–1914.* New York: Charles Scribner's Sons, 1928.

— *The World Crisis. 1915.* New York: Charles Scribner's Sons, 1929.

— *The World Crisis. 1916–1918.* Parts I & II. London: Thornton Butterworth Ltd., 1927.

Clarke, Dudley. *Seven Assignments.* London: Jonathan Cape, 1948.

Clausewitz, Carl von. *On War,* edited and translated by Michael Howard and Peter Paret. Princeton: Princeton University Press, 1976.

Colville, John. *The Churchillians.* London: Weidenfeld & Nicholson, 1981.

Connell, John. *Auchinleck.* London: Cassell & Company Ltd., 1959.

— *Wavell. Scholar and Soldier.* New York: Harcourt, Brace & World, Inc., 1964.

Darwin, Bernard. *The English Public School.* London: Longmans, Green, & Co., 1929.

Deakin, F. W. *Churchill the Historian.* Third Winston Churchill Memorial Lecture. University of Basel, 10 Jan. 1969.

Eade, Charles (ed.). *Churchill by his Contemporaries.* New York: Simon & Schuster, 1954.

Eby, Cecil D. *The Road to Armageddon. The Martial Spirit in English Popular Literature 1870–1914.* Durham and London: Duke University Press, 1987.

Ellis, L. F. *The War in France and Flanders, 1939–1940.* London: H.M.S.O., 1953.

Ensor, R. C. K. *England. 1870–1914.* London: Oxford University Press, 1960.

Funk, Arthur L., "Churchill, Eisenhower, and the French Resistance," *Military Affairs*, Vol. XLV, No. 1 (Feb. 1981).

Foot, M. R. D. *SOE The Special Operations Executive. 1940–46.* New York: University Publications of America, Inc., 1984.

Fussell, Paul. *The Great War and Modern Memory.* New York: Oxford University Press, 1975.

Gilbert, Martin. *Winston Churchill. Volume III. The Challenge of War. 1914–1916.* Boston: Houghton Mifflin Company, 1971.

— *Winston Churchill. Volume IV. The Stricken World. 1916–1922.* Boston: Houghton Mifflin Company, 1975.

— *Winston Churchill. Volume V. The Prophet of Truth. 1922–1939.* Boston: Houghton Mifflin Company, 1977.

— *Winston Churchill. Volume VI. Finest Hour. 1939–1941.* Boston: Houghton Mifflin Company, 1983.

— *Winston Churchill. Volume VII. Road to Victory. 1941–1945.* Boston: Houghton Mifflin Company, 1986.

Girouard, Mark. "When Chivalry Died," *The New Republic*, Vol. 185, No. 13 (30 Sept. 1981).

Goldhamer, Herbert. *The Adviser.* New York: Elsevier, 1978.

Gordon, John W. *The Other Desert War. British Special Forces in North Africa, 1940–1943.* New York: Greenwood Press, 1987.

Haldane, R. A. *The Hidden War.* New York: St. Martin's Press, 1978.

Handel, Michael I. "Intelligence and Deception," *The Journal of Strategic Studies*, Vol. 5, No. 1 (March 1982).

— "Introduction: Strategic and Operational Deception in Historical Perspective," *Strategic and Operational Deception in the Second World War*, ed. Michael Handel. London: Frank Cass, 1987.

— "The Politics of Intelligence," *Intelligence and National Security*. Vol. 2, No. 4 (Oct. 1987).

Harbutt, Fraser J. *The Iron Curtain. Churchill, America and the Origins of the Cold War.* New York: Oxford University Press, 1986.

Harriman, W. Averell and Elie Abel. *Special Envoy to Churchill and Stalin, 1941–1946.* New York: Random House, 1975.

Harrod, R. F. *The Prof. A Personal Memoir of Lord Cherwell.* London: Macmillan & Co., Ltd., 1959.

Hartcup, Guy. *Code Name Mulberry.* New York: Hippocrene Books, Inc., 1977.

Haswell, Jock. *The Intelligence and Deception of the D-Day Landings.* London: B.T. Batsford Ltd., 1979.

Himmelfarb, Gertrude. *Victorian Minds.* New York: Alfred A. Knopf, 1968.

Hinsley, F. H. et al. *British Intelligence in the Second World War. Volume I.* London: H.M.S.O., 1979.

— *British Intelligence in the Second World War. Volume II.* London: H.M.S.O., 1983.

— *British Intelligence in the Second World War. Volume III, Part I.* New York: Cambridge University Press, 1984.

Hodges, Andrew. *Alan Turing: The Enigma.* New York: Simon & Schuster, 1983.

Houghton, Walter E. *The Victorian Frame of Mind. 1830–1870.* New Haven: Yale University Press, 1957.

Howard, Michael. *Grand Strategy. Vol. IV.* London: H.M.S.O., 1972.

— *The Mediterranean Strategy in the Second World War.* New York: Frederick A. Praeger, 1968.

Ismay, Hastings Lionel. *The Memoirs of General Lord Ismay.* New York: The Viking Press, 1960.

James, Robert Rhodes. "The Politician," in *Churchill Revised. A Critical Assessment.* New York: The Dial Press, Inc., 1969.

Johnson, Edgar, "Dickens and the Spirit of the Age," *Victorian Essays,* eds. Warren D. Anderson and Thomas D. Clareson. Oberlin, Ohio: Kent State University Press, 1967.

Jones, R. V. *Most Secret War.* London: Hamish Hamilton, 1978.

Kahn, David. *Kahn on Codes.* New York: Macmillan Publishing Company, 1983.

Kennedy, John. *The Business of War,* ed. Bernard Fergusson. London: Hutchinson & Co., 1957.

Lamb, Richard. *Montgomery in Europe 1943–1945. Success or Failure?* New York: Franklin Watts, 1984.

Lewin, Ronald. *The Chief.* New York: Farrar, Straus, Giroux, 1980.

— *Churchill as Warlord.* New York: Stein & Day, 1973.

— *Ultra Goes to War.* New York: McGraw-Hill, 1978.

Lewis, Julian. "Churchill and the 'Anthrax Bomb'," *Encounter,* Feb. 1982.

Liddell Hart, Basil. "The Military Strategist," in *Churchill Revised. A Critical Assessment.* New York: The Dial Press Inc., 1969.

Macrae, R. Stuart. *Winston Churchill's Toyshop.* New York: Walker & Company, 1971.

Manchester, William. *The Last Lion. Winston Spencer Churchill: Visions of Glory: 1874–1932.* Boston: Little, Brown & Company, 1983.

Masterman, J. C. *The Double Cross System.* New Haven: Yale University Press, 1972.

Marder, Arthur J. *From the Dardanelles to Oran.* London: Oxford University Press, 1974.

— *Winston is Back: Churchill at the Admiralty.* London: Longman, 1972.

McLachlan, Donald. *Room 39. Naval Intelligence in Action 1939–45.* London: Weidenfield & Nicolson, 1968.

Milner-Barry, P. S. "'Action This Day': The Letter from Bletchley Park Crypto-analysts to the Prime Minister, 21 October 1941," *Intelligence and National Security,* Vol. 1, No. 2 (May 1986).

Moran, Lord. *Churchill. Taken from the Diaries of Lord Moran: The Struggle for Survival, 1940–1965.* Boston: Houghton Mifflin Company, 1966.

Morgan, Gerald. "Myth and Reality in the Great Game," *Asian Affairs. Journal of the Royal Central Asian Society,* Vol. 60 (New Series Vol. IV), Part 1 (Feb. 1973).

Morgenthau, Hans J. "Henry Kissinger, Secretary of State," *Encounter,* Nov. 1974.

Mure, David. *Master of Deception.* London: William Kimber, 1980.

Nelson, James, ed. *General Eisenhower on the Military Churchill*. New York: W.W. Norton & Company, Inc., 1970.

Pascal, Blaise. *Pascal's Pensees*. Trans. W.F. Trotter. Introduction by T.E. Eliot. New York: E.P. Dutton, 1958.

Phillips, Janet and Peter. *Victorians at Home and Away*. London: Croom Helm Ltd., 1978.

Plumb, J.H. "The Historian," in *Churchill Revised. A Critical Assessment*. New York: The Dial Press, Inc., 1969.

Roskill, S.W. *Churchill and the Admirals*. New York: William Morrow & Co., Inc., 1978.

Rowse, A.L. *The Later Churchills*. London: Macmillan & Co., Ltd., 1958.

Saunders, H. St. George. *Per Ardua: The Rise of British Air Power 1911–1939*. London: Oxford University Press, 1944.

Schlesinger, Arthur M. *The Age of Roosevelt: The Coming of the New Deal*. Boston: Houghton Mifflin Company, 1959.

Sherwood, Robert. *Roosevelt and Hopkins. An Intimate History*. New York: Harper & Brothers, 1950.

Smith, Frederick Winston Furneaux, 2d Earl of Birkenhead. *The Professor and the Prime Minister*. Boston: Houghton Mifflin Company, 1962.

Snow, C.P. *Science and Government*. Cambridge, Mass.: Harvard University Press, 1961.

— *Variety of Men*. New York: Charles Scribner's Sons, 1967.

Stanford, Alfred. *Force Mulberry*. New York: William Morrow & Co., 1951.

Stewart, Ian. *The Struggle for Crete. 20 May–1 June 1941. A Story of Lost Opportunity*. London: Oxford University Press, 1966.

Storr, Anthony. "The Man," in *Churchill Revised. A Critical Assessment*. New York: The Dial Press, Inc., 1969.

Syrett, David. "The Secret War and the Historians," *Armed Forces and Society*. Vol. 9, No. 2 (Winter 1983).

Thompson, R.W. *The Yankee Marlborough*. London: George Allen & Unwin, Ltd., 1963.

Till, Geoffrey. *Air Power and the Royal Navy 1914–1915*. London: Jane's Publishing Company, 1979.

Tingsten, Herbert. *Victoria and the Victorians*, trans. David Grey and Eva Leckstroem Grey. London: George Allen & Unwin, Ltd., 1972.

Tuchman, Barbara. *The Proud Tower*, 3rd Printing. New York: The Macmillan Company, 1966.

Webb, R.K. *Modern England*. New York: Harper & Row, 1968.

West, Nigel. *MI5. British Secret Intelligence Service Operations 1909–1945*. London: Weidenfeld & Nicolson, 1983.

Wheatley, Dennis. "Deception in World War II," *RUSI*, Volume 121, No. 3 (Sept. 1976).

Wheeler-Bennett, John, ed. *Action This Day. Working with Churchill*. New York: St. Martin's Press, 1969.

Wilkinson, Rupert. *The Prefects*. London: Oxford University Press, 1964.

Woods, Frederick. *Young Winston's Wars. The Original Dispatches of Winston S. Churchill War Correspondent 1897–1900*. New York: Viking Press, 1972.

INDEX

ad hoc committees, 103
ADR (Air Defence Research) sub-
committee, 82, 83, 181
Afrika Korps, 154, 164
Afghanistan, 33
Alanbrooke, General Lord, 18, 88,
89, 92, 96, 98, 125, 127, 129, 130,
131–2, 195n, 210n
Alexander, General Sir Harold (1st
Earl Alexander), 120, 124, 137–8,
141, 170, 213n
Alfred the Great, King, 17, 90
Aliens Subcommittee, 55
amateurism and security, 147–9, 153
Amundsen, Roald, 43
Andrew, Christopher, 78, 153, 188,
200n
Anglo-Persian Convention (1913), 47
Antwerp, Churchill's expedition to
(1914), 48–9, 186
"Anvil", Operation (in southern
France), 168
appeasement, Churchill's opposition
to, 121
Arcadia Conference (1941), 107
Aristotle, 11
Arnold, Dr Thomas, 8, 30
Arrian, History of Alexander the
Great, 85
artificial harbors, 174, 175
Ashanti War, second, 2
Ashley, Maurice, 191n
Asquith, Baroness see Bonham-
Carter, Lady Violet
Asquith, Herbert Henry, 1st Earl of
Oxford, 7, 19, 22, 46, 49, 52, 63,
64, 108, 186
Asquith, Katherine, 71
Asquith, Raymond, 45; "The
Volunteer", 44–5
Astier, Emmanuel d', 214n
Astor, Colonel John Jacob, 43
atomic bomb, 177, 178, 180
Attlee, Clement, 210–11n
Auchinleck, General Sir Claude, 107,
120, 124, 138, 140, 141, 142, 154,
158, 164, 165–6, 211n
Australia, 87, 132
Ava, Lord, 35

Bacon, Francis, Novum Organum,
173
bacteriological and chemical
weapons, 178–9
Baden-Powell, Robert, Lord 39,
198n
Bagehot, Walter, 84, 204–5n
Baldwin, Stanley, 78
Balfour, Arthur James, 7, 10, 75
Balkans, 119, 173
Barbarossa, Operation (German
invasion of USSR), 85, 94, 114,
131, 150, 161, 164
Barham, HMS, loss of, 159
Barrie, J.M., Peter Pan, 17
Battle of Britain, 16, 86–7, 93,
104, 112, 122, 158–9, 174–5, 180;
phoney targets during, 167
The Battle of Dorking (G.T.
Chesney), 55
Battle of the Atlantic, 63, 103–4,
151, 157, 161, 180–1
"Battleaxe", Operation (1941), 126,
165
Beatty, Admiral David, 1st Earl, 59
Beaverbrook, Lord, 214n
Beesly, Patrick, Room 40, 201n
Belgium, German invasion of, 76
Bell A-3 RT scrambling device, 149
Benghazi, 146, 164; fall of, 163, 165
Berlin, Isaiah, 122, 189
Bevan, Colonel John, 169, 170, 171,
173
Birkenhead, Lord, 53, 148; The Last
Lion, 23
Bismarck, 128, 207n; sinking of
(1941), 154
Blenheim, Battle of, 71, 79–80, 120
Blenheim Palace, 12–13, 19, 148;
Column of Victory at, 117

government, wartime, 74–6, 99–116; *ad hoc* committees, 103; advisers, 103; Grand Alliance, 109–16; institutions, 105–9; machinery, 100–5

Government Code and Cypher School (GC and CS), 77, 153–66; *see also* Ultra

Grahame, Kenneth, 40, 42

Grand Alliance, 100, 109–16, 160–1

Graves, Robert, 69

"Great Game", the, 3, 5, 39–40, 54, 186, 187; First World War, 54, 55–65; interwar years, 77–83; Second World War, 143–84, 188

Greece, 107, 132, 137, 149, 164, 170

H_2S (blind bombing device), 174, 181

Habbakuk iceberg bases project, 176

Haggard, H. Rider, 15, 192n

Haig, Douglas, Marshal 1st Earl, 65, 78, 150

Halifax, Lord, 84, 100

Hall, Captain William Reginald "Blinker", 57–8

Hamilton, Ian, 33, 138, 197n

Handel, Professor Michael, ix, 144, 152

Handelsverkehrsbuch (HVB: German code), 56–7

Hankey, Lord, 86

Hardy, Thomas, 41

Harriman, Averell, 92; *Special Envoy to Churchill and Stalin* (with Elie Abel), 167, 206n

Harrow School: bombing of (1940), 32; Churchill at, 12, 21, 24, 30, 31, 32; Songs, 12, 30, 32

Heliograph Hill (Sudan), 40, 56

Hemingway, Ernest, 69

Henry, Colonel, 35

Henty, George Alfred, 14

hero-worship, heroism, 14–15, 33, 34, 42–3, 68, 69–70, 91, 92, 94–5

Hindenburg, President Paul von, 76, 187

Hinsley, F.H., *British Intelligence in the Second World War*, 162

history: Churchill's faith in, 85–7,

110, 121–2; continuity of, 72; romance of, 11–19

Hitler, Adolf, 32, 33, 85, 97, 98, 99, 101, 115, 131–2, 139, 144, 146, 150, 161, 170, 171, 173; Churchill's views on, 92–4; failure of plot against, 162

Hobart, Major-General P.C.S., 71

Hollis, Brigadier (later General Sir) Leslie, 145

Home Front (First World War), 50–1, 53, 73, 74, 117, 186

Home Front (Second World War), 98, 118, 151, 178

Home Guard, 95

Hopkins, Harry, 17, 112–13, 119–20, 152

Houghton, Walter, 191n

House of Commons, 105, 106, 107–9, 111, 123, 127

Howard, Michael, 134

Hughes, Thomas, *Tom Brown's Schooldays*, 30

Huxley, Thomas, 6

Imperialism, British Empire, 6, 75, 87; doubts expressed about, 41–2; linkage between sport and wars to support, 30–1; and patriotism, 42; romance of, 14–17, 34, 42–3; and Victorian wars, 32–40

India, 39; Churchill in, 8, 16, 24, 28, 34, 36, 37, 40

Indian Mutiny, 1

Industrial Intelligence Centre (IIC), 78

Ingoldsby Legends (R.H. Barham), 183

Intelligence/Secret Service, 3, 39–40, 54, 55–60, 143–73; amateurism and security, 147–9, 153; Churchill's manipulation of, 151; cover stories, 159–60, 168, 171; and deception, 167–73; GC and CS, 77, 153–66; "Golden Eggs", 153, 155–62; Industrial Intelligence Centre, 78; levels of war, 162–6; MI-5 Security Service, 145, 146–7; Marlborough, 78–80; Operations Room, 145; organizations, 144–7;